LIVING IN SIN?

Living in Sin?

A Bishop Rethinks Human Sexuality

John Shelby Spong

1817

Harper & Row, Publishers, San Francisco

New York, Grand Rapids, Philadelphia, St. Louis
London, Singapore, Sydney, Tokyo, Toronto

F O R E W O R D

*S*ome people feel that the sexual aspects of human life should be left alone, despite or because of the fact that sex permeates life and influences every aspect of behavior, whether for good or evil. Sex can be called at once the greatest gift to humanity and the greatest enigma of our lives. It is a gift in that it is a singular joy for all beings, and an enigma in its destructive potential for people and their relationships. It is not surprising, therefore, that sex is one of the most difficult aspects of life, and the integration of sex with religion especially so.

The book you are about to read by Bishop John Shelby Spong is remarkable for frankly exploring and firmly dispelling some of the mystery surrounding the biblical writings in relation to appropriate gender roles, traditions about procreational sex, and taboos on homosexuality. The controversy over gender differences and similarities is explored as never before through the eyes of a member of the hierarchy of a major Western Christian tradition. The reader must realize that the author's weaving of religion with science is singular, even in modern times. In allying religious cognition based on faith with scientific cognition based on reality, Bishop Spong offers hope to many who have felt that rational thinking is not welcome in organized religion. One courageous and controversial clergyman has elected to put reality in the pulpit. The reader is taken through the presumptions and incongruities of parts of the Scriptures and given an intelligent alternative to fundamentalist interpretations that lead only to bias, fear, and disgust.

Bishop Spong is an enlightened believer in truth, an intensely devout man and a clergyman with an open mind. There are other clerics of the Judeo-Christian tradition who hold similar views close to the heart, but Bishop Spong has publicly articulated these views. He offers a persuasive alternative in a difficult time. He is a believer in both the historic witness of Christian love and compassion and in the evolving facts of the biological revolution—facts that continue to be forthcoming as a result of scientific progress and that will undoubtedly evoke significant debate among all religious leaders and teachers. A cynic might say that he has failed to uphold a norm of mediocrity.

Living in Sin? deals with some vital problems attendant to the maturation of organized religion in a society that regards sex as something that should be kept hidden. Even the title may evoke these preconceived notions, particularly for those to whom the book is directed: people of faith. Organized religion has had a rough time dealing with sex during recent years. What has evolved might be called a mixture of dogmatic and reactionary thought. It is argued by many that the structure of the family and individual responsibility are dependent on an unchanging system of beliefs about our biological mission on earth. We should, by these people's standards, reproduce efficiently and without variation; to do otherwise is against both natural and divine law. It is no wonder that those who hold to these beliefs are dogmatic about new sexual mores. However, fear about sexual mores always follows ignorance and misconception, and we simply do not have time to approach such a fundamental problem as fear based on ignorance with outmoded dogma.

This rigid construct of what human sexuality should be has perpetuated the myths that have hurt and alienated so many.

Perhaps that is why organized religion, with its erroneous, prescientific beliefs about nature, is so difficult for the scientist to understand—and frightening. As a guidepost to life, religion cannot disregard the lesson of nature: that variation is the creativity of God at the highest level.

The enigma of life is that we are so innately different while trying to remain externally the same to each other. The wonders of genetic manipulation, of behavior modification, and an explanation of the hormonal basis for aggression and sexual preference are about to unfold before us and will doubtless confront our beliefs. If we view these wonders as God's, not ours, given to us as gifts to help us live together, we might realize that science can contribute much to religion. It is not the role of religion to condemn people or to forcibly change the results of a natural process. We need to change the way we think about people and sex. This book gives us a mind-set for change; it is an introduction for a new time.

There is and will always be hypocrisy in religion (as in most institutions), but it is a greater problem for religion to neglect it. If the foundation of religion is a faith fed by mystical, ancient beliefs that are strained in the face of scientific evidence, problems in society will worsen, more of the faithful will be exiled, and divisions will widen. The nonsense associated with the "shunning" of divorced individuals, the ridicule and condemnation of the adolescent's sexual drives as he or she emerges into pubescence, and the isolation of the homosexual are but a few examples of Christian hypocrisy, based on fear, that hide behind scriptural passage and myth. The unique aspect of Bishop Spong's approach is that it confronts hypocrisy and ignorance about sexual perceptions head on. It is not an easy or a pleasant task, but certainly one necessary in this age, and it should allay anxiety in most of its readers, rather than provoke consternation.

Robert G. Lahita, M.D., Ph.D.
Associate Professor
Cornell University Medical College
New York City

DEDICATION

To those people with whom I work most closely:

> Christine Mary Barney
> Denise Games Haines
> Wanda Corwin Hollenbeck
> James William Henry Sell
> Leslie Carl Smith
> John George Zinn

With thanks for their competence, their sense of responsibility, their friendship, their love, and their wonderful ability to laugh at themselves and me.

CONTENTS

PREFACE

*I*n January 1985, responding to questions and concerns expressed to me by the clergy of the Diocese of Newark, I called on the convention of our diocese to authorize a serious study of the changing patterns of family life and human sexuality, and to chart for the church an appropriate response to these patterns.

Many times clergy have shared with me the fact that the standards they reflect in their pastoral ministries differ sharply from the official positions of the church. The church has stated with regularity that genital sexual activity is neither appropriate nor moral except inside the bond of marriage. Yet many, if not most, of the couples coming to our clergy to receive the church's blessing in holy matrimony are in fact actively engaged sexually with each other and, in numerous cases, already living together.

Older parishioners, perhaps divorced or widowed, with increasing frequency have special friends of the opposite sex with whom they share sexual intimacy but with whom they are not even considering marriage. In many instances these people are not on the fringes of church life but are rather quite active, serving in the highest lay offices of local congregations. Many of them have shared their lives openly with their pastors. These pastors, while recognizing the dichotomy, do not find themselves moved to point out the contradictions between the church's teaching and the lives of their parishioners. They are more impressed with the quality of the life that they see being lived out than they are with the moral preachments of the institution they serve.

Still others of our clergy have become so sensitive and open to the realities of the homosexual* minority that they affirm and welcome gay and lesbian individuals and couples into their churches. They do so despite their recognition of the fact that the official stance of their church affirms celibacy as the only moral option open to the gay and lesbian person.

Since practice always precedes theory, these clergy had suggested to me that we as a church might need to look officially at our precepts, theories, and standards to see if they are in fact what we intend to affirm. We need to examine why it is that our pastoral sensitivity so often forces us to set aside the institutional definitions of propriety and morality.

The 111th Annual Convention of the Diocese of Newark, meeting in the heart of that wonderful but oft maligned city, responded to my call by authorizing the appointment of a task force to study these issues, and directed that task force to report its findings to the 112th convention in 1986. This resolution was passed unanimously, and the convention moved on to discuss the ordinary items of clergy salaries and budgets.

As the convention adjourned, one priest approached the podium to make me aware of his interest in being a member

---

*I acknowledge as both a writer and a pastor that some members of the gay and lesbian community object to use of the term "homosexual," likening it to employing the word "negro" for black. Our language about the subject is in a constant state of transition and refinement. I have made every effort to economize use of the word and to find acceptable substitute words, phrases, and images. However, the term is still widely employed in church and society, without derogatory intent or effect. It is simply a word that in both clinical and colloquial circles most people use. In a limited number of cases, I have used the term as a handy way clearly to make a point that should be readily understandable and inoffensive to all audiences of this book.

of this task force: the Reverend Dr. Nelson Thayer, professor of pastoral theology at Drew Theological Seminary in Madison, New Jersey. Drew is an exciting Methodist institution, ecumenical enough to place on its faculty an Episcopal priest and scholar of the stature of Nelson Thayer. Dr. Thayer informed me that he was planning to do some research in this very area as part of his professional work and would welcome the discipline of membership on the task force as a prod to that study.

This proposal was at this time of such minor import that I had given no thought whatsoever to the constituency of the group that I was now authorized to appoint. Yet here, standing before me, was a man I admired greatly, a man who had the respect of many of our clergy and lay people, a priest whose academic and communication skills were noteworthy, asking to be considered for membership. I knew Nelson Thayer to be a pastorally sensitive man, but I had no idea what his ideas or convictions were on any of the specific issues that I had asked to be explored. In one of those intuitive moments that you live to savor joyfully again and again, I said, "Nelson, why don't you chair this task force?" It was a bit of a surprise for him, perhaps more than he was prepared for, but Dr. Thayer accepted that responsibility on the spot, and I thought to myself that such a coincidence of interest, competence, and opportunity had to be God-given.

Several weeks later Dr. Thayer and I sat together to think about membership on the task force. We agreed on a group of sixteen persons to be invited. They included clergy and laity, men and women, whites and blacks, married and divorced persons, unmarried and single persons, professional women and homemakers, and one person who was openly and avowedly homosexual and living in a long-term, permanently committed relationship. Three members of the group had careers in various counseling fields. One was a Rhodes Scholar. Of those invited thirteen accepted, and the group came into being. I met with them at their first meeting to give them their official charge and to tell them why they had been called together. Then I turned the task force over to Nelson Thayer and departed. They were now on their own, able to move in any direction their study would take them, to come to any conclusions they desired, to make any recommendations they wished. Their only formal directive was to report their findings to the diocesan convention in January 1986.

As that date approached, no report was forthcoming. I wondered if this would be one more of those church committees born in enthusiasm but destined to amount to nothing. Dr. Thayer reported to the convention in 1986 that the task force had not completed its work and requested an extension of one year, with the promise of a full report in advance of the 1987 convention, to allow time for convention delegates to be prepared to approve or disapprove it when the convention convened. This request was honored by unanimous vote, and the task force was given another year of life.

Following the 1986 convention, I met once more with the task force to remind them of their charge and to encourage them to pursue their responsibilities. That was the second and only other time that I was to participate in the life of this commission.

Meanwhile, in the fall of 1985, I had been appointed by the presiding bishop of The Episcopal Church, The Right Reverend Edmond Browning, to membership on the Standing Commission on Human Affairs and Health of The Episcopal Church. To this commission is assigned the study of many of the crucial and volatile issues that produce emotional debate in the church, such as abortion, homosexuality, institutional racism, genetic engineering, and others. My particular assignment was to work on issues pertaining to human sexuality. I accepted that task from the chair of the commission, The Right Reverend George Hunt, Bishop of Rhode Island, and began to read widely and deeply in the field.

We decided that we needed to initiate in The Episcopal

Church a consciousness-raising debate on the appropriate influence of new insights into human sexuality, being introduced almost daily from psychology, biology, genetics, molecular biochemistry, and biophysics, on the traditions and time-honored convictions of the church and church people. With the cooperation of the national Episcopal newspaper, we agreed to stage the debate in the pages of *The Episcopalian* through a series of pro and con articles written by the most competent people we could find, who could write with clarity and integrity to support their points of view.

I was asked to write an introduction to the series. That introductory article was originally to have been unsigned, but three attempts to produce an introduction broad enough to satisfy the wide extremes of viewpoint on the commission proved unsatisfactory. Finally I agreed to sign the article, making it clearly the point of view of one member of the commission, so that no one else would have to feel compromised by identification with a piece with which they disagreed. I discovered that what some members of the commission call an "even-handed" approach really means to pretend that there is no change that is legitimate and that therefore there is no need to address the issue. Interestingly enough, upon publication even my signed article produced consternation in some circles, where certain people seemed to resent the fact that I, as a Christian, had a point of view different from theirs.

This series, in addition to my introduction, included paired articles debating the pros and cons of premarital sexual activity, whether or not people of the same gender living in committed relationships should be able to find something other than condemnation in the church's response to their lifestyle, and whether or not there are acceptable options other than marriage or loneliness for single, older adults. The articles were completed by December 1, 1986, and ran in 1987 in the February, March, April, and May issues of *The Episcopalian*. I served as general editor of the series.

During the first week of December 1986, the "Report of

the Task Force on Changing Patterns of Sexuality and Family Life" arrived on my desk. I read it with an unexpected sense of disappointment. My disappointment was not in its content or its style. It was beautifully written, and sensitively engaged the issues. I was frustrated because the report was primarily a pastoral document that called for understanding and more study. I did not understand how its recommendations could be debated in such a way as to come to a decision.

My conviction is that people change their opinions and grow when they are forced in debate to defend their prejudices. I would much rather be on the losing side of a consciousness-raising debate than on the winning side of a debate where the issues elicit little or no opposition. My fear was that this report fell into that latter category, and those fears were enhanced when the report was mailed to the twenty-eight members of the Diocesan Council for their consideration at their December meeting. Dr. Thayer came to that meeting to introduce the report to the Council and to answer their questions—but there were no questions, just words of appreciation for all the work the task force had done on this assignment. By a 28 to 0 vote, the council commended the report to the 113th Annual Convention, scheduled to convene on January 30, 1987.

On January 1, the report become quite public when it was mailed to the six hundred lay and clergy delegates to the convention. Not one letter or telephone call concerning it, either critical or positive, was received from any delegate. All delegates went to one of nine area convocation pre-convention orientation sessions designed to educate them regarding the issues on which they would be asked to vote at the convention. To my knowledge no questions about this report were raised in any of those meetings, except in the convocation of which Dr. Thayer was a member. Even there, it received scant attention.

On January 15, press packets were mailed to the area

newspapers that normally cover our convention. Information on the budget and resolutions, background material on guest speakers (one of whom was our newly elected Presiding Bishop), and data on any reports on which the convention would be asked to act were included in this mailing. Again, there was little or no response.

On Wednesday, January 28, however, Michael J. Kelly, a reporter for the *Bergen Record,* a New Jersey daily whose circulation is basically limited to the populous Bergen County area, called our press officer to say his interest had been raised by the report on sexuality. He asked if he could come by to ask some questions on its background. This request was granted, and the Venerable Leslie Smith, one of my archdeacons, and I met with Mr. Kelly and responded to his questions. On Thursday, January 29, in a front-page story displaying a color photograph of the Bishop of Newark, the *Bergen Record* broke this story under the banner headline "Dissent on Sexual Doctrine." The story stated that the Diocese of Newark proposed the blessing of gay and lesbian couples. The Associated Press immediately picked up the story, sending it out on all wire services across the nation and around the world.

On Friday, January 30, the day our convention opened, we were besieged by television crews from all the national networks, the New York independents, and even Ted Turner's Cable News Network out of Atlanta. Reporters called from Detroit, Oakland, New York, Houston, and Raleigh. *Time* and *Newsweek* both wanted interviews. The press had now made it impossible for this report simply to be filed or ignored. The issues were clearly destined to be debated vigorously. Follow-up stories were sent out on the wire services for the next two days. Television crews were omnipresent for the duration of the convention.

The only official action our convention took on this report was to receive it with gratitude and to commend it to our churches for a year of study. Resolutions coming out of that study were mandated to be presented to the convention of 1988 for vote. That rather mild resolution was lost on the media. In the secular and church press, "The Newark Report," as it came to be called, was debated by official and unofficial groups, by bishops and diocesan conventions, across the land. Stands were taken by various bodies, opposing and affirming a report that the Newark convention itself had only received. I was praised by some, condemned by others.

It so happened that the debate on sexual issues scheduled to run in *The Episcopalian* appeared just two days after our Newark convention. It included the signed introductory article I had written the previous October on changing patterns in human sexuality. The publicity about "The Newark Report" was connected, in many people's minds, to this article written by the Bishop of Newark, although it had been written three months before I even read this report.

The scenario was further complicated by the fact that in November I had accepted an invitation to appear on William F. Buckley, Jr.'s PBS program "Firing Line" to debate the subject of women in the episcopate with a colleague of mine, The Right Reverend William Wantland, Bishop of Eau Claire, Wisconsin. That program had been recorded on January 26, 1987, two days before any of us imagined that "The Newark Report" would create controversy. Since this taping was not aired until March 1, it too was heard as part of the sexuality debate.

For months my mail was so heavy I could not respond to it. I encouraged and engaged in other debates, made numerous television talk-show appearances, continued to read voraciously in the field of sexual ethics, and finally, responding to an invitation, agreed to write this volume and thus to place these questions before the public for debate.

At last I could present the study that had led me to my present conclusions, the background material necessary to understand the issues, and the recommendations that I am led to make, in the medium of a book. Television demands simple answers and quick conclusions. It is a particularly shallow medium. Newspaper coverage permits more details to be included, but it does not endure. Yesterday's newspaper is ever so dated. A book, however, makes a genuine, lasting contribution to a debate. It creates a dialogue with its reader. A book can also focus a church discussion group and inspire sermons, reviews, and reactions both positive and negative, written and verbal. A book can be put on a shelf and taken down at a later date, thus to begin anew to create reaction and response. It is quite obviously my favorite medium of communication.

My readers need to be aware that I recognize that I cannot write or think outside my own frame of reference. I struggle to be objective, to get inside the experience of women, gay men and lesbians, people of color, and those in a different socio-economic situation from my own. But I am a male, shaped by Western civilization. I am a heterosexual, a white, and a hopelessly middle-class person. I do not think that this has affected my scholarship, but it does affect the questions I ask, the way I process data, and the values I assign to various conclusions. I have accordingly had this manuscript read and critiqued by a wide variety of people, in the hope of enlarging its comprehensiveness and edging it toward a higher level of objectivity.

In the preparation of this volume I am indebted to many people. First to Wanda Corwin Hollenbeck, my wonderful secretary, who works as hard and as enthusiastically on a book as I do and whose presence in my office is a genuine and enduring pleasure. Two of the three archdeacons of our diocese, the Venerable Denise G. Haines and the Venerable Leslie C. Smith, served as my primary editors. Archdeacon Haines is a content editor, brilliant and insightful, with a tremendous way with words. She understands their nuances. She and I had previously jointly authored a book, and I am much in her debt. Archdeacon Smith is a former professional book editor. He is the one to whom we turn to settle questions of grammar, word usage, and style. A *cum laude* graduate from seminary, he made a vital contribution to this manuscript. The third archdeacon of our diocese, the Venerable James W. H. Sell, was running our summer camp while the book was being written, but he too interacted with me about my ideas. The two lay executive officers of the diocese, John G. Zinn in finance and Christine M. Barney in administration, picked up an additional load of both work and emotions when the book was being produced. They did it with grace, charm, and good humor that translated into a sustaining support. The other members of our staff—Marge Allenspach, Susan Ayers, Cecil Broner, Rupert Cole, Sharon Collins, Gail Deckenbach, Dale Hart, Olga Hayes, Wendy Hinds, Robert Lanterman, Barbara Lescota, Australia Lightfoot, William Quinlan, and Elizabeth Stone—have all contributed to this book in many intangible ways, and together they make our office a pleasant place to live and work.

Working on the later stages also proved to be an exciting and life-enhancing experience. To Michael Lawrence, my editor, who first suggested this book, and to Rebecca Marnhout, who is the best copy editor with whom I have ever worked, I express my gratitude.

The Bishop of Eau Claire, William Wantland, became my primary debating opponent. A worthy adversary he is, and though I agree with him on very little, I admire and respect him, and I treasure our growing friendship. I would gladly entrust my life to him—but not my vote. Other bishops who have supported my efforts have been George Hunt of Rhode Island, Coleman McGehee of Michigan, William Swing of California, Wesley Frensdorff of Arizona, Paul Moore of New York, John Krumm retired of Southern Ohio, John Burt retired of Ohio, and the Presiding Bishop, Edmond Browning. Some members of the House of Bishops have challenged me deeply and forced me both to defend and to rethink some issues. Primary among these, in addition to Bishop Wantland, have been Gordon Charlton and Maurice Benitez of Texas, Harry Shipps of Georgia, Clarence Pope of Fort Worth, Robert Witcher of Long Island, and Harold Robinson of western New York. I salute with appreciation both groups.

Midway in the preparation of this book, I was privileged to spend an evening discussing these ideas with Dr. and Mrs. Robert Lahita. Dr. Lahita is an associate professor of medicine at the Cornell Medical Center in New York and a member of the faculty of Cornell University Medical College. The area of sexual ethics in which I was working was of great interest to him, and he made available to me books and articles reflecting some of the latest scientific studies. He also cheered the fact that a member of the hierarchy of the church was willing to be open to the scientific world. His previous experience with church leaders led him to feel they were more interested in propaganda than in truth. It was a provocative and memorable evening, so to Bob and Terry Lahita I publicly express my gratitude, with a special thanks to Bob for reading the manuscript and contributing a foreword to this volume.

My mentor and special friend for many years has been The Right Reverend John Elbridge Hines, retired Presiding Bishop of The Episcopal Church. Most of my ideas I have at one time or another discussed with him. His intellect, his wisdom, and his vast experience have greatly enriched my life. Parts of this book were written while visiting with him in Black Mountain, North Carolina. I regard him as the one person I would most like to emulate.

The Diocese of Newark is a unique part of The Episcopal Church. It includes the seven counties of northern New Jersey and is bounded by the Hudson River to the east and the Delaware River to the west. It is one of the largest jurisdictions in the Anglican tradition in America. Within its ranks are some of the finest clergy I have ever known, and some of the most involved, caring, and intelligent lay persons I have ever met. This diocese has a reputation for being controversial that far antedates its present bishop. It comes, I believe, from being willing to be open to the issues of the day and having the courage to address them. I am most grateful that somehow by God's grace I have been privileged to spend the major years of my professional life within this diocese's exciting boundaries. So to the clergy and laity of this diocese I express my thanks.

Finally, I salute my family: my wife, Joan; my daughters Ellen (and her husband, Gus Epps), Katharine (and her husband, Jack Catlett), and Jaquelin (whose life in Germany has minimized my contact with this special young lady). These representatives of the next generation inspire me daily to trust the wisdom that is emerging in their time, and to suggest that the church at large also take that wisdom seriously.

John Shelby Spong
Newark, N.J.
Advent 1987

CHAPTER ONE
Setting the Stage

S ome people will regard this as a book about sex. I regard it as a book about prejudice. For centuries sexual attitudes, sexual taboos, and sexual practices have been used by dominant groups in society to keep others subordinate. Those who possess power define those who are powerless and then impose their own definition on the ones defined. The guiding principle is to ensure the comfort, the convenience, the happiness, and the well-being of the dominant ones.

Behind prejudice there is also fear. We reject that which we cannot manage. We condemn what we do not understand. We set up a means of control to render powerless those dynamic realities we know to be powerful. No aspect of our humanity is invested with more anxieties, yearnings, emotions, and needs than is our sexual nature. So, sex is a major arena in which the prejudice of human beings finds expression.

This fact accounts for the anger and even the violence that erupts when sexual control mechanisms are publicly challenged. Those who organize their lives differently, who adopt values that violate the prevailing sexual taboos, are subject to hate, threat, even attack, and sometimes murder. When the convention of the Diocese of Newark passed a resolution to study the question of church support for committed monogamous relationships between gay or lesbian people, I received thousands of letters—some of which included overt death threats, should I ever find myself in the presence of the writer. Others contained threats that were a bit more oblique; their writers were content to assure me that they would pray for God to curse me with a fatal disease, to strike me with lightning, to allow me to be in a plane crash, or to permit me to fall victim to some other equally effective means of permanent disposal. Gentler critics indicated that they would be content with my resignation. Failing my cooperation in that means of exit, they would press to have me removed from my post as an overseer in the church of God by one of the more familiar medieval methods. Clearly I, or more precisely the Diocese of Newark, had unsettled their security-producing prejudices. Many, whose powers of fantasy were very active, assumed that I had reached conclusions far beyond what is the case.

They also attributed to my presumed conclusions a power that their own convictions did not seem to possess. So they refused to enter the discussion except to condemn, and they were unable to listen to my response. If they had, they would have learned that the only thing about which I am certain is that new data are abroad in our world, demanding to be taken into account. These data, both informational and experiential, raise questions about the way sexuality has been morally and psychologically defined. They are also producing in our time a revolution in sexual thinking and in sexual practice that is unprecedented.

To deny these data is to be both immoral and ignorant. Therefore, this book is a call for Christian people to suspend judgment temporarily, to enter the uncertainty of not knowing, to engage the data, to be part of the debate, to examine sexual prejudices, to redefine values, and thus to help to transform the times. It is an ambitious undertaking, but one worthy of the effort and the risk, for it holds the possibility of renewing us as the body of Christ.

In the debate and in my correspondence, a certain cliché has often been used as if it were self-explanatory. People speak and write about sexuality and moral norms "as revealed in Holy Scripture." They issue with some frequency a call to return to "the sexual morality of the Bible." I find that call difficult to interpret. As this book unfolds, the nature of that difficulty will be explored.

The Bible is a major source feeding the ethical decision making of Christian people, and its message must be taken by Christians with utmost seriousness. But the Bible itself is not free of contradictions, of expressions of prejudice, and of attitudes that have long been abandoned. The same could be said about the ongoing tradition of the Christian church. Church history also reveals sin, prejudice, and misleading appeals to long-abandoned practices. Therefore, arguments that issue from the authority of sacred Scripture or sacred tradition must state what part of Scripture or tradition is being upheld and on what basis that part is retained while other parts are abandoned.

Truth will not be found in simplistic appeals to tradition or in biblical proof-texting. Authoritative claims of infallibility for the papacy, emanating from the Roman Catholic side of Christianity, or of inerrancy for the Scriptures, emanating from some constituencies of the Protestant side of Christianity, are simply not relevant. Such claims have long been dismissed in academic and theological circles, and by thoughtful men and women in the pews as well. These claims remain alive only through the insecurity of Christians who are more concerned with maintaining ecclesiastical power and authority than they are with discerning the truth of God.

The church needs to recognize that in addition to these frightened critics, there is another constituency that is also watching. It is made up of those who believe themselves to be rejected by the church. They are the victims of prejudice, those who have been told in word and deed by the official voices of the ecclesiastical structures that they do not measure up, do not count, or do not belong. When the assumptions by which this group feels judged are challenged by someone from within the church, they also write. Their letters express gratitude, are confessional, recount bitter experiences, and share hurts. They wonder if God or the church has room for them. They, too, are seeking the truth of God. I hope this book will make them aware that they do belong, even as it makes others aware that they exist and do matter.

Because Scripture will be a major issue in this presentation, I begin my task of redefining sexual ethics with a story that, for me, stands forever in the Judeo-Christian tradition as a reminder that human prejudice on any subject cannot be identified with God's will or God's word.

God's call to the church is a call to build a community for all people. Since God's people are diverse in color, size, gender, race, language, age, sexual orientation, and even value systems, an inclusive community is no simple task to develop or to sustain. It is far easier to draw circles and to proclaim that only those who are inside our particular circle will be the recipients of our concern or love, leaving all others potential victims of our prejudice.

Christians are quick to give lip service to the universality proclaimed by the word "all" in Paul's assurance "as in Adam *all* die." Historically, however, we have declined to claim universality for the "all" in the second part of that Pauline phrase, "so in Christ shall *all* be made alive." In the baptismal covenant of *The Book of Common Prayer*, the candidates for baptism and their sponsors are asked, "Will you seek and serve Christ in *all* persons, loving your neighbor as yourself?" and "Will you strive for justice and peace among *all* people, and respect the dignity of *every* human being?" To both questions the response is "I will, with God's help." It is easier to say "all" and "every" than it is to live out the implications of inclusiveness. God's call for an

inclusive community invariably collides with human prejudice, rooted in the human impulse to be secure, to be right, to
claim God's will for human behavior, to justify the ways by
which we diminish others. So it has always been, as the
following biblical narrative, somewhat freely retold, will
certainly reveal.

CHAPTER TWO

A Biblical Call to Inclusiveness

I n the fifth century before the common era, many of the people of Judah found themselves still in captivity in Babylon. They had been carried into exile after defeat at the hands of the army of Nebuchadnezzar in 586 B.C.E.[1]1 It had been a difficult period in Jewish history. The people were deeply infected with what is perhaps the most dangerous tenet of any religious ideology. It is a notion so familiar that it causes neither astonishment nor much criticism. This small, beleaguered nation was absolutely convinced that they were God's specially chosen people. Nearly all their interpretation of their history was couched in an ethos of divine election. Their dominant religious thinking assumed this national ontological definition.

The primary difficulty with believing yourself to be God's specially chosen people is that everyone else becomes God's specially unchosen. One nation cannot be chosen without other nations inevitably being defined as both different and inferior. There is a very fine line between the neutral word "unchosen" and the hostile word "rejected." Inevitably, the hostile word becomes operative when the doctrine of election becomes creedal. Since God has particularly not chosen other people, rejection, hatred and prejudice are justified in the chosen ones, as they model divine behavior as they understand it. In this way the world was divided into the chosen Jews and the unchosen Gentiles. This idea thrived among the Jewish people of the exile. It was reinforced in the period after the Persian general Cyrus conquered Babylon and allowed all captive peoples to return to the homeland that had been lost to them for three generations.

The defeat of the Jewish army, the fall and destruction of Jerusalem, and the exile raised large and troubling theological issues for the captive people. They wondered out loud: "If we are really God's chosen, what does it mean for us to be defeated? Is our God impotent? What does it mean for God's chosen to be homeless for as long as a century? What a strange way for the Holy God to treat God's specially chosen people!" Unable and unwilling to sacrifice the status of being God's elect and desiring to save God from the charge of powerlessness, defeat and exile had to be explained by the people.

And so they were: The defeat and the exile were God's punishment upon a rebellious and unfaithful people, the theologians of the day argued. Covenant is a mutual agreement. God agreed to be Judah's God, and in return the people agreed to obey God's law and God's ritual requirements. Our people failed, they reasoned. We did not obey the Torah; we did not worship God according to the demands of the law. Prodded by their leaders, the exiles resolved: When we return to Judah to rebuild Jerusalem, we will be rigorous in obedience and rigid in ritualistic requirement, lest we face again the vengeance of a wrathful God, disappointed in the elect and willing to punish the chosen nation once again with defeat and exile.

It was such a compelling argument that it produced an effective coalescence of national pride and religious zeal. Evangelical fervor transformed the returning Jewish people into an energized, motivated nation. Political and religious leadership were combined at this moment of Jewish history in the persons of Ezra and Nehemiah. They were to lead the return to their homeland and the reestablishment of their nation.[2]

There was, however, a nagging discomfort about this metaphysical equation designed to preserve God's power and Judah's identity as the chosen people. It placed the blame squarely on the shoulders of the Jews' forebears. Were their ancestors so weak, so inept, so sinful? It was painful to transfer accountability for the disaster onto those who were grandparents and great-grandparents of the chosen people, even if such rationalizations successfully justified the ways of God. The logical questions were then asked: Why were our forebears disobedient? Why did they not obey the law? Why did they not worship properly? Wherein were they vulnerable to sin? Are we also tainted?

As quickly as these questions played in the mind, answers, self-serving and divisive, began to emerge. It was not our ancestors' weakness at all, the returned exiles argued. Some of our forebears had married non-Jewish spouses, who had contaminated us with alien traditions, different values, and corrupting worship services. Foreign elements had polluted the purity of our tradition, compromised the integrity of worship, and were therefore responsible for our defeat and exportation. God's judgment fell on our nation when we condoned these evil, alien practices.

The scapegoat had now been identified: The foreigners were the culprits. God's people, therefore, in the future had to be vigilant to root out and expose any and all foreign elements. The returning Jews vowed: When we restore our nation and our holy city of Jerusalem, when we reestablish in our land the sacred tradition of the past, we must be certain that no foreign elements are allowed. God's chosen people must not be diluted by the presence of those who are not part of the elect. The law must be rigorously obeyed, the ritual practices carried out in scrupulous detail with fastidious correctness. Only in this manner can we guarantee that disaster will not befall us anew.

The theological problem was solved in an interesting and comfortable way. They did not relinquish that sense of being chosen, nor were they forced to entertain a vision of an impotent God. The argument was neat, concise, tight. It also allowed the Jews to avoid facing a hostile world without the confidence that God could be counted on in any future emergency. Fear, fantasy, prejudice, and magic all fed the nationalistic imperatives of the day.

Using the power of this theological mandate, Ezra and Nehemiah led the newly arrived pilgrim people in the renewal of their covenant with God and in an act of rededication to the law. For good measure, these leaders proposed a statute designed to guarantee the racial, ethnic, and religious purity of the rebuilt nation of Judah.

This statute required every Jewish man or woman married to a foreign spouse to divorce and banish the non-Jewish partner from the land. It further required that any "half-breed" children born of that union be banished with the non-Jewish mate. An unwilling Jewish spouse went into exile with the rejected partner and the corrupted children, which meant almost certain death: Aliens were not welcomed into most tribes in that day, and survival apart from a tribe was hardly possible.

The enforcement of the law moved Judah into one of the uglier phases of her national history. Racial purists organized vigilante squads. Bloodlines were checked. Tensions ran high, as the inquisition tore families apart. Personal suffering was extreme. It was an opportunity to destroy political enemies. Banishment was automatic if the authorities could not be convinced of racial purity. The book of Deuteronomy suggests that the search went back ten generations (Deut. 23:3). Judah was to be for the Jews only. God's chosen people must be pure. Foreign elements must be purged. God's worship cannot be distorted with strange and unorthodox practices. No protest was heard against this xenophobia; the hysteria drowned out every objection.

Religious zeal combined with political power to merge into tyranny. Personal liberties and individual, non-conforming values had no protection or platform.

There was, however, at that time one person in Jerusalem who was sufficiently disturbed by the prevailing prejudice to confront it. His only question was, How? What tactics might succeed? Public political attack was doomed to failure. Silence was cowardly. Finally, an idea dawned on him. He would write a story, of the genre of protest literature. It would appear anonymously on the streets of Jerusalem, and by its very charm and persuasive narrative power it would seduce people into both listening to it and discussing it. The central character would be one about whom judgment could not be suspended. The power of this story would be that as people made judgments about the value system under which the central character operated, they would also be making a judgment about themselves. When the narrative was finished, the author arranged to have the town crier read it at the town square, where the people gathered. He was sure that the people would comment and laugh as they listened. Then the point of the story would strike their hearts, and they would see themselves as they really were, and their prejudice would be revealed. What follows is a retelling of the story that anonymous Jewish writer gave to his fellow citizens some twenty-five hundred years ago.

————————————— +++++ —————————————

Once upon a time, in the days of our grandparents many years removed, there was a prophet whose name was Jonah. Jonah was certain that God's love was bound by the limits of his own love, so he assumed that God rejected everyone that Jonah rejected and hated everyone that Jonah hated. With these prejudices firmly in place, Jonah settled into the predictable life of a righteous Hebrew.

But one day God spoke to Jonah and said, "Jonah, I want you to go to the people of Nineveh and preach." Jonah, aghast at this idea, responded with incredulity: "You must be kidding, God! Nineveh is a pagan city. It is the capital of the Assyrians—the scourge of the world. You know that. Why would you want me to preach to the people of Nineveh?"

God was not deterred by Jonah's logic or by his distress, rising as it did out of Jonah's prejudice. With divine patience the demand was repeated, leaving Jonah little recourse. The authoritative command insisted that he do that which he did not want to do and, even worse, believed that he should not do. It was against everything he had been taught. So, Jonah responded in the classic and time-honored way that passive and powerless people have of dealing with authority figures: He said yes, but he meant no. He pretended to acquiesce, all the while hoping that God would soon forget this foolishness and turn the divine attention to some other part of the cosmos.

To show his good faith, Jonah returned to his home and prepared to leave. He packed his suitcase and went down to the seaport, where he booked passage on a boat—not to Nineveh but to Tarshish. It was an honest mistake, he would plead, in case God noticed his ruse. Jonah checked in, went to his stateroom, unpacked his bag, put on his shorts, and went topside with his suntan lotion. Sprawling in a deck chair, he put on his dark glasses and began to read the magazine section of the *Times*. He played the role of a tourist brilliantly. As his boat began its journey into the Mediterranean Sea, Jonah breathed a sigh of relief. He had escaped the divine command, and in so doing had preserved his prejudices intact. Even better, he had saved God from a serious mistake. All went well for the first hour of the voyage.

Then a dark cloud appeared in the sky just above the little boat. It seemed to journey wherever the boat journeyed. No amount of navigational skill could elude it. From that cloud flashes of lightning, claps of thunder, and a torrential rainstorm descended on Jonah's boat. The God-fearing captain, observing this unusual phenomenon, knew exactly what was happening. "God is angry with someone on this boat," he shouted. To identify the culprit the captain used the technology at his disposal. He drew straws. The lot fell on Jonah.

"Jonah, what is this that you have done?" the captain demanded.

"Well," replied Jonah, "God did call me to go preach to the people of Nineveh, but I could not imagine that God meant it. After all, the Ninevites are Gentile people, hardly worthy of God's attention, to say nothing of God's favor."

The captain seemed satisfied with this recital of the facts. It was to his mind a reasonable explanation. Prejudice always seems reasonable to the prejudiced ones. So the captain decided to ride out the storm—but a sharp bolt of lightning and a reverberating clap of thunder greeted that decision. When a large wave broke across the bow of the ship, sliding Jonah's deck chair to the stern and forcing him to grab the guardrail to keep from going overboard, the captain reconsidered.

"On second thought, Jonah," the captain said, "when a sacrifice has to be made and the choice is between you and me, I vote for you." With that, he called three deck hands, and each gripped an arm or a leg. On the count of three, they hurled the hapless Jonah overboard.

God, however, had prepared for this eventuality by creating a great big fish. That fish had been swimming in tandem with the boat, awaiting its moment on center stage. The time had come, and the great mouth of this fish was open to receive the falling, flailing Jonah. Jonah never felt the wetness of the sea. Effortlessly he slid into the unknown and found himself in the confines of a new, but relatively small, Mediterranean condominium.

Jonah had a rather amazing capacity to adapt to new circumstances. He set out to make his living space comfortable. He hung curtains, rearranged the furniture, and settled down to see what might come his way in this strange new chapter of his life. For three days and three nights Jonah remained in the belly of the great fish, until even the great fish could no longer stand Jonah's presence. There was a great primeval belch, and the fish threw up. Out tumbled Jonah, landing on a very convenient sand bar. While Jonah was clearing the water from his ears and the cobwebs from his mind, and trying to make sense out of his bizarre adventures, he heard that familiar voice say, "Jonah, how would you like to go preach to the people of Nineveh?" Jonah knew when he was outmaneuvered. "Okay, God, you win. I'll go."

Persistent Jonah was not through in his debate with God, however. Prejudice never dies easily or speedily. His first attempt to manipulate a powerful authority figure had failed. God had been immovable. His second line of defense is also familiar to those who deal with unyielding authority. "I'll do what you demand, God, but I'll do it in my way. I'll obey the letter of the command but not the spirit. God instructed me to preach to the people of Nineveh, but God did not tell me how to do that preaching or where in Nineveh to preach, so I will preach only in the alleyways and back streets, and I will preach by muttering under my breath. I will obey God on the one hand and achieve my purpose on the other."

Into the alleys and back streets went Jonah, looking disreputable and muttering under his breath, "God says, 'Repent; repent and turn to God.' " He hoped that no one would hear, and then certainly no one would respond. But to his disbelief, the people of Nineveh both heard and responded. By the thousands they poured out of their homes and onto the streets, tearing their clothes, beating their breasts, begging God's forgiveness and asking God's mercy. The whole city was saved.

Jonah was the most successful evangelist of all time. Jonah, however, was in a rage. "God, I knew this would happen. Now you have to forgive these wretched people. Your merciful nature does not allow the destruction of penitent people, so you will save them. Why did you do this, God? Why can your love and mercy not stop at the boundary of my love and mercy? Why do you not hate everybody that I hate? These people do not deserve your love."

Jonah stomped out of the city to sulk on a distant hillside, while the crowds of newly converted Ninevites raised their hands in prayer and praise and the echoes of "Amazing Grace" filtered into the countryside. In disgust Jonah finally fell asleep, only to have bad dreams.

He tossed and turned until dawn. Rousing himself, he became aware that God was strangely absent. During the night, however, God had caused a great tree to grow on the hillside. When the hot desert sun bore down on Jonah, he found refuge beneath that tree's rich green foliage. When the biting desert wind began to blow, Jonah found protection behind its thick trunk. Jonah became attached to that tree in a deep, mysterious way. It seemed to sustain his life and his spirit. When darkness fell, Jonah slept beneath the protective branches of the tree. That night, however, God caused a worm to attack the tree, boring through its trunk and branches and devouring its foliage, until the tree withered and collapsed into the dust. When Jonah awakened and saw that his treasured tree was now dead, he was inconsolable. He wept the bitter tears of grief. His compassion, his pity, and his grief poured out on the tree. Finally, late in that second day, God broke silence and said: "Jonah, is it not rather strange that you can express all this grief and remorse over a tree, and not even a very impressive tree, since it was born in one day and died in another? You have the capacity to feel the pangs of a broken heart over this tree, yet you have no pity and no love for the 120,000 people who dwell in the city of Nineveh, to say nothing of all their cattle."

On this note the book of Jonah ends.

———————————— +++++ ————————————

The genius of this author lay in the fact that his readers would immediately see the distortion in Jonah's character and because the story was being read in a public setting, they would laugh at his rigid, prejudiced viewpoint. They would comment to one another as the story developed, publicly ridiculing Jonah's attitude. Then, with a resounding thump, it would hit them that the stupidity of Jonah was their own stupidity. The narrow-minded bigotry of Jonah was their own narrow-minded bigotry. Their judgment of Jonah was applicable also to themselves. Jonah held up a mirror wherein they looked deeply into their own eyes. Slowly they had to see that God's love is unlimited. God's embrace is not restricted by their embrace. God's grace is not circumscribed by their prejudices and by their definitions.

That is the lesson of Jonah and of those passages of Holy Scripture that call us not only to repentance and obedience but also to inclusiveness. Prejudice erects walls that enclose us in a feeling of security. God beckons us out of our confining lives to a place where we are able to grow into more sensitive and open people, people capable of reflecting the infinite inclusiveness of the God whose invitation is not selective. "Come to me, *all*" (Matt. 11:28), said the Christ of God.

The call to inclusiveness has always been part of the heritage of the Christian church, whether heeded or not. The Divine Commission is an early part of the Christian tradition. "Go . . . make disciples of *all* nations," said Jesus (Matt. 28:19). *Nothing* can "separate us from the love of God in Christ Jesus our Lord," wrote Paul (Rom. 8:39). Presumably, that "nothing" means nothing: no creedal difference, no competing value system, no sexual attitude or practice, no racial or ethnic origin. Nothing. There is an absolute quality to that word that demands inclusiveness. "In Christ shall *all* be made alive" (I Cor. 15:22). Surely that "all" means all.

The church has had to battle itself throughout history to keep its call to inclusiveness intact. In the beginning of

Christian history, even the Gentile Christians were not welcome. The way to Christ was thought to be a single route, a path that led through the Jewish law. Peter championed this principle. Paul challenged him in the name of a universal Christ, and their battle was intense. Its echoes are heard in Galatians and Acts. Paul won, and the church climbed out of the womb of Judaism and into the extensive and diverse Roman Empire, in a move toward universalism. It is important for Western Christians to recognize that the first people to feel the sting of the church's prejudice were our own ancestors—the Gentiles.

They were not to be the only objects of prejudice. The church throughout its history has perceived a God who rejects whatever the church rejects. In almost every instance, it was ignorance that fed prejudice. Whatever the church did not understand, it excluded. For centuries women were not actually members of the church but only "auxiliaries." Others whose ethnicity or economic status caused them to be thought of as "foreigners" were relegated to the galleries of churches and allowed to serve only in subservient roles. In South Carolina, in the early years of the twentieth century, the leaders of The Episcopal Church debated with both seriousness and intensity whether a black man was human enough to be ordained and commissioned to serve as a suffragan bishop for "colored work."[3]

All sorts of people were victims of the church's prejudice. Left-handed people were called "the devil's children" by church leaders. People who committed suicide were refused burial from within the walls of the church. Mental illness made people different and, therefore, feared and rejected. Divorced persons who remarried also were not welcome at the church's altars, for the failure to keep one's marriage vows was thought to be an almost unforgivable sin. In incident after incident, on issue after issue, throughout the history of the church the attitude of Jonah has been the attitude of the church. God's love was understood to be given and withheld just as those who spoke for God to the world gave and withheld their love. In the sweep of history the barriers guarding exclusiveness have been challenged and dismantled time after time by an ever-deepening under-standing of the love of God—a love powerful enough even to challenge the prejudices enshrined in Holy Scripture. Beyond the comfort level of human life, there is always a Nineveh that calls us to set aside our fear and be open to the humanity in those we reject. Nineveh beckons today in the lives of those who do not fit the church's narrow definition of sexual morality. Such persons elicit from the religious establishment much the same response that the people of Nineveh elicited from Jonah. I believe that God is calling the church today to go to these men and women, so that God can show the church what God once showed Jonah, namely that God's love and acceptance are not bound by the limits of our love and acceptance.

Notes

1. Throughout this book I will use B.C.E. (before the common era) and C.E. (the common era) instead of the more familiar B.C. (before Christ) and A.D. (*anno Domini*). I do it as a way of being inclusive of those religious traditions, and most especially of my Jewish brothers and sisters, who feel violated by the Christian assumption that they alone can define the meaning of time.
2. See the books of Ezra and Nehemiah in the Hebrew Scriptures.
3. See *The Journal of the Diocese of South Carolina,* Episcopal Church, 1915–1930.

CHAPTER THREE

The Sexual Revolution

Strange things are happening in our world. Women, breaking the stereotypes of the ages, are entering into every field of human endeavor. India, Israel, the Philippines, Norway, and Great Britain have all been governed by an elected female head of state in this century. Environmental problems, leaping over the boundaries of nation states, have created universal anxiety about the destruction of our atmosphere's protective ozone layer; nuclear power plant accidents; strontium 90 pollution; the effect of pesticides on the life of rivers, lakes and oceans; and the impact of overpopulation. Demonstrations around the world are growing, as aroused people protest the arms race. The use of military power to preserve national integrity or a particular political and economic system is no longer a rational option, in an atomic era.

Women's rights, environmental protection, and world peace at first glance seem to be the concerns of three separate interest groups. Some observers, however, see them as deeply related. The feminist movement is surely related to a changing awareness of human sexuality and to the unwillingness of half of the human population to accept the sexual definitions of a previous age. Environmental concerns are linked to feminism also: We live on Mother Earth, and the call to stop violating her and to seek a harmonious way to live with nature is deeply related to the growing respect for the feminine in life. The peace and disarmament movement also has this feminist dimension. At its very core, the peace movement raises questions about the meaning of war, which since the dawn of civilization has been a ritualized sexual activity demonstrating virility. It is the ultimate expression of that competitive masculine quality that the male-dominated world has extolled as virtuous for thousands of years. Today it is questioned continually.

So beneath the surface these three movements appear to be connected, to be rising out of the same rebellion against the patterns of the past. Beneath the symptoms we perceive a challenge to all previous models of self-understanding, a change in all the stereotypes by which life has been organized, and a call to human beings to be something different in a different kind of world. The old order is passing away.

At the heart of these swirling tides of change there is a primary shift in the understanding of the proper balance of power between men and women. The organizing rule of life in the past has been the patriarchal mind-set. Patriarchal principles, accepted as "the way things are," formed patriarchal prejudices that then reinforced the principles. That mind-set gave us kings, male deities, and the sexual stereotypes of dominant man and submissive woman. That patriarchal world, unchallenged for thousands of years, is colliding with the new understanding of life emerging on every side. Fritjof Capra, the philosopher-physicist, observing the signs of our times writes, "We have reached the end of the reign of male domination."[1] In language influenced by Eastern religious thought, he argues that the masculine "yang," having moved to its ultimate limit, now is in full retreat before the feminine "yin." In the new age the feminine moon will shine as brightly as the masculine sun. The male drive to conquer and subdue the earth must recede before the recognition that such a conquest is not the path to success but to death. Survival will depend on learning to live in harmony with Mother Nature. Harmony with nature will replace conquest of nature. The male mentality, ever seeking to exert its power and control over all of life, finally achieved the scientific breakthrough of splitting the atom. With that knowledge the masculine spirit has developed a weapon that renders meaningless and absurd all the war games that boys and men have played since the dawn of the patriarchal era. Interdependence, not domination of others, will be the newly perceived pathway to life.

Most cogently, the patriarchal definition of masculinity is now perceived to have been instrumental in killing many men's ability to feel emotion. The patriarchal definition of femininity has denied the female almost all her strengths, save her sexuality that men have exploited in numbers of ways. The patriarchal mentality is almost inevitably homophobic, for gay men threaten the prevailing definitions of maleness, and lesbian women refuse to flatter dominant males by conveying to them any sense of needing that which they are, or that which they have to give.

The quest for survival of the human race has brought all of these definitions under serious question. As the need to change becomes more urgent, every sexual pattern based upon these definitions will begin to fall. The patriarchally defined marriage began to fail in this century as the divorce rate soared. The patriarchal double-standard of premarital sexual behavior, prescribing sexual abstinence for women and sexual experimentation for men, has largely been abandoned. The patriarchal assumption that everyone needs to be married has become inoperative, and the single population has risen dramatically in our time. Patriarchal condemnation of homosexuality has been countered by a growing willingness on the part of gays and lesbians to claim their identities and to be themselves, openly and honestly.

This openness has forced this generation to deal with its

sexual prejudices as never before. This shift in consciousness away from patriarchal prejudices has also demanded a redefinition of God. The God of traditional Western religious thought has been a male deity designed to affirm the very assumptions that are destined to pass away. On various levels, all of us are aware of these changes and in varying ways we are all responding to them. The emotional range of our response is wide, running from welcoming enthusiasm to hostile condemnation. Both responses signal the importance and the reality of the changes. With these broad brush strokes in place, I will now fill in the details of my premises.

Before the patterns of change began to penetrate our minds, life was thought to be divinely ordered. Almost everyone had a designated place in which they were willing, if not always content, to live. A familiar church catechism caught this concept when it taught its adherents to say, "to do my duty in that state [place] of life unto which it shall please God to call me."[2]

By godly decree, the role of woman in the past was clear. She was created for marriage and motherhood. She was to be the keeper of the hearth, the rearer of children, obedient and loyal to her husband. If she did not marry she was viewed as a failure, called pejoratively "an old maid," and generally pitied. Before marriage, at least in the dominant strand of the social order, she was expected to be chaste. Elaborate control or chaperone systems were developed to guarantee that chastity. The typical male expected his spouse to be virgin at marriage and faithful after marriage. Her goodness and success as a woman were determined by how well she satisfied these expectations.

The role of the man in that era was also equally well defined: His task was to be the breadwinner. His masculine power was defined largely by the effectiveness with which he competed in order to carry out this assignment. He was the patriarch, the king of his household, the decision maker, and his wife and children were expected to serve him. A male occupation was usually chosen for him, within very specific limits set by his father. Most often it related to the task historically performed by the males in his unit of society, which up to the industrial revolution in the nineteenth century was usually agricultural in nature, the land being the backbone of the economy. When particular skills were required, an apprenticeship program was developed. That, too, had a patriarchal shape based on the relationship of master and servant. All of life was molded by the hierarchical values of the patriarchy.

The formal schooling that did exist for the general population also bore the stamp of the patriarchal mind-set. The schoolmaster was a father-substitute who possessed ultimate authority in the classroom. Strict discipline, including corporal punishment, was the order of the day. The curriculum differed according to the sexual stereotypes of the day. Boys were taught math, science, and philosophy; girls were taught music, poetry, and fine arts.

A lid was set on how much education a girl really needed. Colleges, at their beginnings, were reserved primarily for a few privileged men. When the occupation of schoolteacher was finally opened to women (it paid too poorly to attract enough men), training schools for teachers were established. In time these would evolve into women's colleges. Coeducational schools were unimaginable. Men and women were thought to be so vastly different in nature that no educational track could be designed to fit both. Female institutions of higher learning, originally called "teacher's colleges," took quite seriously the task of guarding and protecting the virtue and the reputation of their students via many heavy-handed rules and regulations. Administrators and faculty regarded themselves as *in loco parentis*.

In that day and time no one would have suggested that marriage should be a relationship of peers. The wife was much more like an honored servant, with bedroom duty and privileges. She was not expected to be able to engage her husband in significant conversation. For her to have opinions about politics, history, or business was simply not appropriate, since those topics were clearly in the male domain.

This understanding of human life was functioning when the Constitution of the United States was written. The citizens who made up the body politic were landowners, presumed to be men since in most states women could not own property. Women, slaves, children, and poor tenant farmers did not share in the ownership and franchise of this nation. Since this order of life was believed to have been ordained by God and built into his creation, it was unquestioned. To rebel against it was to rebel against the "Father" God. "As it was in the beginning, is now and ever shall be," was part of the language of regimentation. Change in the social order was to be resisted.

In Illinois in 1873, a woman named Myra Bradford wanted to practice law. She passed all the required examinations but was nonetheless forbidden to practice, for that necessitated an official license from her state that was not forthcoming. She sued. The case went all the way to the Supreme Court where, by an 8 to 1 vote, her petition was denied. Justice Joseph Bradley, writing the majority opinion, stated that "the natural proper timidity and delicacy which belongs to the female sex evidently unfits it for many of the occupations of civil life. The constitution of the family organization which is founded in the divine ordinance as well as in the nature of things indicates the domestic sphere as that which properly belongs to the domain and function of womanhood. The paramount destiny and mission of women is to fulfill the noble and benign office of wife and mother."[3] To that mentality change has certainly come. Today, women not only practice law in Illinois, but a woman sits on the Supreme Court of the United States, making its 1873 decision visually inoperative. "The divine ordinance" to which Justice Bradley referred no longer seems either divine or eternal.

In a quest for more civic privilege and authority, women began their fight for the vote shortly after the Constitution was adopted. Following the American Civil War, the franchise was extended to newly emancipated black men with the passage of the Fifteenth Amendment to the Constitution in 1870. This fueled the suffrage movement among women, who argued that they, like the former slaves, could no longer be regarded as illiterate or irresponsible property. The holders of power first laughed, then got angry, then resisted vigorously, but all to no avail.

The women's suffrage movement grew, as increasingly independent women began to swell the professional ranks of schoolteachers, nurses, and secretaries and started their upward economic climb. Finally, in 1920, the Nineteenth Amendment to the Constitution was ratified, giving women the power of the ballot box, an essential component of full citizenship. Twelve years later a woman named Frances Perkins received a cabinet appointment from a newly elected president. Within only sixty-three years a woman was nominated for the vice-presidency of the United States by one of the two major American political parties. The entire political arena of this nation, with its moral ambiguities and intrigues, was now open to women. The patriarchal structure of life, once so dominant that it ruled with little challenge, began visibly fading. When the order of the past collapsed, the stereotypical roles of male and female on which that order was built were not sustainable. The changes wrought eroded traditional sex roles and altered the balance of power between the sexes, giving birth to the sexual revolution of the twentieth century.

When this revolution began to crack patriarchal patterns of morality, there was an immediate outcry and a rush to repair the breach. The circles of masculine power, especially the circles of religious power, insisted that the existing moral codes were immutable. Like the Ten Commandments, they were carved in stone and were quite permanent. God's law was universal and more stable even than the "Law of the Medes and the Persians." Religious myths invariably depicted the deity writing down the rules by which the covenanting people agreed to live. These rules were then invested with the dignity of being expressions of the sacred will of God,[4] making any change in the prevailing practice a violation of God's will.

But the change continued despite this resistance, condemnation, and the appeal to the divine order. Something was emerging that could not be stopped. The moral codes governing sexual behavior are today being rewritten in both practice and law, quite unaffected by the voices that seek to contain, control, or condemn. One seminary dean recently wrote that any attempt to rethink ethics, or to change the paternal nature of God, or to surrender the exclusive claim that one small group possesses the only truth, must be "countered at every level."[5] Such stances are as grandly impotent as Don Quixote's tilting at windmills. The world, with its values, its definitions, is changing not because people are becoming immoral but because the human understanding of life is changing. In the words of one nineteenth-century hymn, "New occasions teach new duties,/Time makes ancient good uncouth."[6] One can hardly expect all sexual stereotypes to change without a resulting change in sexual behavior. With dynamic new perceptions of truth arising from scientific investigations, and new insights from changing historic perspectives, sexual patterns were destined to be in flux.

Of course, moral patterns never were quite the way those who call us to reaffirm "traditional morality" think they were. Marriage, for example, was not ever universally required to legitimize sexual activity, even in Western Christian society. In some nations of the Western world, older and sexually experienced women were expected to initiate young post-pubescent boys into the mysteries of lovemaking. This would prepare a young man to be a gentle and effective lover with his virgin bride. In less structured ways, men were never required to wait until marriage for sex. Prostitutes, servants, lower-class women, and women of oppressed racial minorities were regularly used as sexual objects by socially prominent young men. Only the woman (and only certain women, at that) was required to "save herself for marriage," and marriage in fact bound only the sexual activity of the wife to her husband, not vice versa.

The true agenda of marriage at its inception was by far more economic than it was moral. The woman would produce the heirs to the man's wealth and property. Among the upper classes, who really made the rules, the virgin status of one's bride and the faithfulness of the married woman were the only guarantees a man had that his heir would be legitimate and therefore the one to whom he could pass on his fortune. As one wag suggested, the essential difference between knowledge and faith is that in childbirth the woman knows the baby is hers, while the man only has faith. The only way faith could be changed into indisputable knowledge for the man was through strong moral prohibitions on female extramarital sex and the organization of society to prevent a wife from having any opportunity to be indiscreet. Religious, cultural, political, and economic institutions provided those prohibitions.

This is why marriage was never demanded or enforced, even by the church, among the lower classes until very late in Western history. The peasants had no wealth to preserve, so they never developed any great need for a marriage ceremony to cement restrictions around the wife. In seventeenth-century England, for example, the vast majority of couples who brought their children to be baptized were listed in English church registers as having common-law marriages. Without benefit of clergy, lower-class men and women simply began living together. The church, at least in England, participated in these patterns for centuries. In the past, the world was not as concerned about sexual morality as many of today's moralizers imagine.

In time, however, the stated moral norm of monogamous marriage did gain ascendency and was saluted as good and proper, and it did serve as a stabilizer of life and a sanctifier of the home. The prime beneficiaries of that system were content to allow it to be thought of as an expression of the will of God, a mark of good breeding, or even as the only behavior pattern assumed to be moral.

Irresistibly, though, the forces of change that would forever shape the institution of marriage were gathering momentum. One rather impersonal agent of change was the steady but sure decline in the average age for the onset of puberty. In the seventeenth and eighteenth centuries, it was not unusual for young girls to commence their menstrual cycles as late as ages sixteen and seventeen. Through better diet and health care the age at puberty for boys and girls has been dropping on an average of six months every fifty to one hundred years.[7] Today's young people become sexually mature significantly earlier than did their great-great-grand-mothers and grandfathers. Most young girls in today's society begin menstruating by the end of the twelfth or thirteenth year of their lives.

If there had been no other changes, this alone would have greatly lengthened the period between puberty and marriage, unless the age of marriage dropped correspondingly. In fact, exactly the opposite has occurred. While natural forces lowered the age of puberty, cultural forces have postponed the age of marriage, principal among them the opening of educational opportunities to women, the increasing length of time required to complete an education, and the requirement of higher and higher levels of expertise for both men and women.

My mother, who was born in 1907, had her formal schooling halted six weeks into the ninth grade by my grandfather, who believed it was a waste of time to educate girls. The women in my mother's generation who went to college were few indeed. My daughters, who were born in 1955, 1958, and 1959, were part of a generation in which women went to college in almost equal numbers with men. Each of my daughters attended universities that had been coeducational less than a decade.

Today, when puberty has been separated from marriage by ten or more years, can cultural and moral norms continue to insist that the only proper sexual outlet is inside marriage? That places ethical norms into conflict with biological reality. Moral law must be in harmony with nature. Have we as a society stopped to weigh the impact on sexual morality of these changes?

Another factor changing sexual ethics today was the technological breakthrough producing reliable birth control methods. The fear of pregnancy has in the past been a powerful deterrent to non-marital sexual activity. The desire to limit and control pregnancy is as ancient as human indiscretion and temptation. Male withdrawal before orgasm was described as early as in the book of Genesis, in the story of Onan (Gen. 38). From ancient times "safe" and "fertile" periods were tracked. Medicines were ingested and barrier devices were fashioned, but all were, by and large, ineffective. Fear of pregnancy kept the woman chaste. That fear was supported by a powerful cultural condemnation of the adulterous woman who bore a child out of wedlock. Nathaniel Hawthorne explored the fury of this condemnation in *The Scarlet Letter* (1850).

This same fear of pregnancy also served to encourage the taking of mistresses, as a sexual outlet for the male. A woman who had already borne five or six children may have felt more relieved than betrayed when her husband took on a new romantic interest. The role of mistress was eventually institutionalized in many countries and ceased to be a matter of popular moral concern. Of course, the proper woman was guarded sexually and never given the opportunity to take a lover on the side with tacit approval from the community. But twentieth-century innovations in birth control—what Madonna Kolbenschlag calls "the great emancipator" of women[8]—doomed the old sexual economy.

With the resulting equalization of the sexes, what was sauce for the gander became sauce for the goose. All of those outlets that male-dominated society had set up to protect and control the female, while accommodating the male's desire for additional sexual outlets, were called into question. No longer was a mistress a male necessity, under the guise of providing him a sexual outlet that did not risk an unwanted pregnancy for his wife. A man could quite literally cleave to his wife in faithfulness and mutual pleasure without such a fear. The development of effective birth control might have been the means whereby monogamy was finally established as the operative as well as the theoretical pattern of sexual behavior. But men, having never been bound sexually and having little inclination toward such binding, declined to allow this technological breakthrough to limit them in any way. The woman, though, having been imprisoned for centuries inside a male-dominated system, discovered sexual freedom and socio-political equality simultaneously.

The sexual revolution was on. The forces of change gathered, the pace accelerated, the tide became inexorable. Woman's suffrage; increased educational opportunities for women; coeducational colleges that refused to oversee private behavior; the development of the nuclear family necessitating apartments for unmarried singles where no parental eyes could stare; the social mobility, assisted by ever-improving transportation systems, which increased anonymity; the entry of women into the work force; the opening of executive and professional ranks to women—all these combined with effective birth control to change the shape of history. These were the forces that dismantled the patriarchal control system, and the reasons why the moral norms of a bygone era are not holding.

Of course the moralists, most of whose public voices were male, expressed grave concern. The world they knew and loved, the world that had served them well, was and is dying. The era of male domination is on its way out.

When the social systems of the past fail, when yesterday's prohibitions fall, it is easy to believe that moral anarchy and even insanity will soon follow. The excesses that invariably accompany times of revolutionary change are sometimes enough to convince many that such an age has already arrived. In time, however, new laws and guidelines for self-restraint collect around newly perceived values, enabling them to flourish and to work for good. That is surely happening today. In both religious and secular circles the lesson has been learned that promiscuous sexual behavior is destructive spiritually and emotionally as well as physically—that no sexual encounter can be so casual that it has no effect. The whole social order has backed away from the sexual experimentation that was so commonplace at the height of the revolution.

The alternative of returning to the sexual patterns of the distant past, however, is no longer open to us. There can be and will be no return to the values and virtues of that patriarchal age in which what most people define as "traditional" moral norms were developed. More and more, we will witness the expansion of that gray area bounded by promiscuity on one side and sex only inside marriage on the other. Most people will live inside this area of relativity, of uncertainty, of various levels of commitment and various kinds of sexual practices. It will be in the gray area that new values will need to be formulated.

What men and women are engaged in today is a battle to redefine who they are—in a new era, with new knowledge and new consciousness. The call to the church in this era is a call to be present with its people in that expanding gray center of life, to assist in the search for behavior patterns that will enhance the lives of all people. The time has come for the church, if it wishes to have any credibility as a relevant institution, to look at the issues of single people, divorcing people, post-married people, and gay and lesbian people from a point of view removed from the patriarchal patterns of the past, and to help these people find a path that leads to a life-affirming holiness. Is it too much to think that those gifts might come from the church? I think not.

Notes

1. Fritjof Capra, *The Turning Point* (New York: Simon & Schuster, 1982), pp. 35-39.
2. The Episcopal Church, *The Book of Common Prayer* (Greenwich, Conn.: Seabury Press, 1928), p. 580.
3. Supreme Court case of Bradford vs. the State of Illinois, 1873.
4. John S. Spong and Denise G. Haines, *Beyond Moralism* (San Francisco: Harper & Row, 1986).
5. John H. Rodgers, "The Seed and The Harvest," *Trinity School for Ministry* 3, no. 6 (July 1987).
6. James Russell Lowell, "Once to Every Man and Nation," 1845. It is interesting to note that The Episcopal Church did not use this hymn in its revised hymnal, put out in 1982. Not only were the words sexist, but the editorial committee did not believe that the divine moment for choice comes only "once to every man and nation."
7. Janice Delany, Emily Toth, and Mary Jane Lupton, *The Curse: A Cultural History of Menstruation* (New York: Dutton, 1976).
8. Madonna Kolbenschlag, *Kiss Sleeping Beauty Good-Bye* (San Francisco: Harper & Row, 1988).

CHAPTER FOUR

Divorce: Not Always Evil

A dominance-subordinance relationship is the model by which marriage is understood in a patriarchal society. Forces that destabilize the underpinnings of the patriarchal society will also contribute to the breakdown of the institution of marriage, as that society has interpreted it. That indeed is going on at this moment, as the divorce rate indicates.

From an almost imperceptible beginning several centuries ago, the shift in the power differential between the sexes has accelerated to a breakneck speed in our generation. In the space of one decade the whole society has come to be sensitive to sexist, non-inclusive language. The media speak of firefighters and chairwomen; churches refer to sons and daughters of a God who is being imaged with maternal as well as paternal qualities. Professional positions that fifty years ago no one could have imagined being filled by women have now been opened to them. Patriarchal models of marriage are likewise in retreat. Before discussing the high incidence of divorce, it would be well to look at both causes and symptoms in the process of change. Perhaps the high divorce rate represents something positive rather than negative for human life.

In the latter years of the nineteenth century, the invention of the microscope allowed the human eye (a male eye it certainly was) to see an ovum for the first time. The existence of the ovum had long been assumed, but it had never been seen. This conjunction of theory and data was a dramatic moment in human history, with ramifications far beyond the scientific. It established once and for all the fact that the woman was a partner equal in every way to the man in the reproductive process. As commonplace as that assumption is today, its recent origins will come as a surprise.

It seems apparent from myth, taboo, and folklore that in prehistoric times the connection between sexual intercourse and pregnancy was not comprehended. Jean Auel, in her carefully researched novels about Neanderthal life,[1] suggests that the common wisdom among Neanderthal people was that in some strange way the "spirit" of the male was caught by the female and produced the babe in her womb. The period of nine months between conception and delivery was simply too long for their primitive cause-and-effect understanding of human life. All they knew was that women produced babies and somehow shared in the power of the earth mother.

With the rise of patriarchy some seven to ten thousand years ago, the role of the woman as the recipient of the child's spirit diminished in the popular mind. In the Mediterranean countries at the dawn of the Christian era, the accepted view of reproduction was that the whole potential child existed in the spermatozoon of the male. He planted this child in the neutral womb of his mate, who added nothing to the genetic makeup of the infant but served only as the incubator for the man's child. (Our language reflects this inaccurate view of conception: We still refer to the role of women in childbearing by saying things like "She had his baby" or "She gave him three beautiful children.") However, she was also somehow thought to be responsible for the sex of the child. A woman who did not produce a son for her husband was quite blameworthy. Not to produce a son indicated that her female nature was not "receptive" enough—and to be barren meant that the woman was an inadequate receptacle.

This distinctively male bias informs the Christian myth of the virgin birth of Jesus. For Jesus to be God's Son, only the man had to be removed from the reproduction process. It did not compromise the early Christians' claim of a divine origin for Jesus if his mother was human, since the woman provided only the womb that received and nurtured the developing fetus.

When the mutuality of the genetic process came to be understood, then the choice of a man's mate began to be a far more important decision. Not only did he marry into a family with a particular socio-economic status, but he also married into a chromosome pool that would in part determine the individual potential of each child. That is why the actual sight of the ovum through the microscope lens was a watershed moment in the journey toward sexual equality. The status of married women could not have improved until their coequal role in reproduction had been established.

This power shift has even been noted liturgically. There was once a time when most Christian marriage ceremonies required the bride to promise to love, honor, and obey her husband. Obedience is a quality appropriate to the master-slave or the parent-child or even the master-pet relationship. It certainly is not appropriate to a mutual or peer relationship. Indeed, only a society that believes women to be inferior to men would require of the woman an oath of obedience to her husband. This vow has now been deleted from most wedding ceremonies, or has at least become optional since the early part of the twentieth century.

Other subtle hints of female second-class status were not so easily expunged. Until well into the decade of the seventies, in *The Book of Common Prayer* the bride was asked to "give her troth" while the groom was requested only to "pledge" his troth. In the climax to the traditional wedding ceremony, the officiating minister, acknowledging that the union had been accomplished, said, "I pronounce you man and wife." Presumably, the groom was a man before the ceremony, so the liturgical action had not changed his identity. The woman, however, had become a new thing: a wife, with all of the attached legal control mechanisms. Newer liturgies have since equalized the commitment, so that both partners now say something like "This is my solemn vow" and are pronounced "husband and wife."

But these are essentially only cosmetic changes, since the ultimate symbol of female degradation in marriage has persisted, in the form of the officiating minister's question, "Who gives this woman to be married to this man?" Normally, the father of the bride, who had marched his daughter down the aisle, responded, "I do," and so one man gave the woman away to another man. One does not give away what one does not own. By implication the bride was her father's property and as such she could be given, sometimes even sold for a bride's price or dowry, to another man. As sensitivities have risen, this embarrassing liturgical anachronism has been changed a little. The father may now say, "Her mother and I do," or the parents might say together, "We do." The 1979 edition of *The Book of Common Prayer* changes the word "give" to the word "present" and suggests that the man may be presented along with the woman. But the liturgy has never included the question, "Who gives this man to be married to this woman?" because that would challenge the very assumptions about patriarchal marriage the liturgy has been designed to uphold.

Since for most of recorded history women in large measure lacked economic power and the political and social means to achieve it, they had to rely upon marriage as their primary means to gain security. A wife was thus a kept woman. No matter how unsatisfying or impossible the marriage relationship might become, divorce was usually worse for the woman. The courts were male-controlled. Female judges are a twentieth-century phenomenon, as are female lawyers and female jurors. For those few cases that did reach the divorce courts, the basic economic unfairness of this system was addressed through the imposition of alimony and child-care subsidies, though these might not be forthcoming if the woman was perceived to be blameworthy. The divorced woman could then live on court-ordered payments from her ex-spouse. So even in her divorced state, she remained a kept woman. Moreover, the courts were both inefficient and uninterested in enforcing divorce settlements, so the divorced woman quite frequently lived with chronic uncertainty and in poverty.

Ownership of capital was rarely transferred in a divorce settlement from husband to wife. The woman's inability to deal adequately with investments was assumed, making such arrangements seem foolish. Into many a divorce settlement was also written a proviso that alimony payments would cease if the divorced spouse ever remarried. The implication was that when another man assumed economic responsibility for the divorced woman, presumably in exchange for her domestic contributions and her sexual favors, the obligation of the original husband would come to an end.

Under these conditions, women in particular avoided divorce. The woman would endure behavior that was sometimes abusive; she would absorb the attacks on her dignity that her husband's infidelity, sometimes quite blatant, would heap upon her; but economic survival demanded that she remain in the oppressive marriage. The primary initiator of divorce in this era was the man. Occasionally the woman's family might be of such financial and social standing that she could dare to demand divorce. However, even in some of those cases her inheritance from her own family had been placed at the time of the marriage under her husband's control. So few job opportunities awaited the unattached woman that domestic service, sweatshops, or prostitution were sometimes her only alternatives to remaining in a cruel marriage.

Slowly but surely, in this last century, the economic independence of women has risen, and in proportion the patriarchal conditions of marriage have decreased. When World War II drained the supply of men into the armed forces, women enjoyed a dramatic increase in economic power. Suddenly, working outside the home was not demeaning. It became a woman's patriotic duty, and in answer to the call she even took on heavy industrial jobs that once were strictly male turf. Western propaganda legitimized the unprecedented situation, extolling the virtues of "Rosie the Riveter."

Even the armed forces were integrated by women during World War II. Women performed secretarial and maintenance jobs, which released more soldiers and sailors for the manly art of war. (No one thought that these women's corps would become permanent or that they would in time produce women generals and colonels, admirals and captains, but indeed that has now happened.) There was also a very male-informed wartime expectation that when the fighting ceased and things returned to normal, the women would retire to home and hearth, gladly handing these responsibilities back over to the men. Little did people realize what a taste of economic power would do to women's yearnings for independence.

After World War II the college rush began in earnest, as young men and returning veterans sought to expand their horizons through higher education. Women would not be denied this opportunity. State universities were sued to stop discriminating and to admit women. The segregated, state-supported women's colleges declined in status. Eventually the all-female private colleges began admitting men. Today the once-strong academic bastions of male dominance have a high percentage of female students. With the fall of such symbols of gender discrimination as the famed sexually segregated eating clubs on the prestige campuses, it became clear that eventually women would invade the professional graduate schools and the schools of business, engineering, medicine, and law.

A woman was no longer limited to being a secretary or even an administrative assistant, nurse, dental hygienist, or paralegal. The tide of equality was coming in strongly. Nothing could hold it back. Today there are women bank presidents and vice-presidents, women attorney generals and district attorneys, women scientists and astronauts, women surgeons and medical school professors, women clergy. Women are now present in almost every decision-making function in our society.

We have even developed sex-neuter terms to describe the emerging egalitarian members of this new world. They are called yuppies (young upwardly mobile professionals), muppies (middle-aged upwardly mobile professionals), and dinks (double income, no kids). Mandatory economic dependency for women, as a class, has ended. Even alimony is gradually disappearing, and a division of property has taken its place. The prevailing assumption is that today's men and women are equally capable in most cases of earning an adequate living, so the accumulated capital wealth is shared equally. (That assumption is not accurate in many cases, however. Single women and their children now make up the majority of poor households in our society.)

When mutuality is a factor in the marriage relationship, when equal opportunity is available in education, earning capacity, and social standing, then marriage becomes a very different entity from what it was in more patriarchal times. Marriage has increasingly become a partnership that implies peership. It projects a new and different image that affects every aspect of our common life.

Sexual partners come together to meet the needs of not just one person but of both partners. Women today are presumed to need, want, and enjoy sex as much or as little as men. That was not assumed in previous centuries, when young brides were instructed by their mothers in their sexual duty. "Just close your eyes and think of England" was the classic Victorian premarital advice. Mutual pleasure in the sex act, with the accent on mutual, is now extolled in all the sex manuals as the ultimate goal, the *sine qua non* of good sex. Expectations about sharing and egalitarian patterns of behavior are pushing the patriarchal order of yesterday off the center stage of human expectations.

Marriage is ceasing to be a power relationship between two unequal persons. Increasingly it is seen as a relationship between two persons who want to create a new life together, share sexual pleasure, work in concert for the economic well-being of the family unit, and be partners in planning their older years together. In such a relationship the possibility of open conflict will necessarily be greater. One person can no longer end the discussion by imposing unilaterally upon the other. In a partnership marriage, the oath of fidelity and care for the well-being of the other will bind both partners, or it will bind neither.

If one partner wants to enter into an extramarital sexual liaison, the opportunity to escape the gossip of the local community, in this highly mobile society, is now equally available to both man and woman. Briefcase-carrying women on business trips are a common sight at airports across the land. Motels, once the favorite place for the traveling man to arrange a secret tryst, are now catering more and more to the presence of professional women.

As the woman's economic power rises, industry after industry has shaped its products and its advertisements to meet its newly discovered female constituency. The major economic decisions of the family, once the male domain, are now made by both men and women. Even such destructive habits as smoking have become equalized. No longer do the men retire to the library to smoke cigars and carry on business talk after a meal, while the women converse over coffee in the parlor—it's cocktails and cigarettes all around now, for those who partake.

The opportunity to divorce a spouse is now also shared between men and women. Although I do not want to promote divorce, I do recognize that it must be equally available to husband and wife. Once it was an option basically only for the man. That is a fundamental change in the sexual power structure. At the very least it means that our society has successfully doubled the number of people who are able to contemplate and carry through on a divorce. For that reason alone the divorce rate would be rising.

There are other reasons, however, for the increased frequency of divorce. With the decline of concern about patriarchally defined property, the stigma against divorce has lessened. When Adlai Stevenson, Jr., ran for president of the United States in 1952 and 1956, much was made of the fact that he was a divorced man. He never remarried, so he avoided offending any decision-making ecclesiastical body by seeking to enter a second marriage. This nation, however, was not certain it could allow a divorced man into the White House. Yet less than twenty years later it accepted the fact that Gerald Ford was married to a divorced woman, and one administration after that America twice elected a divorced and remarried man, Ronald Reagan, to the presidency. His marital status was not once an issue. The queen of England and the Pope both royally received him and his second wife. This was something Wallis Simpson did not receive from English royalty, nor did Henry VIII receive it from the papacy.

Today, divorced persons are regularly remarried in Anglican, Protestant, and Roman Catholic liturgies. Often the official church position is still, in varying degrees, against divorce and remarriage. In practice, the fact remains that with carefully constructed word changes (i.e., divorce becomes annulment) and a willingness to go through a laborious and costly process, almost anyone who wishes can be remarried, with that person's church conveying its blessing.

It is fascinating to reflect on how the male-dominated church has historically regarded divorce. Divorce was the only failure, indiscretion, or sin that was incorporated into official canon law. The church felt no need to have canons on murder, bank robbery, child molesting, or arson. Only the divorced and remarried person was punished by automatic excommunication. Divorce threatened the structure of life and the power of the church in a serious and disturbing way. One does not waste energy either institutionally or individually in confronting issues that are of no consequence. The church confronted divorce, legislated against it, punished those who participated in it, purged its ranks of those who moved beyond it into a second marriage, and made sexual abstinence the only option for the divorced.

Today, despite threats and loud protests from the official voices of organized religion, divorce has become not just legal but almost commonplace. That frequency of marital fracture is hardly to be applauded, but it is also not to be condemned. Divorce has some very positive values that must be isolated and supported, as well as destructive potential that needs to be minimized.

The necessary stance for the church today, it seems to me, is to take both marriage and divorce quite seriously. The church should recognize and state quite openly that divorce is not an unforgivable sin, nor is it always tragic; indeed, in some instances divorce is and can be positive and good. After having done all it can to fulfill its vow to support the marriage, the church also needs to undergird divorcing persons when they make that decision. Passive, benign rejection is neither helpful nor compassionate.

The gifts that help a modern marriage succeed are mutual attentiveness, the ability to practice self-sacrifice, and a willingness to negotiate. Negotiation requires flexibility and presumes an equality of power to shape the final decision.

Divorce becomes one alternative to conflict that cannot be resolved, in that it can be chosen equally by either partner. As such it is morally neuter and does not merit the automatic response of condemnation from the church. Divorce has become part of the cost that society must pay for the emancipation of women. An early reversal of the high divorce rate would require, I believe, suppression of the growing equality between the sexes. That is too expensive a price. The church accepts this fact in practice. Approximately half of all the marriages performed in my episcopal jurisdiction are of divorced persons. It is time we stated positively that divorcing people are not always evil, not always sinful, not always to be condemned. Sometimes divorce is the way to an abundant new life for one or both of the formally linked partners.

Women are discovering that not only are they free to leave a destructive marriage without ruining their lives—they may choose not to be married at all. Further, women who want children may opt to raise them as a single parent. Marriage is no longer the universal vocation. Women are discovering in their careers the emotional fulfillment that men have long known could be there. Those women able to achieve economic independence may find marriage a career detriment and a financial liability. Should they be forced by the expectations of society into marriage for the sake of companionship and for the gratification of sexual needs? Similarly, motherhood is no longer a woman's biological destiny. Her choice not to bear or raise children, or to do so apart from a primary relationship, further shakes the rationale that undergirds the institution of patriarchal marriage.

This issue of whether to marry is posed poignantly for those divorced women and men in whom the hurt of a failed marriage remains. Such persons are more aware than most of the trauma of divorce. There may be an unwillingness to become vulnerable to that hurt again, yet no one loses the need for companionship, admiration, and affection. What might the nature of a relationship be if a divorced woman or man is neither able nor willing to make an avowed commitment? Is marriage the only relationship in which the intimacy of sexual love can be shared at every stage of life? That issue will be looked at in depth in chapter 13. Suffice it now to say that marriage is not in the life plan of many single adults, for a wide variety of good and sufficient reasons. That fact needs to be affirmed.

These unmarried adults are not and will not be bound by the moralistic judgments of the past that guaranteed a dependent status for the woman. They do not fit into conventional molds nor are they willing to try to. For the most part they are not promiscuous; promiscuity is the lifestyle of a very small percentage of people. A responsible relationship is more frequently the case. Can this not be held up as good by a just society and a church committed to moral standards?

The pursuit of separate but equally demanding careers has brought a new tension to marriage. When that tension causes a marriage to break up, who is to say that the divorcing couple is wrong and the repressive system of the past is right? What moral issues need to be faced? Does the group of people for whom marriage is an asset have a right to impose the standard that enhances their lives upon those people who have chosen a different path? Is there only one lifestyle that is moral? What makes it so? From whence comes the assumption that sex inside marriage is always holy? Marriage does not make sex holy, the quality of the relationship does. Is sex outside marriage always sinful? What happens when we apply the biblical standard of judging the tree by its fruit? Suppose the manifestations of a committed but unmarried relationship are love, joy, and peace, while bitterness, pain, and hurt are the products of a legal marriage. In what qualities does holiness reside? Can traditional morality be adapted so that the good things it sought to ensure with its particular prohibitions and affirmations might still be accomplished inside a new set of affirmations and prohibitions that are appropriate to the contemporary values that have been embraced by both men and women?

For the church to have no word for this significant group in our society except a word of condemnation is unworthy. For the church to speak judgmentally and moralistically, without giving the slightest indication that the positive and good forces that fuel the changing mores have been grasped or understood, is itself immoral. For the church not to recognize that its traditional moral codes rise out of, enforce, and interpret a system of male oppression of women is irresponsible.

Inside the struggle for integrity and meaning and amid changing circumstances is the place the church needs to be. The church will have an authoritative voice in that arena, however, only as long as people perceive that the primary message the church proclaims is not a threadbare and pious call to return to the moral conclusions of the past, without regard for those who have been and would be again traditionally the victims of those conclusions.

I, for one, am no longer willing to acknowledge the claim that morality has been frozen in an era that primarily served the dominant male. Nor do I share a sense of regret that this moral understanding is passing away. I dare, rather, to claim that a new morality is emerging that does manifest the fruits of the Spirit and that is built on the foundation of the mutuality of the sexes. In the name of all those who will benefit from this emerging consciousness, I welcome the new day and believe that the God who continues to call new possibilities into being will look out upon this new creation and pronounce it good.

Notes

[1] Jean M. Auel, *The Clan of the Cave Bear* (New York: Crown, 1980); *The Valley of the Horses* (New York: Crown, 1982); *The Mammoth Hunters* (New York: Crown, 1985).

CHAPTER FIVE

Homosexuality: A Part of Life, Not a Curse

The verb "to be" is the key verb in every human language. We use it to describe that which is of our very essence. If I have a broken leg I do not say, "I am a broken leg." But if my leg has been amputated, I might well say, "I am an amputee." The amputation has redefined my being. I might say, "I have measles" to explain a rash, or "I have cancer" to explain a physical pain. The verb "to be" is used when we say, "I am tall," "I am blue eyed," "I am male," or "I am female." It is employed to describe the essential characteristics of life over which we have no control, or that which is so much a part of our identity that we cannot think of ourselves apart from it.

Language reveals far more than we imagine when we say, "I am heterosexual," or "I am gay", or "I am a lesbian." We now know that homosexuality is part of the essential nature of approximately 10 percent of the population. Statistically this means that in the United States of America, homosexuality is the sexual orientation of some twenty-eight million citizens. It means that every time one hundred people gather in a church anywhere in this nation, the mathematical probability is that ten of them are gay or lesbian persons. It means that no one of us ever goes through a day encountering or transacting business with as few as ten people without the probability that one of those ten is a homosexual person. It means that in every core family or extended family, when the circle expands to ten persons, there is a mathematical probability that one member will be gay or lesbian. The gay and lesbian population is all around us, touching our lives at numerous points, receiving our love and friendship, serving us with professional competence in a myriad of ways, even listening to and laughing at our jokes and our not-so-subtle innuendos about homosexuality.

In prior generations these homosexual individuals have lived in silence, hiding in the shadows or blending unnoticed into the majority society. Today gay and lesbian persons are emerging from their closets, identifying themselves publicly, and demanding justice, recognition, and acceptance. They represent one additional factor in the changing sexual landscape. No treatment of human sexuality can avoid confrontation with the prevailing cultural prejudices against gay and lesbian people, nor can the ever-present phenomenon of homosexuality itself be ignored.

Homosexuality has been diagnosed in the past as a mental sickness, a medical model that persists in the minds of many. Homosexuality as an illness, however, began to be questioned with the publication of the Kinsey reports in 1948 and 1953.[1] That questioning grew until the board of trustees of the American Psychiatric Association officially removed it in 1973 from the second edition of *The Diagnostic and Statistical Manual of Mental Disorders*. As the manual explains the decision,

The crucial issue in determining whether or not homosexuality per se should be regarded as a mental disorder is . . . its consequences and the definition of mental disorder. A significant proportion of homosexuals are apparently satisfied with their sexual orientation, show no significant signs of manifest psychopathology . . . and are able to function socially and occupationally with no impairment. If one uses the criteria of *distress* or *disability*, homosexuality per se is not a mental disorder. If one uses the criterion of *disadvantage,* it is not at all clear that homosexuality is a disadvantage in all cultures or subcultures.[2]

Anthropological studies affirm that latter conclusion. There have been some primitive societies in which male homosexuality, far from being treated as a perversion to be shunned, was looked upon as an honor, even as a special blessing from the deity. The homosexual man quite often was assigned the role of the shaman or holy man. He was sometimes thought of as a third sex and given tribal permission to wear female clothes and to perform, liturgically, acts that outside the liturgy would be thought of as belonging to the female domain.[3]

The lesbian received no such honors as far as anthropological studies indicate. As a subjected member of society, she was forced to undergo the regular sexual rituals of the tribe, to mate, and to reproduce, with or without her consent. It was and is more difficult to discern her as separate and distinct in the society. Even our prejudice has a patriarchal stamp.

The modern, prevailing notion that homosexuality is a mental disorder is rooted in Sigmund Freud's theory that it is an aberration that occurs when normal development is somehow distorted between the ages of four and nine.[4] Others, inspired by Freud, speculated on the psychic makeup and influence of the primary adults (usually the parents) in the maturation of the gay or lesbian person. This was a particularly cruel theory, for it placed on the parents blame for what was thought to be a neurotic development, and it fed the guilt and rejection that so often characterized the relationship of a homosexual son or daughter with his or her parents. Nonetheless, because these early medical theories promoted homosexuality as an illness of maladjustment, there was hope of cure. Psychoanalysis in the medical community, or prayer therapy and faith healing in the religious community, were the proffered treatments. A behavior pattern that is maladaptive or learned can presumably be changed into what the majority regards as wholeness.

Continued research in this area, however, has not produced such a cure. Instead it has increasingly falsified the idea that homosexuality is a mental illness. Many researchers believe that not one shred of reproducible evidence has come to light to substantiate clinically the illness theory. If, as is the case today, leading medical practitioners are no longer able to call homosexuality an illness, it then seems inappropriate for official church bodies to continue to pass resolutions based on this discredited medical premise. The church is either failing to realize its ignorance or is acting as if its leaders are privy to some special source of expertise.

There are others who judge homosexuality as a perversion deliberately chosen by those of a depraved or sinful nature. Many heterosexual people cannot imagine that homosexual lovemaking could be pleasurable; some even say they are revolted at the thought of it. Members of the dominant sexual orientation reason that what is normal for them is also natural; if something is not normal for them it must be deviant and, thus, depraved. A variation of this conclusion argues that since homosexual behavior is "unnatural," it is contrary to the order of creation. Behind this pronouncement are stereotypic definitions of masculinity and femininity that reflect the rigid gender categories that arise out of patriarchal society. "Natural" sex is based on the complimentary aspects of male and female genitalia. But the urgent question is, How important are the genitalia to sexual desire?

Rosemary Ruether has argued that men and women possess equally the physical apparatus necessary for emotional intimacy.[5] But human thinking has been so influenced by patriarchal values that the male-female relationship can be imagined only in terms of a power equation involving domination and subjection. Female receptivity to male penetration in the sex act has become a paradigm and a synonym for the natural. In this scheme, heterosexual activity is defined as the only valid expression of love. A corollary of this assumption suggests that the man has a gender-specific capacity for decisive action and the woman has a gender-specific capacity for passive intuition—a sixth sense, if you will.

We are moving away from that mentality. Personhood emerges not out of an imposed sexual role but out of the human ability to hear, feel, think, and relate. None of these abilities requires sex organs of any shape or description. Men and women alike have the physiology necessary to speak and hear, to love and be loved. Personal unity comes, Dr. Ruether attests, when one connects "the many parts of the self through multiple relationships with other people."[6] There is nothing unnatural about any shared love, even between two of the same gender, if that experience calls both partners into a fuller state of being. Can a religious tradition that has long practiced circumcision and institutionalized celibacy ever dismiss any other practice on the basis of its unnaturalness?

Contemporary research is today uncovering new facts that are producing a rising conviction that homosexuality, far from being a sickness, sin, perversion, or unnatural act, is a healthy, natural, and affirming form of human sexuality for some people. This research is still in its infancy, relatively speaking, but it has demonstrated a capacity to confront and challenge sexual fear and prejudice that has become entrenched by centuries of repetition. Only in the last few decades have we begun to understand such things as the structure and various functions of the brain, to say nothing of the importance of chromosomes. Discoveries in these areas have had a dramatic effect on our knowledge of human behavior. Specifically, research consistently seems to support the assertion that sexual orientation is not a matter of choice; that it is not related to any environmental influence; that it is not the result of an overbearing mother or an effeminate or absent father or a seductive sexual encounter. Some researchers are finding that certain biochemical events during prenatal life may determine adult sexual orientation, and that once set it is not amenable to change. Though new data are being gathered almost daily, few people working in the area of brain research expect these conclusions to be overturned.

Despite centuries of belief to the contrary, it is slowly dawning on us that the seat of sexual arousal is the brain, not the genitalia. To put it bluntly, this means that the brain is the primary sex organ of the body. A person's sexual orientation and what he or she finds sexually exciting are functions of that person's brain. An understanding of these new findings in the field of human sexuality must therefore begin with a look at modern discoveries about neurophysiology and its role in human learning.

In the animal world the line between male and female is not as rigid as many sex-role ideologues would have us believe. A report on issues concerning homosexuality produced by the Lutheran Church in America in 1986 cited some fascinating biological studies documenting this:

Among some species of fish, particularly the coral reef fish, a virtual sex change will occur in order to ensure reproduction. If a male is suddenly removed from his female partners, the most aggressive female first acts as the male, then functions as the male, and eventually even produces sperm. Among guinea pigs, the total repertoire of sexual behavior occurs at that moment when the adult female presents herself to the male for mounting and ejaculation. This experience is changed dramatically when the pregnant female guinea pig is treated with androgens or androgen blockers. In the case of the former, when the female offspring reaches maturity, she mounts other females; in the latter case, the male offspring presents himself for mounting to other males. Apart from this reversal, no other behavior inappropriate to gender was observed.[7]

These data would seem to indicate that sexual orientation and the behavior that arises from that orientation has a neurobiological explanation.

This conclusion has been further enforced by experimentation on rhesus monkeys. Tests reveal that when testosterone is blocked from male fetuses in utero, it produces behavior in the male offspring traditionally associated with the female monkey. This, despite the fact that no abnormal hormone balance registers after birth, nor does any subsequent hormone treatment change the monkey's activities to behavior more appropriate to the male of the species. These experiments suggest that a chemical process sets the nature of an unalterable sexual response in the brain during gestation. Or, to be quite specific, the "sexing of the brain" is a prenatal occurrence over which neither the fetus nor the parent has any control whatsoever.

These conclusions have been further augmented by the work of Gunter Dörner, director of the Institute of Experimental Endocrinology at the University of Humboldt in East Berlin. When the scientific community began to understand that it was the hypothalamus, located beneath the thalamus in the brain, that controlled the output of the hormones, Dörner set out to find in the hypothalamus of rats what he took to be different male and female sex centers. His experiments revealed that if rats did not get enough of their appropriate sex hormone during development these sex centers would be formed differently, creating in males the sexual behavior of females and vice versa.

From these data Dörner argued that sexual orientation in a human fetus is also the result of a neurochemical hormone process that occurs in the womb. Male and female homosexuality, he contended, are caused by the prenatal effect on the brain of varying amounts of a main male sex hormone, testosterone. The relative quantity of testosterone available during critical periods of fetal brain development stamps the yet to be born infant with a masculine or feminine orientation, usually but not always in accordance with the genetic sex of the fetus. This is true, he argued, not just in human beings but in monkeys, rats, guinea pigs, birds, and practically everywhere in nature. It remains a fact that among higher mammals homosexuality is found in roughly the same statistical percentages as is found among *Homo sapiens*.[8]

Dörner performed a series of experiments to test his hypothesis. Male rats were deprived of testosterone during the critical fetal period of sexual differentiation in the brain. As predicted, this process produced homosexual behaviors in the adult male rats. Encouraged by this result, he went a step further. Dörner reasoned that if these rats possessed feminized brains, injection with estrogen would produce from the brain a surge of the ovulation hormone known as luteinizing hormone (LH), as if in response to a signal from a nonexistent ovary. When this test was carried out, the predicted response occurred. The same test was then performed on male homosexual human beings, with identical results. The brains of the homosexual males in this experiment responded to the estrogen injection with an LH hormone surge, while the brains of a control group of heterosexual males did not. Dörner believed this demon-strated that the brains of male homosexuals had been, in fact, feminized prior to birth, and that homosexuality is thus physiologically determined by biochemical variables.[9] If true, this finding constitutes a powerful step forward in demonstrating the source and explanation for the reality of homosexuality.

Unfortunately, Dörner, out of an apparent bias, began to draw conclusions that were not justified by his research and that brought him quickly into conflict with the German medical establishment. Dörner saw homosexuality as something to be purged from human life by stopping it before it is formed. So, he literalized his conclusions and sought to devise a means to prevent in utero the formation of persons with homosexual orientations. In this process he went far beyond what his data could support. Critics, reacting to this excess, also tended to dismiss his findings. His findings, however, if not conclusive, are substantial and provocative. It is in the application of his findings that Dörner skates on very thin ice. He has tried to draw conclusions that are beyond the scope of his data. He could not recognize that a homosexual orientation might be both normal and valuable to the development of humanity. To understand its cause is not a call to devise a means to prevent it. Some things are better left to the evolutionary process that has carried us from single cells to self-consciousness over a period of hundreds of millions of years. The improper use of data does not mean that the data are inaccurate. Dörner's findings need to be taken seriously.

The story of the Dominican Republic children, recorded by Jo Durden-Smith and Diane de Simone, provides a striking additional confirmation of the thesis that the brain is "sexed" irrevocably before birth and that post-birth experiences cannot reprogram the brain in an alternate sexual direction. The story is so unusual that I will allow these authors to tell it themselves.

In the early 1970s, away from public attention, the descendants of Amaranta Ternera were discovered. And the controversy in science began.

Amaranta Ternera—we have changed, by request, her name and the names of her relatives—was born 130 years ago in the southwest corner of the Dominican Republic. There was nothing wrong with Amaranta, so far as we know; she seems to have led a normal and ordinary life. But there *was* something wrong with the genes she left behind her in her children. And there *is* something wrong with a number of her descendants. Seven generations later, Amaranta's genes have been located in twenty-three families in three separate villages. And in thirty-eight different individuals in these families the strange inheritance that Amaranta passed down to them has been expressed. These thirty-eight were born, to all appearances, as girls. They grew up as girls. And they became boys at puberty.

Take the ten children of Gerineldo and Pilar Babilonia, for example. Four of them have been through this extraordinary transformation. The eldest, Prudencio, was born with an apparent vagina and female body-shape, just like his next sister-brother, Matilda. Prudencio was christened Prudencia. And he grew up, Pilar says, tied to his mother's apron strings, kept apart from the village boys and helping with women's work. But then something strange began to happen to his body. His voice began to deepen. At around the age of twelve, his "clitoris" grew into a penis and two hidden testicles descended into a scrotum formed by the lips of his "vagina." He became a male. "He changed his clothes," says his father Gerineldo, "which the neighbors just had to get used to. And he fell in love with a girl almost immediately." Today Prudencio is in his early thirties. Like his brother Matilda, now Mateo, he is a brawny, elaborately muscled man. He is sexually potent and he lives with his wife in the United States. Like seventeen of the eighteen children studied by a group headed by Cornell University's Julianne Imperato-McGinley—all of whom, she says, were raised unambiguously as girls—Prudencio seems to have had no problem adjusting to male gender, male sexual orientation and male roles.

It is this which makes Prudencio and the other Dominican children important. *They seem to have had no problem adjusting to male gender, male sexual orientation and male roles.* Prudencio and the others are genetically male. But what they have inherited from Amaranta is not a general insensitivity to testosterone, but an inability to process it on to *another* hormone, dihydrotestosterone, which is responsible, in the male fetus, for shaping the male genitalia. In the absence of these, the Dominican children were born looking like girls and they were raised as girls. At puberty, though, their bodies were pervaded by a new rush of male hormones to which they were sensitive. Their male parts—which had been waiting in the wings, so to speak—finally established themselves. And nature finished the job it had earlier botched.

The children, though, did not have the psychological breakdown that the conventional wisdoms predict they should have had. This is crucial, for it *must* mean one of three things. Either the children were really raised as boys from the beginning. Or they were raised, at least, with a great deal of confusion about what gender they were, in which case one might expect them to have a disturbed sexuality as adults. Or they were born with a masculinized brain already established before birth in their "female" bodies, a male brain that slipped comfortably into male expressions when their bodies changed at puberty. By this argument, not only the body is sexed at birth but *also* the brain. And by this argument, nature, in gender behavior, is every bit as important as nurture. Learning, in fact, may have little to do with it.

The parents, as we have said—and Julianne Imperato-McGinley—insist that the Dominican children were raised unambiguously as girls. This means that the third hypothesis—that their brains were masculinized before birth by the main male hormone testosterone—must be taken very seriously.[10]

These accounts individually and collectively support the scientific claim that sexual orientation is, in all probability, a matter of the prenatal "sexing of the brain"; that homosexuality is thus a given fact in the nature of a significant portion of people; and that it is unchangeable once set. It is not genetic in nature, therefore it cannot be "bred out" of the species. The only argument remaining is whether or not this represents a malfunction in the natural process of fetal development or is instead a normal variation serving a purpose in the evolutionary process that has not yet been identified. However, any process of nature that occurs one time out of every ten can hardly be called a malfunction. Nature is far too exact, I believe, to admit that level of mistake. We are driven to the realization that what we have long viewed as a moral issue is in fact an ontological issue. Homosexuality is an issue of being itself.

When we turn to the field of genetics we find some additional studies helpful to our understanding of sexuality. There are twenty-three pairs of chromosomes in the nucleus of each human cell. Only one pair are sex chromosomes. Women have a double X set of sex chromosomes; men have an unmatched set labeled XY. Gender is determined at the moment of conception by the man when either an X or a Y sperm unites with the X chromosome in the ovum. The Y chromosome is responsible for the development of the testicles during the seventh week of gestation. Once formed, the testicles' Sertoli cells secrete a substance which *inhibits* the development of the female reproductive system. Thus, the biological structure of human life is oriented toward the development of females. The Y chromosome, which produces the testicles, interrupts and interferes with that process, allowing males with external genitalia to be born instead of females with internal genitalia.[11]

Variations on this regular genetic pattern do occur. Once in every five thousand births, for example, an individual is born with only one sex chromosome, a single X. That person is always female, but she has no ovaries. Still another variation is found in Klinefelter's Syndrome, where the person possesses three chromosomes: XXY. The resulting sterile male may develop some female characteristics; sometimes in the past these people made their livings in circus freak shows. The XYY variation is not necessarily a sterile male, but persons so shaped genetically tend to have a pronounced tendency toward aggression that has been identified in some studies of people with super-aggressive behavior that sometimes becomes antisocial. Nature's mistakes may be humanly tragic, but not for the species as a whole, since many aberrancies of sexual genotype lack the reproductive capacity.

I have verified that my conclusions possess high levels of probability with the help of Dr. Robert Lahita, associate professor of medicine at Cornell Medical Center in New York City. He became interested in this issue through his work in determining why certain diseases, such as lupus erythematosus, primarily affect women while others, such as dyslexia and autism, primarily affect men. He, like many scientists, has been distressed that official church bodies make decisions and ethical pronouncements based upon premises that are not supported by the scientific community. I share his distress. Sanctified ignorance is still ignorance.

Since the evidence points to the conclusion that homosexual persons do not choose their sexual orientation, cannot change it, and constitute a quite normal but minority expression of human sexuality, it is clear that heterosexual prejudice against homosexuals must take its place alongside witchcraft, slavery, and other ignorant beliefs and oppressive institutions that we have abandoned.

Some people fear that accepting this stance will mean that critical judgment must be suspended from all forms of homosexual behavior. That, too, is an irrational manifestation of prejudice. All forms of heterosexual behavior do not receive approval just because we affirm the goodness of heterosexuality. Any sexual behavior can be destructive, exploitative, predatory, or promiscuous, and therefore evil, regardless of the sexes of the parties involved. Whenever any of those conditions exist, a word of moral judgment needs to be spoken. The difficulty comes when a society evaluates heterosexuality per se as good and homosexuality per se as evil. Such moral absolutes eventuate in preferential ethical treatment for heterosexuals: Distinctions will be made for heterosexual people between life-giving and life-destroying behavior, while any and all patterns of sexual behavior arising from a homosexual orientation are condemned as sinful. Such a moral position leaves gay and lesbian persons with no options save denial or suppression. Indeed, many an ecclesiastical body has suggested that these are in fact the only moral choices open to homosexually oriented people. Perhaps we need to be reminded that large numbers of heterosexual people engage in promiscuity, prostitution, rape, child molestation, incest, and every conceivable form of sadomasochism. Further, by refusing to accept any homosexual behavior as normal, this homophobic society drives many gay and lesbian people into the very behavior patterns that the straight world most fears and condemns.

Prejudice always defines its victims negatively, blanketing them with stereotypes that hide from view their individual humanity. This principle was illustrated for me recently when I had to deal with a church that had called a woman to be its rector (or pastor). The lay leaders of this congregation were very proud of this courageous selection, unprecedented in the life of their parish and still unusual for the church at large. However, this particular pastor proved not to be a good choice on a number of levels. Within a short time of her coming a departure was negotiated, and the church began a search for a new pastor. When the name of a second woman candidate was proposed, the search committee chair announced rather firmly that the committee could not consider a female prospect this time. "We tried that and it failed," he asserted. Around the table there were nods of general agreement.

"If you had had an unsatisfactory male pastor," I inquired, "would you now be saying 'We had a male minister and he just didn't work out, so we will not consider another male?'" There was silence in the room. Prejudice always masquerades as rationality until it is exposed.

Prejudice is enforced and reinforced by the corporate wisdom of the community in which it is upheld, until it is thought to be God's self-evident truth. Prejudice withers only when two things occur: when new knowledge undercuts its intellectual basis and when people begin to observe and experience in those they reject a distinction between behavior that is destructive and behavior that is life giving. A strong signal that a prejudice is becoming moribund is communicated when the victimized group refuses to accept being defined by others as evil. All of us should welcome the cry of "gay pride." It is the emotional equivalent of "Black is beautiful." Self-acceptance, a defiance of the definition of the majority, is now a major force at work in the gay and lesbian world.

Even conservative expressions of Christianity show signs these days of being influenced by the movement toward acceptance of gay and lesbian persons—quite a change, considering the history of church attitudes toward them. So widely was homosexuality condemned in the early days of this century that it was rarely even mentioned in ecclesiastical gatherings. One does not debate such self-evident evils as murder, rape, arson, and child molesting. Homosexuality was once thought of as being in such a category.

As it has become more difficult to define evil quite so simply, perceptions have changed and judgment on this and a whole host of moral categories has begun to be tempered. Today almost every church body responding to this debate has passed some sort of justifying resolution designed to alleviate the sense of dis-ease that continued prejudice against gay and lesbian people is beginning to create. The earliest of these resolutions were couched in the sweet rhetoric of piety. Homosexual persons were declared to be the children of God and commended to the pastoral ministry of the church. That stance satisfied the church for a decade or so, because no one bothered to define "pastoral ministry." One patronizing form this attitude took was the suggestion that the church should "love the sinner while it hates the sin." Funny how it was that none of those defined as sinners experienced that love. Most gay and lesbian people learned not to trust the church's pastoral sensitivity to members of a group that the church corporately rejects. Despite the negativity in this type resolution, however, it still represented a small step forward. At least the prejudice was having to be defended—a sure sign that it was beginning to waver. It also indicated that the issue was now important enough to demand consideration.

The second stage in the debate came when the civil rights and economic well-being of the homosexual population were threatened. Then the church, ever on the side of the victim, passed resolutions designed to urge justice before the law when dealing with *all* people, even homosexual people. A person should not be fired for being gay or lesbian, the church asserted. A person could not be physically abused just because of his or her sexual orientation. Gay and lesbian persons should be granted a bank loan with the same ease and at the same interest rate as anyone else with a similar financial history. Churches felt quite proud of these "liberal" resolutions. Once again, they did not press the implications of these actions. Consider the economic penalty a gay or lesbian person pays when not able to claim his or her mate as a dependent under the internal revenue code, or the lack of legal status of gay and lesbian people if their partners die intestate. Can such practices be just when 10 percent of the population cannot marry according to the laws of the state? If a mortgage is sought by a gay or lesbian couple to buy a home in our particular neighborhood, are we still quite so open?

Politicians seeking election quite often have to address the various political ramifications of prejudice against homosexuality. Championing the cause of the gay and lesbian population is not the way to collect winning votes. The negative emotions that such campaigns release usually burn brightly until they expend themselves in their own excesses. Even the witch hunts in Salem, Massachusetts, in the seventeenth century finally ended in public revulsion. Until that happened, however, many women were charged, tried, convicted, imprisoned, and even executed for witchcraft—so it has been with sickening frequency whenever homosexuality has been raised as a political issue. Yet as costly as these episodes are, they are part of the process that alters public consciousness. Persecution of minority people always seems to mark the time of transition. When the restraints that the majority places on those who they believe are evil become evil themselves, then men and women of conscience revise their thinking and take action on behalf of the victims to guarantee, at a minimum, their civil rights. Most church groups today have moved at least to this second stage.

The next step follows on the heels of the decision to end persecution. It is a strange step, in that it is appealing despite an incredible level of naïveté. It is articulated in those resolutions and statements from church leaders and official bodies specifying that a distinction is to be drawn between sexual orientation and sexual behavior. They suggest that since one might not be able to choose one's sexual orientation, that orientation cannot be considered sinful. But since one can choose how to act no matter what one's ontological orientation, and since the sexual acts of the homosexually oriented person are evil, they are therefore not allowable inside the sanctions of the church. So if you are born with a homosexual predisposition, you cannot act on the basis of this predisposition. Your sexual energy must be contained, suppressed, sublimated.

The positive thing about this sort of resolution is that it signals a dawning realization that homosexuality is not an orientation that is chosen but rather a reality that is given. Once that watershed truth is accepted, the attitudes and behaviors of heterosexuals do begin to adapt, just as they adapted when we stopped thinking that left-handedness was abnormal. It is certainly a step forward to recognize that a minority characteristic might not necessarily be abnormal but rather a reflection of the rich variety of human life. As the realization that one cannot choose one's sexual orientation any more than one can choose to be right-handed begins to win its way, certain prejudicial words and phrases begin to drop from our vocabulary. "Sexual preference" is one such phrase, implying that one can stand at a crossroads and decide whether to become heterosexual or homosexual.

However, before extolling too highly this kind of resolution, let me point out its incredible naïveté. It suggests that those who have a homosexual orientation also have a capacity to refrain from all sexual activity. It assumes that this 10 percent of the population can or will be willing to affirm and accept the vocation of celibacy that someone other than themselves has approved for them.

Those who know anything about celibacy know that true celibacy is a rare and unique vocation to which few are called. This vocation or lifestyle cannot be imposed involuntarily. The experience of the Roman Catholic church, which requires celibacy of its priests, is that even with all the external structure of the priestly life—the unique clergy dress, the rigid prayer disciplines, the aloof paternal titles, the cultivated image of set-apartness—the life of true celibacy is difficult to sustain, and the vow of celibacy is still broken with dismaying regularity. Yet those who support resolutions of this genre act as if celibacy can be mandated for the gay and lesbian population. Acceptance of this imposed celibacy becomes the price gays and lesbians must pay to receive the church's blessing upon their lives. Imagine the response that would be forthcoming if some ecclesiastical body, in the name of God and morality, announced that henceforth an arbitrary 10 percent of the heterosexual world would have to live in sexual abstinence if it wished to participate in or be blessed by that church. It is almost unbelievable that this level of logic informs the majority viewpoint of solemn assemblies of influential and well-meaning bishops, representative clergy and lay people, or even seminary faculties where higher learning is presumed to prevail.

Nevertheless, this point of view, with all its ambiguity and naïveté, is still an expression of forward movement, but quite obviously it cannot be the concluding word in the debate. It finally sinks into its own internal contradictions and unrealistic expectations.

In time a new understanding of the origin of homosexuality will cause us to lose the irrational anxiety that our children might be seduced into a homosexual lifestyle by some chance encounter. Witch hunts aimed at removing "those people" from positions where they might be quite influential in the lives of our children will be revealed for what they are and will cease. No longer will our own anxiety overwhelm us when we have a fantasy or dream that we fear might be an expression of latent homosexuality. No longer will men have to hide their softer, yielding sides and women their athletic competence, in order to make sure no one suspects them of an evil orientation.

The next stage is being entered when we begin to regard both the homosexual orientation and the heterosexual orientation in and of themselves as neither good nor evil, but only as real and true. Both aspects of human sexuality will ultimately be seen as natural. The recognition is growing that there is a majority orientation and a minority orientation and that both have roles in the enrichment of human life. This change will take time, for ignorance and fear are both tenacious, and prejudice covers human irrationality, making it difficult and frightening to relinquish.

Once the naturalness of majority and minority orientations is established, and the expectation of celibacy for gay and lesbian people is removed, the question of the moment will then become, How does a gay or lesbian person lead a responsible sexual life? Surely the laws of church and state must give equal protection and affirmation to this group. Our pious conditional resolutions binding moral homosexuality to celibacy reveal nothing less than an irrational belief in a sadistic God, in the light of new knowledge. This God created gay and lesbian people only to punish them. God made them in creation complete with sexual drive and then said that morality demanded that this drive be repressed. Once again we are confronted with the dictum that bad biology and bad biochemistry result in bad theology.

The traditional position of the church, based on the false premise that loving sexual expressions between persons of the same gender are always evil, must come face to face with the evil this stance has itself created. How can the fullness of life be achieved when some of God's children are barraged by consistent messages proclaiming them to be immoral? How can any person, in the face of constant disparagement, ever develop a positive self-image? We cannot really give ourselves in a loving commitment to others unless we believe that we have some value. Two broken, fragile egos that are daily downgraded and humiliated will not be able to sustain each other easily in a mutually monogamous relationship. The lack of community support and the necessity to hide a relationship from public life puts enormous strain on a couple's psychological resources.

In turning away from its self-righteous condemnation and grudging allowances, the church might first confess its own hardness of heart: "Lord have mercy upon us and forgive us for that evil judgment that has twisted and distorted your sons and daughters in every generation of your church's life."

Second, the church must set about the task of rethinking the ethics of human sexuality. I will develop this idea in a specific way in chapter 15. Suffice it to be stated now that the intimacy of love, the legitimacy of a publicly recognized relationship, the joy of companionship, and the peace of a life without secrets are not to be denied to anyone in his or her pursuit of happiness and the abundance of life about which the gospel speaks (see John 10:10).

The issue of what is permissible behavior in public life contrasted with private life comes to a head in the church's rules for ordination. Should the church ordain a gay person who is neither duplicitous nor celibate? The question itself, when publicly debated, indicates a leap forward in ethical consciousness. The fact remains, however, that there have always been gay people among the ordained and in religious orders. For two thousand years the church has had gay clergy in numbers far beyond what most people have dared to imagine. They have occupied every position in every ecclesiastical hierarchy. They have assisted in the fashioning of the doctrine, discipline, worship, and ecclesiastical dress of the church. When celibacy was mandated as the only proper lifestyle for the ordained, in the twelfth century, the doors were opened for gay males to find in the church's priesthood a legitimizing place where their single status would be turned from a liability to a virtue and where their lives could experience creativity and community. If gay people were excised from the ordained ministry throughout the church's history, enormous gaps would appear, perhaps as much as 80 percent in certain periods of history. Indeed, there was a time when all under the vows of celibacy were suspected of being gay.[12]

The argument now about whether or not gay people should be ordained is, in one sense, almost ludicrous. The outcome of the debate will not change the constituency; it will change the public face of the church. Moralistic voices want to keep "the secret." The Roman Catholic church, among others, goes so far as to suspend, expel, or silence members of its clergy who publicly admit their preference for the same gender.[13]

Of course gay people should be considered without prejudice for the ordination process. They should be screened like all other candidates, with a view toward examining the integrity of their calls, the gifts they have to bring to the church, and their intelligence, sensitivity, devotion to God, willingness to work, and competence to handle their sexual energy with responsibility and commitment.

Would a particular congregation call or accept a gay or lesbian pastor who had formed a monogamous, loving relationship and who did not want either to abandon that partner or to live a lie? It is happening at this moment, but primarily in cities and urban areas where anonymity in the larger community is possible. I personally know such clergy, who have the loving support of their people, and I do see the gospel of Jesus Christ being lived out in those congregations.

I applaud these clerics, their partners, and the people of their churches for having the ability to transcend the prejudice that still surrounds us on every side.

Regrettably, there are others who live at this moment in a fear that will not allow openness. They operate under various protective covers, always wondering whom they can trust. Some have shared their life stories with me. My support for them in their heroic struggle to live in both love and integrity is firm. They have taught me much. I am in their debt.

Some will read these words and suggest vigorously that this stance puts me as a bishop into opposition with the official stand of the church I represent, and to the historic position of the church catholic. They are correct. I am a minority voice in that ecclesiastical structure. That minority is growing, as new knowledge permeates the whole society. It will not be minority forever. The church has changed its mind many times in history and will do so again. The deeper question is the one that calls the authority of our sacred story, the Bible, into question. Does this point of view not fly in the face of Holy Scripture? Are not all of the issues raised thus far dealt with authoritatively in the Bible? Those are powerful questions for Christian people to consider. They are worthy of the serious attention that indeed they shall receive in the next section of this book.

Notes

1. Alfred Kinsey et al., *Sexual Behavior in the Human Male* (Philadelphia: Saunders, 1948); *Sexual Behavior in the Human Female* (Philadelphia: Saunders, 1953).
2. John Fortunato, "Should the Church Bless and Affirm Committed Gay Relationships?" *The Episcopalian,* April 1987.
3. John S. Spong, *Into the Whirlwind* (San Francisco: Harper & Row, 1983), chapter 8.
4. Sigmund Freud, *Three Contributions to the Theory of Sex* (New York: Dutton, 1962); *Totem and Taboo* (New York: Vintage Press, 1946).
5. Rosemary Ruether, "From Machismo to Maturity," in Edward Batchelor, Jr., *Homosexuality and Ethics* (New York: Pilgrim Press, 1980), pp. 28ff.
6. Ibid.

7. The Advisory Committee of Issues Relating to Homosexuality, *A Study of Issues Concerning Homosexuality* (New York: Division for Mission in North America, Lutheran Church in America, 1986), p. 21.

8. Jo Durden-Smith and Diane de Simone, *Sex and the Brain* (New York: Arbor House, 1983), p. 101.

9. Ibid, p. 128.

10. Ibid, pp. 104-6.

11. *A Study of Issues*, p. 21.

12. Spong, *Into the Whirlwind*, chapter 8.

13. John J. McNeill, "Homosexuality—The Challenge to the Church," *The Christian Century* 104, no. 8 (March 1987): 242-46.

CHAPTER SIX

An Ambiguous Symbol of Authority

A re you trying to rewrite the Bible?" "If the Bible says it is wrong, then it is wrong!" These sentiments, framed in a thousand different ways, represent the reactions of frightened religious people who feel that somehow I am threatening the values by which they live. Those values and the Bible are inexorably linked in their minds. It is therefore important for me to engage the Bible quite specifically, as the debate rages about sexual matters.

The Bible is one of those ambiguous symbols of authority that history has overlaid with a fascinating mystique. For many, to be able to quote the Bible in support of their opinion is to be justified, vindicated, proud, and right. For some, the debate is closed once it is clear that the Bible is on their side. Official church pronouncements, recognizing this, tend to be laced liberally with biblical proof texts. Much of the influence of the revival preachers of yesterday and the electronic preachers of today comes from the authority of that open Bible in their hands and their assertion that in that book is found the "inerrant word of God" that answers every question. Such a word is final, perfect, and above all not affected by the changes and chances of mortal life that are threatening the audiences to which these men appeal. The Scriptures, when literalized and proclaimed with certainty, bring a sense of stability and security to those who resist every change. There is great comfort in this attitude.

Yet that is only half of the truth about this book. The power of the Bible is such that it has also been considered an ally by those who have championed the forces of change. In almost every dramatic confrontation on the key issues in Western history, the Bible has been quoted on both sides of the conflict. For years the Bible was used to justify the prevailing political idea known as the divine right of kings. But it was also used as a powerful weapon in the hands of those who led the revolution against royalty, as Oliver Cromwell's rebellion attests. Abraham Lincoln and Jefferson Davis both appealed to the Bible as support for their attitudes toward black people, and to give moral authority to their different sides during America's bloodiest war.

It should therefore come as no surprise that as changes in the conventional patterns of sexual behavior force their way into the public awareness, the Bible is quoted by both conservatives and liberals in the conflict. But because ours is an increasingly secularized age, this debate reveals some noteworthy differences. The first is that the church no longer holds the power over people's minds that it once held. This means that the ranks of the ecclesiastical liberals have become quite thin. Those who have despaired of ever reforming the church have quietly dropped out of organized religion altogether. Many of the voices advocating a new day for sexual ethics are those of people who have moved significantly away from contact with things religious. They are now citizens of the secular city. Their dignity has been offended once too often by ecclesiastical pronouncements on sexual matters that are out of touch with modern reality, or that seem blissfully unaware that women, in particular, can no longer be defined by the stereotypes of another century. They are not going to be bludgeoned by any church or church leader into giving up birth control or refusing to use abortion as a legal option for reproductive choice. Nor are they impressed when male preachers, quoting a literal Bible, remind them of the values of yesteryear or speak nostalgically about the virtues of the "traditional family." In their minds that family, consisting of a working father, a home-bound mother, two children, and a dog, no longer exists. These people have in large measure learned to live without the church as a major force in their lives, and they quite frankly no longer want to be bothered with what they view as religious prejudice or even religious ignorance. A secular world in which the church has no effective power is a new thing.

On the other hand, those conservative voices of the religious establishment, convinced that the secular world has become the devil's playground, seem to become more and more shrill with every passing day. They approach what they regard as the challenge to morality with disturbingly high levels of hostility and anger that reveal their runaway anxiety and insecurity. Their attitudes belie the claim they make that certainty and righteousness are theirs as Christians. The changes in sexual behavior patterns that are occurring threaten religious influence and undermine religious authority. Leaders of the church, like leaders of any threatened institution, move vigorously to repair the breach in their armor. Even well-educated church leaders who would not want to be identified with fundamentalism are happy to claim the conclusion of the fundamentalists, if their purposes are thereby served. One bishop, for example, recently took umbrage with me for writing that among the Episcopal bishops in America there are representatives of every theological and ecclesiastical style of church life: charismatic, evangelical, liberal, conservative, Anglo-Catholic, and fundamentalist. It was this last category that upset him. He wrote that he did not know any fundamentalists in The Episcopal Church's House of Bishops. In the next paragraph, however, he stated his belief in the literal historicity of the birth narratives of Matthew and Luke by saying, "If God had decided to be born of a virgin, that would be no problem for Him [*sic*]." When I pointed out that he held on this issue a fundamentalist position that would not be supported by reputable biblical scholars, either Catholic or Protestant, he was shocked but not silenced.

So the lines of this debate have hardened. There is very little interaction beyond the mutual hurling of anathemas across the chasm. Unless bridges can be erected over this widening breach, the fate of this volume will not be to initiate a dialogue but to be ignored by the secular society and condemned by the religious establishment.

The only way I know to begin the task of bridge building is to allow the world to hear Christian voices that are different from the norm, but that take this present world as seriously as the secular society does and that cannot be legitimately dismissed as godless, as the religious right is prone to do.

In this section of the book I seek to initiate the bridge-building process. First, I will focus on the Bible, freeing that sacred source from its literalistic imprisonment, then I will make proposals that will demonstrate new moral options in this brave new world.

This is not an attack on the integrity of the Bible, as the religious right will surely contend. It is rather an attack on a literalistic and magical view of Holy Scripture that I believe imprisons the real truth of the Bible. Unless we succeed in supplanting fundamentalistic interpretations of the Bible, the Bible itself will be rendered impotent and valueless in a very short period of time.

This is a dangerous undertaking for a member of the church hierarchy. But that is also the source of this book's power, if indeed it is to have any. For I do take seriously the treasures of our faith. I will explore in depth exactly what the Bible says about sexuality, women, homosexuality, marriage, divorce, and adultery. The results should amaze the secular society and infuriate some religious conservatives, as it becomes clear that the Bible will not support the things for which its support has been claimed through the ages.

CHAPTER SEVEN

The Case Against Literalism

When I was in the seventh grade I received my first personal Bible as a Christmas present from my mother. It looked the way a Bible was supposed to look. It had a floppy leather cover, tissue-paper pages with gold edges, a limited concordance in the back, and numerous maps of the Holy Land in biblical times. Each page had two columns of text, a layout only used, in my experience, for dictionaries or encyclopedias, neither of which are meant to be read in any continuous way. The text was divided not just into short chapters but into even shorter verses, and wherever Jesus was determined to be the speaker in that text the words were printed in red ink. It was the "Authorized Version," which of course meant the King James Bible. After all, this was 1943, and all those "modern" versions had not yet been printed.

The fact that this was considered an appropriate Christmas present (I also received that Christmas a large, wall-sized framed picture of Jesus) to give to a twelve-year-old boy is a clear statement of the values of my family. I was thrilled. My mother had invested our large family Bible with an aura of holiness. It was seldom read, but it was always respected. It stayed in prominent view on the coffee table, and one did not place a glass, cup, or any other object on top of it.

Inside the sacred bindings of that family Bible my own name had been solemnly entered along with my date of birth and baptism, the names of my parents, and some other pertinent personal data. Several lines higher on the page was the record of my parents' marriage and the names of their parents, only one of whom had I ever known. Somehow this book bound the generations and related us to the eternal God, whom we referred to without hesitation as our "heavenly Father."

In proper response to this special Christmas gift, I vowed to read a chapter of the Bible each day. So began my love affair with this book. I still read the Bible every day, and at a rate designed to enable me to complete the text of both Testaments as well as the Apocrypha once every two years.

Throughout my life I have read the Bible on many different levels, ranging from the magical to the scholarly. I learned much of its content in Sunday school and in the vacation Bible schools that were part of my regular childhood summer routine. I took two courses in Bible for credit in the public schools of Charlotte, North Carolina. (Teaching Bible in public schools had not at that time been declared unconstitutional.) Both courses were taught by a gentle fundamentalist lady who wore no makeup because "it violates the word of God." Her scholarship might have been lacking, but her love for the Lord was not. She could mesmerize her class by narrating the exciting Bible narratives of Joseph, Moses, Elijah, and Paul, or the story of the cross. She believed in memory work, and to this day I can quote in their King James "original" large chunks of Scripture. My love for the Bible, born in those early years, has remained with me for all of my life, even if my original shallow view of Scripture has not.

My literalistic approach to the Bible died in late adolescence under the onslaught of a great secular state university. The death of literalism, however, did not bring with it, as it seems to do for so many, a death of my interest in biblical study.

While at theological seminary I yearned to get as deeply as possible into biblical studies. I was thrilled with the insights of higher criticism. My introduction to the Hebrew Scriptures, which I then rather insensitively referred to as the "Old Testament," was exciting beyond measure, coming to me through the skillful mind of Robert O. Kevin. The Christian Scriptures, however, with the exception of the Johannine literature and the Gospel of Mark, were not well presented. They were assigned to the junior members of the faculty, for whom they were not a priority. I was not deterred, however, and began my own book-by-book study of Matthew, Luke, Acts, Paul, the pastoral epistles, the general epistles, and Revelation, to compensate for this faculty inadequacy.

After graduation my first parochial assignment was to a parish just off the campus of Duke University. The congregation was composed of young people struggling to reconcile the biblical superstitions of their childhood Sunday school lessons with the challenge of modern education. It was an assignment made in heaven for me, and I grabbed it with gusto and enjoyed some success at it.

The Bible became more and more central to the development of my ministry. For twelve years in two large congregations I taught an adult Bible class for one hour each Sunday before the primary worship service. For six of those years that class was broadcast on a local radio station. I was determined in that forum to communicate with lay people my own enthusiasm for biblical scholarship and higher criticism. Most of them responded eagerly, and in fact the class became a community conversation piece. Those who could not admit any possibility other than literalism began to look for other churches in which to worship. But for every person who left, ten new people came, drawn by the hope that church does not have to be an anti-intellectual experience.

I would spend an entire year on a single book of the Bible, such as Genesis, Exodus, or Mark. I spent three years on the Luke-Acts corpus, two years on the Johannine literature, and one year on the Pauline Epistles. I would read extensively in preparation for these lectures and would revel in new insights. I still have the tapes of those classes, and the study notes that helped me prepare for each lecture are filed away by the year in large folders.

It was these years of study, teaching, and dialogue that brought me to the point where I am willing to be quite public about my search for the depths of truth that I believe the Bible contains. I know that I speak not for myself alone but also for all of those Christians whose faith is strengthened rather than weakened by biblical scholarship. When the debate in the church on changing sexual patterns became a debate about the proper way to use the Bible in sexual decision making, I had the distinct feeling that my entire life had been but a preparation for this moment.

The Bible did not drop out of heaven fully written. That seems obvious, yet so many use the Bible as if it had. The first step, therefore, in understanding the Bible is to explore pre-biblical history, to look at the antecedents of Scripture, to isolate and explore the documents that lie behind the Bible.

The major strands of tradition that come together in the Torah (the first five books of the Hebrew Scriptures) number four. Each is unique, descriptive of the values of its time and place, and reflective of the social, political, and economic realities that produced it. To quote the Torah without being aware of these primary textual distinctions is to presume that every verse is objective and of equal import. There is less truth than naïveté in such an approach.

The Judeo-Christian tradition has its origin in the call of Abraham to leave Ur of the Chaldees to form a new people (Gen. 12). Abraham was a shadowy figure who, if he was actually an individual in history, lived sometime around 1800 B.C.E. Two things are remarkable about that date. First, the earliest narrative about Abraham did not achieve written form until somewhere around 920 B.C.E., or some nine hundred years after he was supposed to have lived. This means that the story of Abraham was handed down orally, probably around the campfire, from parents to children for more than twenty-five generations. It has the coloration of tribal legend. In the light of this, how literal are we willing to be about such episodes as the sacrifice of Isaac, the jealousy between Sarah and Hagar, and the relationship between Abraham and Lot?

The second thing worth noting is that the earliest possible date of Abraham's moment in history would still make our faith story less than four thousand years old. When one considers the present astrophysical estimate that our planet is between four and five billion years old, and the current anthropological conviction that recognizable, if primitive, human life has been on this planet for between one and two million years, then a faith story born in 1800 B.C.E. is not ancient but relatively new and modern. If that faith story is literalized and claimed as the exclusive bearer of God's inerrant and infallible plan of salvation, one must wonder why a gracious God would leave human beings in both ignorance and sin for 99.9 percent of the time that they have inhabited the earth. One must also wonder at the wisdom of a God who would allow "false" or "pagan" religious systems such as Buddhism and Hinduism to develop simultaneously on this tiny globe. These other ancient religious systems have always had more combined members than the Christianity that we claim is the "only saving truth." So at the first moment of comprehensive insight, the security-producing assertion of exclusivity that undergirds biblical authority begins to sink into the sea of the relativity of all truth.

When we focus on the first written document to be woven

into the Bible, other insights demand examination. This primal strand of biblical material is known as the Yahwist narrative, because it refers to God by the name Yahweh. It was produced in the southern kingdom of Judah. Jerusalem, the capital of Judah, was the holy city in which the royal house of David ruled. The Yahwist narrative was a court history, written to serve the best interests of the royal tradition of hierarchical authority. It portrayed a God who would speak and deal only with those anointed leaders of God's choice. Moses was God's political instrument, and Aaron, Moses' brother, was the divinely designated priestly leader. On God's behalf these leaders mediated God's demands and God's invitation to the people to enter a covenant. The God Yahweh did not communicate directly with the people. God spoke to the people only through Moses and Aaron, and ultimately only Moses spoke directly to God. Priestly leadership in this period of Hebrew history was derived from political leadership, and political leadership was derived directly from God. Aaron discovered his secondary priestly status in the golden calf episode (Gen. 32) and when he tried to lead a conspiracy against Moses (Num. 12).

The historians in David's court who wrote the Yahwist narrative were quite sure that no authority rivaled the authority of God's chosen political leader. To rebel against the king or the royal family was tantamount to rebelling against God. Indeed, the people came into a covenant relationship with God only by being part of that nation with whom God had established a bond with the ruling elite. To be near God, to share in God's true revelation, required communion with the divinely established hierarchy through which God drew near to the people. This point of view was used in later centuries to buttress Paul's argument against rebellion (Rom. 13), to support the institutions of royalty, and to build those hierarchical churches on the catholic side of Christianity, in whose theology God speaks to the people through the ordained, in particular the infallible papacy of Roman Catholicism. Rebellion, revolution, or reformation are simply wrong, if God is identified with the ruling tradition. That was the Jerusalem point of view, as expressed in the initial strand of pre-biblical material. The Yahwist narrative might well be called the Hebrew *Iliad*.

The second narrative that antedates the Bible is known as the Elohist document, because it refers to God by the name Elohim. It is usually dated around 750 B.C.E. and was composed as a sacred history of Israel in the northern kingdom around the capital of Samaria. The northern kingdom had separated from Judah when its people had successfully rebelled against the royal house of David in the closing years of the tenth century B.C.E. Jeroboam, a brilliant military leader, had demanded certain reforms of the young king Rehoboam, grandson of King David and Bathsheba (I Kings 12:3-5). When these reforms were not forthcoming, he led a revolution that ended with a division of the once united realm into Israel in the north and Judah in the south. Jeroboam was installed as king in the northern kingdom. In time the city of Samaria was built, to be the new capital to rival Jerusalem (I Kings 16:24).

Jeroboam was empowered by the people in his challenge to the divinely appointed royal authority. There was, therefore, in the northern kingdom no divinely established royal family and no temple adjacent to the royal palace as the visible symbol of God's presence. Since the people chose and empowered the king, he was a constitutional monarch who either pleased the people or ran the risk of being overthrown. The job security of the king of the northern kingdom was never very high, and no stable royal line ever developed.

The story of the northern kingdom's history rose out of this experience and was informed by the new set of social values, and varied widely from the account of the Yahwist writer. The people remembered the events at Sinai somewhat differently from the way Judah recollected them. The

Elohist writer believed that God had made a covenant with the whole nation, not just with the leadership. The people then had chosen Moses and Aaron to represent them before God. Their leaders had thus received their power and authority from the people, not from God. Those to whom power has been given can just as easily become those from whom power has been withdrawn. Rebellion against the leader was not construed to be rebellion against God. The Elohist tradition is not only one source of the democratic process that vests power in the people who elect, but also of that sense of congregationalism that marks Protestant Christianity today. This was the incipient beginning of the "priesthood of all believers," of a tradition that refuses to accept the unrepresentative decisions and excessive claims of an ecclesiastical or political hierarchy. Since the northern kingdom viewed the patriarch Joseph as its primary ancestor, he was portrayed in their folklore as Jacob's favorite child, on whom Jacob lavished gifts and attention, including the coat of many colors. Joseph's mother was portrayed as Jacob's most beloved wife. The Elohist document was a social and political narrative designed to extol the ancestors of the ones writing the story and to develop a sense of history in the long, distinguished, and sometimes perilous sacred saga of the people of the north. The Elohist narrative might well be called the Hebrew *Odyssey*.

In the year 721 B.C.E. the city of Samaria fell to the army of the Assyrians. The people of the north were dispersed into exile, never to reassemble as a nation. A few managed to escape to the southern kingdom. Judah, though also defeated, had played its political cards more adroitly, and exchanged vassalage to Assyria for some vestiges of continued independence. At least its citizens were not transported to Nineveh. Among the treasures preserved by those few northerners who escaped the Assyrian plague by fleeing to Judah was the sacred story of the Elohist writer.

The narrative was brought to Jerusalem, where it joined the Yahwist document to become two versions of the sacred history of a once united people. In time the Yahwist and Elohist versions were merged into a single narrative that is identified as the Yahwist-Elohist document.

The knitting together of the two sacred stories did not produce an exact fit, but it did provide a sense of shared ancestry. The division of the kingdom was historically legitimized by giving their common forebear, Jacob, two wives—each destined to be the mother of half of the nation. In one of the sacred stories Joseph was sold into slavery to the Midianites, by his brothers. In the other he was sold to the Ishmaelites (Gen. 37). Though dissimilar, both versions appear in the blended story, and the contradiction is ignored regularly by those who claim inerrancy for the "Word." There is one version of the Ten Commandments from the Elohist tradition in Exodus 20 and a different version from the Yahwist narrative in Exodus 34. Perhaps the attempt to take cognizance of these two irreconcilable accounts helped to create the narrative that portrayed Moses smashing the tablets of stone and having to return to the top of Sinai to ask God to write them down a second time. In any event, the editorial task of putting the larger sacred story together was done in Jerusalem sometime in that century between the fall of Samaria in 721 B.C.E. and the reign of King Josiah, which began in 639 B.C.E.; for it was in the time of Josiah that a third document came to light and joined the sacred saga.

Josiah was probably the most popular king in Judah, after the division of the kingdom. He was a devoted worshiper of Yahweh and possessed a charismatic flair. Because of his deep religious convictions, he ordered some renovations and repairs done on the temple in Jerusalem in 621 B.C.E. In the walls, whether by design or accident (we will never know), there was discovered a new book of the law purported to have been written by Moses (II Kings 22).[1] It was given the name "the second law," or in Greek the *deutero-nomos*. We call it the book of Deuteronomy. King Josiah had the text brought to him. After he read it, he initiated a thoroughgoing reform of the religious life of Judah that came to be known as the Deuteronomic reform. He first called together a sacred assembly at which he read the new word of the Lord through Moses and then informed the people that changes in the realm based on the new commands of this book would be instituted immediately. Most of the changes were aimed at centralizing the authority of the Jerusalem priesthood in the religious life of the nation. Following this reform, Jerusalem alone was the appropriate place for the Passover, and the desired place for circumcision, presentation, and bar mitzvah. The Passover pilgrims coming to Jerusalem at the time of the Last Supper were following a tradition that began with Josiah's reforms. It was not long before Deuteronomy (with its third version of the Ten Commandments in chapter 5) was grafted onto Judah's growing sacred story to produce the Yahwist-Elohist-Deuteronomic account. This was the narrative that some thirty-five years later the Jews took with them into exile in Babylon in 586 B.C.E.

No experience shaped the religious life of the Jewish people more profoundly than the exile. Their nation was defeated by the armies of Babylon, their people were marched off into exile, and their concept of God was both expanded and narrowed almost simultaneously. Under the driving leadership of Ezekiel and a group of priests, the Jewishness of these exiled people was made indelible on their bodies (if they were male) by mandatory circumcision, and in their hearts and minds through strict observance of the law and cultic practices of their tradition. Sabbath day observance and dietary regulations, both designed to create Jewish separateness, were rigidly enforced. Synagogues, as the places where people in exile could keep alive their faith and practice, made their entrance into human history. But most important, for our purposes, a massive rewriting of the Jewish sacred story was undertaken by a school of priests.

This revision doubled the length of the Torah and heightened the cultic traditions against which the prophets had long spoken. Indeed, the age of the prophets had all but ended.

It was this rewritten, theologically conservative, rigidly legal version of Judah's sacred history that Ezra and Nehemiah carried back with them when they came to rebuild Jerusalem in the fifth century B.C.E. It was this rewriting of the law that later produced Sadducees and Pharisees. But it was also this rewriting that guaranteed Jewish survival as an identifiable people in history. In seven great stanzas, the priestly writers added as an introductory chapter to their sacred story what is now the first and most familiar creation story. This narrative was designed primarily to raise the Sabbath to prominence and to bind it in Jewish observance as a mark of identity. It was the priestly writers who added the cultic commentary to the familiar Elohist version of the Ten Commandments in Exodus 20, so that motives and reasons were given for refraining from idolatry, obeying parents, and observing the Sabbath, and by which coveting was more thoroughly defined. It was the priestly editors who recast the flood story so that Noah took seven pairs of clean animals and only one pair of unclean animals into the ark. This enabled Noah and his family to keep the law during those 40 to 150 days and still have food to eat, as well as the ability to make the proper sacrificial offering that worship required without destroying any single species (Gen. 7). The story of the wandering in the wilderness also was retold by the priestly writers so that Moses and the people of Israel did not violate the Sabbath by gathering the breadlike substance, manna, on the seventh day (Exod. 16).

In contradistinction to the priestly editors was the simultaneous work of Second Isa. (Isa. 40–55). This prophet called Judah out of its tribal identity by sketching for its people a universal vocation, while the priestly writers were driving the nation more deeply into its tribal nature by identifying God with their national aspirations. Second Isaiah was destined, at least for the time being, to be a "voice crying in the wilderness." This latter priestly influence extended into the period of the Maccabees and even into the years of Jesus, when effective political and religious leadership in Jerusalem was merged into a single office and vested in the high priest.

Without awareness of the original source and motivations of a text in the Torah, the Bible cannot be used with integrity, nor can it be quoted in debate to prove some point that in all probability the original authors would never have considered. The inconsistencies within the biblical tradition are especially clear in a comparison of the historical books of Samuel and Kings with the later, rewritten history of the same events by the Chronicler. The two versions cannot be reconciled.

Compare the account of the death of King David in I Kings 1 with the account of his death in I Chronicles 28–29. In the I Kings version the aging monarch was suffering chills, and no amount of blankets could warm his body. His advisors set out to discover the most beautiful maiden in the land (this was the first Miss Israel contest), who would have the privilege of lying in the arms of her king to warm his body with her own. Abishag the Shunammite was the winner, and she entered Jewish folklore and fantasy, inspiring such later passages as the Song of Songs. It was a realistic and human story. Quite different was the narrative in I Chronicles, written centuries after Kings. By this time David had been idealized as the superpatriot, the exemplary Jewish prototype, the ultimate authority on liturgy and Torah. He ordered the officials of Israel to his death bed to impart his final words of wisdom. They were treated by King David to a long monologue rehearsing his reasons for not building the temple in Jerusalem and giving detailed directions about how that temple must be built and how the priests and the

Levites were to behave. It is a strange and wondrous contrast.

Those who support biblical inerrancy must struggle either to reconcile the two accounts or, at the very least, to say which is accurate. Unfortunately, these mental exercises miss the meaning of both accounts. When a text is approached with the wrong questions, it yields nothing but the wrong answers. Unfortunately, however, that is the way many people approach the Bible. In such biblical ignorance every new insight or scientific breakthrough is perceived to be an erosion of the authority of Scripture.

When one turns from the Hebrew to the Christian Scriptures, the issues of scholarship do not change. There is a tendency among some well-meaning moderates to dismiss the excesses of the Hebrew Scriptures but to cling steadfastly to the "New" Testament as the true, inerrant Word of God. That point of view also cannot be sustained. In the twenty-seven books of the New Testament inconsistencies abound. There are also a number of identifiable sources, some of which are antecedents to the Gospel narratives. Mark may have been written as a whole, but few scholars believe the other three Gospels were. Matthew used Mark, a document known as Q or Quelle, and a special additional source known as M, to compose his Gospel. Luke also used Mark and Q, but he used them in a way very different from the way Matthew used them. Luke also had his special private source that we call L, which may have been, indeed probably was, a series of sources, some written and some oral. Luke may have been written in an original shorter version that we call proto-Luke, expanded some years later with the addition of the birth narrative and Mark. A cursory look at the elaborate dating process at the beginning of Luke's chapter 3 causes many to surmise that his original story began there. The accounts in John of the wedding in Cana of Galilee, the woman taken in adultery, and the Galilean resurrection narrative seem to some scholars to have come from other sources.

We are also conditioned by the present form of Holy Scripture to read Paul through the filter of the Gospels. We may realize intellectually that Paul lived, wrote, and died before any Gospel had been composed, but still be unaware of our own internal blending processes. In the Pauline corpus, for example, Paul never tells the story of his conversion. The Damascus road narrative was created by the author of Acts more than thirty years after Paul's death. That story quite obviously met some of the author's political needs in the early struggles of the Christian church. I am not sure, however, that Paul would recognize that account as a part of his life story.

Contemporary scholarship has now divided the Pauline corpus into authentic and pseudo-Pauline writings. Romans, I and II Corinthians, Galatians, Philippians, Colossians, I and II Thessalonians, and Philemon are now considered genuinely Pauline. Ephesians, I and II Timothy, Titus, and Hebrews are no longer attributed to Paul. So when quoting the New Testament, does one assign the same weight to a passage from I Timothy, now known with certainty not to be Pauline, that one might assign to Romans? Is the authority of Scripture in the person of the author or in the community that assigns authority to its sacred story?

Early Christians assumed the former. That is why they claimed apostolic authorship for post-apostolic works. Since we know these books not to be apostolic, their argument will not suffice today. If the authority is in the community, then the right to change, revise, and render inoperative various parts of the Scripture must also be vested in the community. When pseudo-Paul writes in II Timothy that "all scripture is inspired by God" (II Tim. 3:16), a text much beloved by fundamentalists, it does not occur to today's reader that when that verse was written the author was referring to the Hebrew Scriptures. At that moment in history no Christian writings had obtained the status of Scripture, and the New

Testament itself had not yet come into being. The struggle the church went through before deciding which sacred writings were scriptural and which were not was yet to come. Some very popular Christian writings, such as the Gospel of Thomas, the Epistle of Barnabas, and the Shepherd of Hermas, were not finally included in the canon of Scripture. At least one book that was included—the Epistle of James—was, according to no less a Christian figure than Martin Luther, a serious mistake.

The writing of the books included in the Hebrew Bible range in time from 920 B.C.E. to 135 B.C.E. The time span for the Christian Bible begins with Paul's letters in 49 C.E. and concludes with II Peter sometime before 150 C.E. Can any verse from any book be quoted out of its context and with any integrity be applied to an issue being debated in the world some nineteen hundred years later? Yet that is the way Christians have used the Bible, again and again.

Even on subjects as basic to Christian theology as our understanding of who Jesus is or what happened on the first Easter, there is great confusion in the biblical texts themselves. A quick chronological rearrangement of the New Testament makes this quite obvious.

Paul, who did all of his writing between 49 and 62 C.E., simply proclaimed the presence of God in the person of Jesus. He did not explain it or justify it and he certainly did not do any systematic theologizing about it. "God was in Christ reconciling the world to himself," he stated (II Cor. 5:19). He believed that salvation had been achieved in Jesus. God had declared Jesus to be God's Son by the Holy Spirit at the moment of resurrection (Rom. 1:4). Doctrines of the Incarnation or the Trinity would have been inconceivable to the Jewish Paul, both of them requiring a Greek ontology that he would have found quite foreign.[2] Paul represented the first stage of christological thinking, the stage of proclamation.

By the time the Gospel of Mark was written, however

(65–70 C.E.), people were beginning to ask how it was that God was in Christ. Mark provided the popular answer at this early stage of theological thinking. His answer was that God entered Jesus at baptism. The heavens opened and the Spirit descended on Jesus like a dove, and God claimed Jesus as God's own. So from resurrection in Paul to baptism in Mark, the moment in which God named Jesus God's Son had begun its journey. Mark's baptism story is a version of what later came to be called "adoptionism" and was condemned as heresy. Yet for perhaps as long as two decades Mark, with what the church later was to call an inadequate and even heretical understanding of the nature of Jesus, was the only written Gospel in existence among Christian people.

Some twenty to twenty-five years later, Matthew and Luke were written. By this time it was no longer considered adequate to suggest that God adopted Jesus into a special relationship at his baptism. So, both Luke and Matthew added narratives to Mark's story (Matt. 1–2; Luke 1–2) that suggest that God and Jesus came into some identification with each other not at the time of his baptism, when Jesus was already a grown man, but at the very moment of conception. He was "conceived by the Holy Spirit, born of the virgin Mary." Christological thinking had reached a new plateau. Eventually even this view came to be regarded as inadequate.

By the time the Fourth Gospel was written, around the turn of the century, the moment of conception had been recognized as too finite and limited to be the point of divine/human identity in Jesus. John dismissed the virgin birth narratives, about which he had certainly heard, and substituted his hymn to the divine Logos: "In the beginning was the word [logos] . . . and the Word became flesh and dwelt among us" (John 1:1, 14). The moment God and Jesus came into mutual identity was not at the resurrection, as Paul had thought, nor at the baptism, as Mark had believed. It was not even in the moment of conception, as Matthew and Luke had suggested. God was in Christ or Christ was in God from the beginning of time. John had completed the backward journey of the moment of divine/human merger in Christ.

Who is right? Perhaps they all were. Who is literally correct? Perhaps no one is, nor can anyone ever be when trying to capture God or the Christ in the vehicle of human words. How then can the Bible be the authoritative instrument by which our faith is validated? It cannot be unless and until a literalistic approach to the Bible is surrendered. The Christ of Mark, who urged those who saw his mighty acts to keep silent lest the messianic secret be revealed prematurely, simply cannot be reconciled with the Johannine Christ, who walked around in public saying such incredible things as "I am the bread of life," "I am the living water," and "The Father and I are one." On a literal level they cannot both be correct.

The same sort of incongruities are found when the Easter moment is explored chronologically through the pages of Scripture. Paul is still the one who proclaims "God raised Jesus." Paul always used the passive verb form. He did not narrate a single resurrection detail. He provided lists of those who witnessed that exaltation. Proclamation, not narration, was the original form of the resurrection kerygma.[3]

Mark, the first Gospel to be written, gave a very scant Easter account, so scant that early Christians kept trying to embellish it with additional details. In Mark there were no appearance narratives of the risen Christ. The women confronted the empty tomb, heard from the young man the resurrection message with its promise of a Galilean rendezvous, and then fled the garden in fear. That was all there was to Mark's story of Easter. Matthew added greatly to the details, the magic, and the miraculous. Matthew provided us with an earthquake, soldiers falling into a dead stupor, an angel descending from heaven, graves being opened, saints rising to walk the streets of Jerusalem, and Jesus actually being seen by the women in the garden. The only time, however, that the disciples saw the risen Christ in Matthew's account, he was the already ascended and glorified Christ who appeared out of heaven on a Galilean mountaintop to give the Divine Commission.

Luke changed Mark's resurrection messenger from a young man into two obviously supernatural angels. Luke omitted the account of the women seeing the risen Lord in the garden and denied that there was a Galilean tradition of Jesus' appearance at all. He opposed the implication in Mark and in Matthew that resurrection and ascension were a single action, and separated them by forty days. He used the ascension to close off the resurrection appearances, all of which he said occurred only in the environs of Jerusalem.

John reestablished the resurrection/ascension as a single moment, expanded the physical details of the risen body to include the invitation to touch his wounds and handle his body, and had Jesus join the disciples to eat fish by the Sea of Galilee. The Fourth Gospel also added the Pentecost experience to Easter day, denying the Lukan tradition that separated the two events by a substantial period of time.

Who was right? When details are in opposition, proponents of the two sides of the contradiction cannot both be right. If the church cannot agree in its own sacred book on the details of who Christ is or what happened on the first Easter, are we dealing with something that lends itself to a literal interpretation of anything? If those two central events cannot be literalized by Holy Scripture, can anything meet the test of literalization? If the Bible does not conform to the rules of literal truth, then can its words be used in any literal way to settle any dispute in Christendom? Is the proof-text method of applying the Bible ever appropriate? Indeed, quoting the Bible to prove a point in some dispute is both an inadequate and an inept response to any issue. In the Bible there are conflicting accounts of creation, conflicting versions of the Ten Commandments, conflicting under-standings of who Jesus is and was, conflicting details concerning what happened on the first Easter, conflicting views on the meaning of Pentecost, and even on when, or if, the end of the world will come. Despite the fact that these conflicts and alternatives are present in Scripture, there are still some who insist that the Bible is inerrant and that its texts can be quoted to define and support a wide variety of moral activities.

Once literalism has been set aside as a basis for biblical interpretation, the more subtle issues of biblical scholarship can be explored. No author is objective or devoid of agenda, so a legitimate question to ask of the biblical text is, Why was this story preserved? Why was it so important in 920 B.C.E. to tell the story of Abraham's call to journey into what is now Palestine to establish a new nation? Did it have anything to do with the fact that these Hebrews fleeing from slavery and oppression in Egypt were experienced by the other people who were settled in Palestine as a marauding, pillaging wave of unwanted immigrants? To justify conquest of that land, did they not have to establish a prior claim of ownership which, in fact, the story of the call of Abraham provided for them? Why was Jacob given two wives and two concubines? Was it not to establish kinship and common history among the migrant bands of Semitic people who came together at a place called Kadesh to form a covenant? (See various references to Kadesh in Numbers, Deuteronomy, and Joshua.) All these Semitic peoples had probably not been slaves in Egypt, so they did not all have in common whatever the Red Sea experience was. But they joined their histories formed an alliance, worked together in the conquest of Canaan, and wrote a Red Sea motif into the story of the crossing of the Jordan River, so that all could share the moment of defining exodus.

Why were such things as Jesus' words "render to Caesar" remembered? Was not religious/political loyalty a major issue in the struggle of the early church for survival, caught as it was between synagogue and Caesar? No text is neutral; it has been preserved because it answered a question, settled a dispute, or met some need of the community that chose to remember it.

Another question that must be asked of a biblical passage is framed variously: Who is the enemy? What is the threat? Why the hostility? When the biblical narrative tells a murderous tale in which the prophets of Yahweh destroy the prophets of Baal, what is the issue and the underlying motive? Is it analogous to a denominational schism or a church fight? Since the Bible is written from the point of view of the Yahweh worshipers, the sensitive reader knows that there is more to its stories than meets the eye. A search for the real issue becomes vital. What was the root of the rivalry between Israel and the Philistines? How did the Exodus fit into Egypt's history? What did the Jewish concept of the promised land mean to Canaan's original inhabitants? What was the attitude of the Romans toward the conquered province of Judea, and what caused that attitude? When the author of I Timothy says, "I forbid women to speak in church," from where does the anger spring? Who is speaking where? One never prohibits what no one has ever thought of doing. The truth is probably that somewhere male authority was being challenged and the structures of control were cracking. The various strands and books of the Bible take one side of a two-sided or even possibly a many-sided dialogue. A student of that written work will make every effort to discern the dialogic partners to whom the words were directed. Without that, the literal words will be distorted.

Once the audience and the issues are discerned, the interpreter must explore the assumptions of the writer. Sometimes they are obvious, sometimes hidden. Even when obvious, we sometimes remain blind to them until society begins to ask new and provocative questions. For example, when the story of the ascension was written by Luke, few people questioned the cosmological assumptions of the author. The earth was flat, the sky was a dome over the earth, and the abode of God was above the dome. So when Jesus returned to God after the events of Good Friday and Easter, he simply had to rise beyond the sky. But in a space age where the sky is not a dome but an infinite void, Luke's cosmological assumptions become obvious because they are now obsolete. The limitation on literalized Truth in the story becomes obvious. Matthew records Jesus in the Sermon on the Mount saying, "You have heard that it was said, 'You shall not commit adultery.' But, I say to you that every one who looks at a woman lustfully has already committed adultery with her in his heart" (Matt. 5:27-28). Reading this, one becomes aware that either the audience was all male or that the author assumes that men are by definition the lusters and women are the lusted-after. The male bias is apparent. When this generation reaches a point where it no longer shares the social and intellectual assumptions that inform and shape the biblical narrative, will we still continue to treat the Scriptures authoritatively? That is a serious issue present before the church.

Sometimes even the most straightforward moral directives are, on further study, not so simple after all. For example, most people believe that the Bible states without equivocation, particularly in the Ten Commandments, that murder is wrong, stealing is wrong, bearing false witness is wrong, adultery is wrong. There is no question here about the meaning of these biblical imperatives—right? Wrong! What the Bible really says is that these things are wrong for a Jew to do to a Jew, but a close reading of the text will reveal that when Jews dealt with their enemies, then lying, killing, stealing, and raping were all acceptable forms of tribal behavior. In war the common pattern was to kill the men, claim the booty, and kidnap the women for sexual sport and servitude. In the Exodus account of the confrontation between Moses and Pharaoh, Moses delighted in bearing false witness, promising the Pharaoh that the Hebrews would only go a day's journey into the wilderness to offer sacrifices to their God (Exod. 5:1ff.). Neither Moses nor Pharaoh really believed that story. When the escape from Egypt did occur, the Hebrews robbed the Egyptians blind—and they did it gleefully (Exod. 12:36). When they were on the other side of the Red Sea, they rejoiced to see the Egyptians dead on the shore (Exod. 14:30). You shall not bear false witness! You shall not steal! You shall not kill! Not applicable, the Hebrews would assert, except in intra-Jewish relationships.

The tribal limit on the moral law of Scripture was graphically expressed in a Deuteronomic text which reads, "You shall not eat anything that dies of itself; you may give it to the alien who is within your towns . . . or you may sell it to a foreigner" (Deut. 14:21). So much for universally applied moral precepts!

We have a holy book into which we have read much and out of which we have quoted, probably inappropriately, for almost two thousand years. Since I will be presenting some new proposals in this volume, I will find myself opposed by those who use the Bible as a weapon to defend tradition. These critics are the spiritual heirs of those who have used this book throughout history to support the status quo whenever an emerging new consciousness promised to bring about changes in the social and economic order. A book that was quoted to justify slavery when slavery was in danger of being outlawed, and to support segregation when that evil system was beginning to crumble, and to keep women suppressed when women began to claim full membership and citizenship rights, will surely be quoted today to condemn changing sexual mores and the experimental patterns in family life that are being tested, and to justify the condemnation of homosexual persons when these historic victims of prejudice begin to assert their right to be themselves.

To counter this, I will go deeply into Holy Scripture to examine in detail specific texts that continue to be frequently used to keep women "in their place" and to return gay and lesbian people to the darkness of their closets. In a real sense, the debate in the church about issues of human sexuality is a debate over the authority of Scripture and over the role of both Scripture and the church in sustaining the ignorance that is the basis of prejudice. I welcome the opportunity to enter the biblical battleground.

Notes

1. Richard E. Friedman argues in his fascinating book *Who Wrote The Bible?* (New York: Summit Books, 1987) that the author of the Deuteronomic material was none other than Jeremiah.
2. This point is made in detail in chapter 3 of my book *Into the Whirlwind* (San Francisco: Harper & Row, 1983).
3. I go into a much fuller explanation of this in my book *The Easter Moment* (San Francisco: Harper & Row, 1987).

CHAPTER EIGHT

The Biblical Attitude Toward Women

*T*here is no doubt about the fact that the Bible is biased against women. The only questions are, Why, and out of what does that bias emerge? That is the nature of the inquiry to be pursued in this chapter.

Throughout the Hebrew Scriptures an intense battle was constantly being waged between the followers of Yahweh and the followers of another religious tradition that was variously called idolatry, Baal worship, or the worship of the fertility gods that were so popular at the local shrines throughout the land. To understand how the Bible defined women, it is necessary to understand this religious conflict, for in addition to theological issues profound sexual issues were also at stake here.

The Yahwist tradition was not ancient, as religious systems go, but it was destined to play a powerful role in the history of the world. It emerged with the stories centering around the patriarch Abraham. It came to self-consciousness during the Exodus, under Moses. It was the religious force that solidified Judah so well that its people survived an exile of almost a century. The cohesiveness of Yahweh worship empowered the people of Judah to return and rebuild their nation following the exile.

The Hebrew Bible was written primarily by the worshipers

of Yahweh. It was a chronicle of the great actions they believed Yahweh had performed for the people. The Yahwists had a vested interest in heightening and embellishing the details that enhanced Yahweh's power. So we read of incredible moments in Jewish history that can only be explained by the divine presence of Yahweh, working on behalf of his chosen people. There were the plagues in Egypt, the parting of the waters of the Red Sea, the manna sent from heaven to feed the wandering people in the wilderness, the crossing of the Jordan River, the destruction of the walls of Jericho, the conquest of Canaan, and many, many others. But despite these dramatic accounts of divine favor and intervention, Yahwism was never the only religion in Israel. The biblical narrative reveals that the people of Israel and Judah fell back again and again into the popular religions of the region, defined variously as idolatry, the worship of a golden calf, or Baal worship.

This pattern of religious infidelity brings up other questions, equally provocative but seldom asked. The Bible does not hesitate to show us the reason why Yahweh might have great appeal among the people, but what was the appeal of what the Bible calls idolatry? Wherein lay the power of this religious tradition that Yahwism never fully succeeded in suppressing? Who was Baal? Why did this Baal so threaten a prophet of Yahweh named Elijah that after the showdown on Mount Carmel he murdered all of Baal's prophets? (I Kings 18:40). Do people in religious conflict kill those who have nothing to commend them? Why could the followers of Yahweh not break the hold of these deities on the people of the covenant?

As late as the seventh century B.C.E. the power of these local shrines was still so strong that the reforms mandated by the newly discovered book of Deuteronomy called for the enforcement of their closing. From that time forward the reformers designated the temple in Jerusalem as the sole determiner of true worship, the Vatican of ancient Judah. Do people oppress, close down, or obliterate religious traditions that are not rivaling them for supremacy? If these traditions were in fact "nothing," as the words of the Yahwists asserted, why did the followers of Yahweh seem so threatened by them?

Even the rigorous Deuteronomic reforms appear to have failed to purify the worship of the Jewish people, for there was still another attempt in the fifth century B.C.E., under Ezra, to root out from Judah yet once again alien but popular religious practices. If one reads behind the lines of Holy Scripture, it becomes apparent that the worship of Yahweh was locked in a titanic and never-ending struggle against a vital enemy. The echoes of that struggle are present in the stories, the rules, the stereotypes, the prohibitions, and the myths. Indeed, they are present on almost every page of the Hebrew Scriptures. Until we identify the hidden appeal of the enemy that created such a spirited competition with the Yahweh tradition, we will not understand the driving passion of the Scriptures.

Yahweh's principle rival was identified most frequently in the Bible by the name Baal. Baal was the male consort to the female deity Asherah. The religion of Asherah-Baal was a nature religion—a fertility cult tied to the cycles of the seasons and the fecundity of the soil and womb. This goddess-god couple was worshiped in local shrines with explicitly sexual liturgies that included both male and female prostitutes.

Yahwism was a new religious development that challenged entrenched Baalism in a battle that lasted until Yahwism finally became dominant, if not fully victorious, among the Jewish people. That victory was not achieved easily, and until it was secure the Yahwists expended great energy trying to eradicate every vestige of their enemy's former power. It was as if the followers of Yahweh feared that the power of this goddess of fertility and her consort might someday return and reclaim preeminence, at Yahweh's expense.

Yahweh was a solitary male god who did not need a female partner to create life. He created instead by speaking the Word. His Spirit was the essential principle of life itself. Baal worship, on the other hand, was intensely sexual, with the sexual power of reproduction honored as the source of life. In the Yahwist tradition the masculinity of God was all important—Yahweh had created nature and was the Lord of nature. In the Baal tradition the feminine fertility principle was an equal to her male consort in the bringing of life into being. The female deity was identified with nature and sought to call people into harmony with nature.

Given the intense rivalry of these two traditions, it stands to reason that the Hebrew Bible, written by the Yahwists, would have an overwhelming male bias. If the followers of Yahweh were engaged in a struggle to destroy the fertility goddess who was Yahweh's primary rival, would they not be prone to denigrate any value or contributions that might be associated with a female deity? Would not women, vital to a fertility religion as representatives of the mother goddess, also be devalued by the Yahwist tradition? This is exactly what happened, and it is out of this struggle that the biblical writers adopted the pervasive anti-female bias that permeates every page of their Scriptures. This anti-female bias not only won the day among the Hebrews but also passed uncritically into Christianity. Through Christianity that male bias has spread throughout the Western world. Whenever the bias was questioned at any time in history, the response came that God had willed it, for this is what the Bible taught. There is no doubt that the Bible taught an aggressive male superiority, but did God will that? Was that God's purpose? Does the sexist prejudice in the Bible reflect the mind of God? Those issues I believe are open to serious question.

To place this into an even earlier and more universal

context, let us journey back into the shadows of prehistoric human life and examine whatever we can discover there about the earliest forms of human worship.

Anthropologists seem certain that the first deity worshiped by human beings was a goddess, not a god. Reverence was given to the deity as the mother of all things living, and she was identified with the earth or the soil. The earth to this day is feminine in every language and mythology the world over. Mother Nature is her pale modern descendant.

The earliest records of the human endeavor reveal that there was little or no distinction made between human life and the rest of the natural world. The original human saw itself only as part of the world of nature, bound to a particular place. To leave the sacred soil that nurtured, fed, and protected primitive human life was, quite literally, to commit suicide. Hence the land itself as the giver of life was deified. The primary analogy by which these creatures understood human life was sexual, and for that reason the woman, the obvious bearer of the new life, was primary. She was created in the image of the earth mother, the source of life. Men were quite secondary. Out of the womb of the earth mother came plants and the other gifts of life. Into the womb of the earth mother at burial went her children and her products; the vital life force of the divine mother had ceased to be present in them. Because the connection between sexual intercourse and childbirth had not yet been discerned, the women of the tribe held the real power. Even the biological life of the male was continued only by the woman. Her fertility gave birth to the individual and gave immortality to the tribe. Because the woman was the essential source of life, God was conceived in primarily female images.

In addition to the reproductive gift of life itself, the man was also drawn to the woman for sexual pleasure and for sexual release. If contemporary studies on Neanderthal life are accurate, sexual intercourse appears to have been understood primarily as a liturgical act whereby the male honored the divine mother by opening the channel through which the mother's gift of new life could be born. Impregnation by the male was not an idea that had yet been imagined.

When the connection between coitus and childbirth was established, the status of the man began to rise. He was then perceived to be crucial to the reproductive process that guaranteed life. The original Mother Earth goddess then came to be complimented by a consort, first thought of as the Father Sky god. The rain coming from the sky was the divine semen sent to impregnate Mother Earth so that life could come forth. Both men and women at that time continued to be defined in terms of the soil and the reproductive processes of nature. There was still no sense of an "I" and no sense of being an entity separate from nature itself (or herself).

Worship in that period of history when the deity was still female (although now accompanied by a male consort) was designed to celebrate and re-create that maternal aspect of the human life and to call people into harmony with the natural forces. The place of the mother in society was still primary. Human beings always form their understanding of God out of their own values, needs, and self-understanding. We do make God in our own image. We deify whatever we perceive to be the source of security and awe, and the giver of life and death. In the earliest period of human history this source of security and giver of life was female, so the original understanding of the deity was primarily feminine.

Herbert W. Richardson in his book *Nun, Witch and Playmate* writes that this maternal understanding of both God and human life prevailed until the dawning of self-consciousness, when a division appeared in human life between the natural instinct and the emerging ego that dared to stand against that instinct. Humanity began to perceive a difference between a person and the soil that sustained that person.[1] The moment we separated ourselves from the soil was also the moment at which reflective thought, and therefore human history, began. At some point some creature freed himself or herself from total immersion in nature, from complete identity with a place, and by an overt act of the will left home and tribe to undertake a life of his or her own, or as we might say today, to seek his or her fortune. A journey opens every great epic and every great religious narrative. That moment produces a new consciousness that brings about a new definition of every aspect of life. When human life is defined in a new way, the God worshiped by that human life will also be defined in a new way. Anthropological studies indicate that this volitional level of self-consciousness was not part of the human experience prior to 7000 B.C.E., but it had become the almost universal human experience by the year 1000 B.C.E. It is not coincidental that most of the major human religious systems were also born in that period of human history. They were the direct by-products of this process of redefinition.

The story of Abraham can be understood anew within this framework. Abraham, a man, left his home, breaking his identity with a place called Ur of the Chaldees in about 1800 B.C.E. By an act of will overcoming the need for security, he journeyed to a new place in response to the perceived call of a deity who also was not bound to Abraham's previous space. Indeed, this God called Abraham to leave home. The personal ego of a human being had reached the point in the evolutionary process where it could challenge and finally replace the definitions operative within nature religions. Will had replaced instinct as the primary motivator of human behavior. A new level of humanity had been achieved.

One symbol of this shift was that human sacrifice, a ritual activity prominent in fertility religions and designed to appease Mother Nature, was largely abandoned. Human life no longer had to feed the appetite of a fertility goddess. This motif is expressed in the most vivid story of the Abraham saga. Abraham, about to sacrifice his firstborn son Isaac, was stopped by the God who called him to journey. Child sacrifice was to be no longer necessary. Abraham realized that this God was no longer circumscribed by the reproductive process of nature. This God rather called Abraham to continue his journey to separate himself from nature and place, to celebrate his own life and the life of his son, and to build a new nation that would in the beginning at least be nomadic. Human beings now proceeded to carve their existence out of nature and to force nature to serve human life above all else.

When human activity moves from identifying with nature to the conquering of nature, then the human understanding of God will reflect that change. Survival will become less a function of the reproductive capabilities of the woman and more a function of the man's ability to make nature meet his needs. Those who seek dominion over Mother Nature will be the ones who hear a male god give to human life the order to subdue nature, the realm of the goddess. In this context a female deity becomes both anachronistic and anathema, and a male deity who has power over all natural forces replaces her. Yet one cannot displace the female goddess without also displacing her incarnation, the female human being. When the female deity faded, so also did the status of the woman. The struggle for food, the need for protection, the advancement of civilization had come to require the strength of the man. As male dominance grew, so the concept of a male god gained strength. After a fierce struggle that lasted perhaps two millennia, the female deity departed the human scene, at least in the West, to hibernate until the struggle for survival once again required her particular attributes.

It was the descendants of this Abraham, out of this transition moment of human history, who crafted the stories of creation that have shaped the sexual stereotypes of our civilization. Their myths of the beginning reflected the struggle between the masculine Yahweh and the fertility cults of Asherah and Baal. The God who called Israel out of

Egypt, just as he called Abraham out of Ur, would confront, engage, and attempt to annihilate the agricultural and fertility deities of the land of Canaan. The successful suppression of fertility worship, with its female deity, was part of the background of the surviving creation story, in which the goddess Eve, mother of all living, consorts with evil and is banished forever from paradise by the superior male god. There follows the biblical insistence on the totally masculine nature of God and the corresponding assignment of divine (i.e., male) prerogatives to men, who alone, the myth argues, are created in the image of this God.

The God of the biblical creation narrative was a solitary male who was understood not as a father but as a king. A father must be complemented by a mother to produce life, which schema would keep the fertility cycle intact. A king, however, could rule over his realm in majestic, lonely splendor. No queen shared status with the king in the ancient world. Indeed, the king would normally preside over a harem where the women lived and loved according to his sole command. The biblical God was envisioned as masculine, without a sexual equal. That is the central principle of monotheism as opposed to bitheism. In bitheism creativity is sexual and therefore demands both the male and female deities. In monotheism creation is volitional, the product of mind and spirit, and is therefore an expression of a self-contained masculinity.

As the horizons of human life continued to expand beyond the natural land-connected processes of survival, the role of the male also expanded. Since God was male, only a human male could properly model this God as the representative holy person. Woman, now unfit to represent the deity, increasingly was confined to the family space of hearth and home. Taboos were developed that limited her capacity to expand her world by inhibiting her participation in the hunt, the fight, the activities of trade, or any civic role of authority, all of which became male responsibilities. Indeed, the woman was thought of as a possession of the man. Throughout the history of warfare she was transferred as property and booty, part of the spoils to which the victor in war was due.

The ancient cities founded by the patriarchal clans had three civic institutions: the palace, the temple, and the wall. All three enforced male dominance and all found expression in the biblical narratives. In the palace the king formulated the laws that were the foundation on which the social grouping of the clan was organized. In the temple the male priesthood designed the rituals that transformed the king's rulings into mythical cosmic acts that stamped the law with a divine intention. The liturgy of that temple included a commemoration of the time their god gave the people his law. Since law was the means by which people escaped the cycles of nature to follow their own wills, these liturgies celebrated that moment of transition in human history.[2]

To the liturgy that recalled the giving of the law was added the liturgy of kingly enthronement. The ritual of enthronement served to unite the cosmic god with that god's people and to break the power of their identity with Mother Nature. Worship was the servant of the hierarchy of the tribe. Church and state were never separate. In the period of Israel's royal history, the king's temple in Jerusalem was the true church and the center of Yahwism. The rivalry between the royal temple and the popular local shrines was nothing less than a rivalry between the enthronement rituals designed to extol kingly and therefore masculine power and the rituals of the fertility cults designed to enable the common people to lapse back into their nature identities that emphasized male and female sexuality. Beyond the king's control, popular worship continually lapsed into the rituals of fertility.

At the wall the soldiers, released from agricultural tasks by the organization and diversification of tribal life, were charged with the task of defending the city against their enemies. Annually they went forth in a holy war that celebrated masculine power and reconnected them to their monarchical male god. The narrative of David and Bathsheba began with the revealing words "In the spring of the year, the time when kings go forth to battle" (II Sam. 11:1). War itself was a ritual of male dominance. It offered men the opportunity to prove their courage. It separated them from the women, who roused in them feelings of sexuality and weakness that lured them from their male pursuits. In warfare they felt virile and potent.

The older biblical creation story, recorded in the second chapter of Genesis, reflected this period of the rise of male dominance. The newer creation story in the first chapter of Genesis was less misogynist, but it still portrayed an exclusively male God who fashioned the universe.

In both creation accounts Yahweh spoke and called life instantaneously into being. Yahweh always stood above or outside of nature. Since nature was female, God could not be bound by it. Even the sun and the moon, once natural deities of male and female description, were Yahweh's creations (Gen. 1:16). God was the craftsman who separated light from darkness, divided the firmament, created nature's power, and made it serve him. Man was made from a clod of earth. He was not the offspring of a woman; he was the work of the master craftsman, the male God. The ties of blood, soil, and nature were thus broken in this creation myth. This craftsman-technician God had assumed the power of the earth mother goddess. Man was made to have dominion over the earth, not to worship it. Procreation and parenting were replaced with concepts of lordship and covenant. The story of life could now escape the cycles of reproduction. History thus became for the first time a human possibility.

This transition from nature to history was not an easy one. The fertility cults provided the security of the known. Action based on the strength of the ego pushed humans into the unknown, into a journey. Since the memory of the past tugged at the edges of the human awareness, the temptation to reclaim the security of the past had to be resisted. One way of dealing with that was to take the security of the past, the identity with nature, out of the past and project it into a future hope. So, the development of human self-consciousness on one level was perceived as "the fall," and the future kingdom of God was envisioned as the goal toward which history was driven. The perceived need for salvation now had a focus.

These are some of the sociocultural truths not so deeply hidden in the creation myths of the Jewish people. These myths had to deal in a new way with the woman. Reversing the obvious pattern of nature, the most ancient creation story in the Bible had the woman created out of the body of the man, as a subhuman but higher than animal helpmate for the male. The dragon who appeared as the female power in so many Middle Eastern myths became, in this story, the snake who brought temptation and was condemned by the male deity to crawl on its belly for all time. The woman who proves to be the downfall of the race was last in creation and first in sin, or as Letty Russell observed, a "twice cursed creature."[3] The authors and carriers of this myth were strongly motivated to make the woman a powerless secondary person. The God who created had defeated and replaced the goddess who procreated. Since the power of female deity was not then fully dissipated, she had to be controlled or mastered, castigated or put down fiercely.

Throughout the religious mythology of the Bible there was tension between these two elements. It was portrayed as a struggle between reason and nature, between an imposed order and an uncontrollable raging chaos. The dragons of the sea, Rahab and Leviathan, that appear so often in Hebrew Scriptures (Pss. 74:12-17; 89:9-12; Job 26:12-13; Isa. 51:9-10) were the ever-present symbols of the female power of darkness, variations of the serpent symbol that always threatened to undo the ordered creation. Eve, who was not accorded the status of being an original part of the created world, was depicted as the one who threatened to undo creation by identifying with the chaos over which the male God hovered to bring order. It was the woman who forced the banishment of the first family from the garden, making the conquering of nature in order to earn one's living the destiny of the male. To know pain in childbirth was the price the woman paid for being evil.

This anti-female myth of creation is reflected in prohibitions on fertile women, who were required to participate in cleansing rituals after menstruation and childbirth. The sacred covenant that provided the framework of biblical history was something between the men and their male god. The women of Israel related to God only insofar as they stayed in relationship with their men. Not surprisingly, therefore, the law of Sinai was addressed only to men. Women had few legal rights in that society. In the Decalogue (Exod. 20) the woman was mentioned in the same breath as the ox, adultery was defined as an act that violated another man's property, and coveting was perceived to be an activity in which only men could engage.

The ramifications of the sexual assumptions found in the creation myths inform the remainder of the Bible also. In Holy Scripture the man had absolute power over the woman's life and over her body. She existed only for his pleasure and to meet his needs. The founding patriarch Abraham demonstrated this on two occasions when, to save his own life, he offered his wife Sarah first to the Pharaoh (Gen. 12) and later to Abimelech, the king of Gerar (Gen. 20). His son Isaac learned to do this from Abraham and repeated the process in Gerar by offering his wife Rebekkah to the same king Abimelech (Gen. 26). We call that "pimping" today, but the Bible took no offense at it, for the woman was not worthy of any consideration. When Sarah could not conceive a child she gave her maid, Hagar, to Abraham to be a surrogate mother for his son (Gen. 16). Only

Abraham's continued line, not Sarah's continued dignity, was important. Time and again in the biblical narrative the barrenness of the woman was interpreted as her fault and her shame. Her sole purpose apparently was to bear children and to serve her husband. From her earlier position of honor as mother of the race, woman was downgraded to being only a passive womb where the offspring of the male could be nurtured to full-term. If she could not carry the man's child, if her body expelled his sperm (as menstruation was thought to do), then she had little other worth. Leah, Jacob's first wife, was portrayed as hoping that her success in presenting Jacob with sons would cause him to love her. The Bible provides us with the story of Hannah praying to be given a child so that her shame might be taken away (I Sam. 1) and with the account of the barren wife of Manoah, mother of Samson by God's intervention (Judg. 13) but nonetheless so insignificant that her name was not even given in the narrative. However the temptress Delilah, who stole Samson's masculine power, was certainly named (Judg. 16). Like Eve, she contaminated the purity of male creation, stealing the male's power and turning order into evil chaos.

Women were defined in the Bible almost entirely in terms of their sexual function. Provisions were even made in the Torah to assure that the woman would be blamed when "a spirit of jealousy came upon a man." The Torah even went so far as to prescribe a method whereby the woman could be tested for her responsibility in creating the man's jealousy (Num. 5). The law also prohibited women from inheriting property (Num. 36) and declared women incompetent to make vows or to enter into contracts (Num. 30). An additional insight into the biblical attitude toward women can be found in Numbers, where instructions were given in how the Israelites were to treat Midianite prisoners at the end of a victorious battle: All the males were to be killed; all the women who were not virgins were to be killed; but the men of Israel were free to keep for themselves all the women who were virgins. If there is any question as to the fact that the Bible was addressed to a male audience to protect male values, it is invalidated by the injunction "A woman who grabs a man by his private parts shall have her hand cut off" (Deut. 25).

When we seek biblical guidance on the issues of human sexuality today, we discover that despite the frequent quotation of the Bible in the defense of conventional morality, the Bible presents us with ambiguous, contradictory, and sometimes absolutely unacceptable standards for making sexual judgments today. On one side, no sexual practice was condemned more completely in the Bible than the sin of adultery. It was one of the commandments to which was added the death penalty (Deut. 22:22). The story of the woman taken in adultery (John 8:1-11) gives evidence that this penalty was still a possibility in Jesus' time. But on the other side, we must recognize that the prohibition of adultery, as the writers of the Bible understood it, bound primarily the woman. Adultery in the Bible was defined as sex with a married woman. The marital status of the man was irrelevant. If the woman was not married, sexual relations with her were not adulterous. Women were the possessions of the primary male in their lives (see the story of Judah and Tamar in Gen. 38 and the story of the Levite's concubine in Judg. 19). If someone other than a woman's husband took from her the sexual pleasures she had to give, then that man was both robbing her husband of something that belonged to him alone and tampering with his line of succession.

The second thing to note about adultery in the Bible is that the prevailing marital pattern of the times was not monogamy but polygamy. What does adultery mean when one man can possess an unlimited number of women for his own amusement? How can an injunction based on these premises be used to define morality today?

When we move on into the Christian Scriptures, polygamy

disappears but the second-class status of women does not. Paul repeated the masculine distortions of the biblical creation myth by asserting that man only "is the image and glory of God. . . . Man was not made from woman, but woman from man. Neither was man created for woman, but woman for man" (I Cor. 11:7-9). He further prohibited a woman from speaking in church (I Cor. 14:34ff.), since she was a subordinate creature, that is, not fully human. This anti-female polemic became even more strident by the time the pseudo-Pauline letters to Timothy and to the church in Ephesus were written. "Let a woman learn in silence with all submissiveness," the letter to Timothy states; "I permit no woman to teach or to have authority over men" (I Tim. 2:11-12). This author went on to blame women once again for sin and to suggest that a woman's salvation would come "through bearing children, if she continues in faith and love and holiness, with modesty" (I Tim. 2:15). The author of Ephesians exhorted wives to submit themselves to their husbands as unto the Lord, "for the husband is the head of the wife as Christ is the head of the church" (Eph. 5:23).

There were throughout the biblical story some exceptions to the patriarchal rules that seemed ever ready to keep women in their place. Some women in the sacred drama did rise to positions of power. Miriam's intervention saved Moses' life (Exod. 2); she continued to be involved in matters of state (Num. 12). Deborah exercised important political and military leadership twenty-seven hundred years before Joan of Arc (Judg. 4). Ruth's faithfulness to the law of her husband's religion was so complete that she was grafted into the covenant people and became the great-great-grandmother of King David (Ruth 4:18-22). Queen Esther put faithfulness to God before her own life and won for her people a mighty victory in the continuing war against human prejudice (Esther 1-10). Judith's clever strategy defeated her enemy by turning sexuality into a weapon of war (see the book of Judith in the Apocrypha).

In the Christian story all four Gospels assert that a group of women were the first people to receive the Easter announcement of the resurrection. Luke's Gospel portrays Mary, Jesus' mother, as the primary witness to the true meaning of his life as God's special self-revelation. Women seem to have been the financial supporters of the apostolic band and were primary leaders in Paul's embryonic church.[4]

Despite these exceptions, however, the patriarchal definitions of men and women are predominant throughout the pages of our sacred story from Genesis to Revelation. In light of all this, what does it mean, in the midst of a sexual revolution, when people call on the church and world to return to the sexual morality of the Bible? Both the religious and ethical directives of the Bible were formulated out of a patriarchal understanding of life, with the interests of men being primary. Are we willing to return to these destructive definitions of both men and women? Do we desire to hold up the biblical image of dominance and submission as the Christian model for male-female relationships in our time?

If the Bible has nothing more than the letter of literalism to offer to our understanding of human sexuality today, then I must say that I stand ready to reject the Bible in favor of something that is more human, more humane, more life giving, and, dare I say, more godlike. I do believe, however, that there is a spirit beneath the letter that brings the Bible forward in time with integrity. That spirit must be sought with diligence. Without it the Bible will not be for our times a source of life or a guide in the area of sexual ethics.

Notes

1. Herbert W. Richardson, *Nun, Witch and Playmate* (New York: Edwin Mellen Press, 1971).
2. For details of how this developed in Israel, see chapters 2 and 3 of *Beyond*

Moralism, John S. Spong and Denise G. Haines (San Francisco: Harper & Row, 1986).
3. Letty M. Russell, "Woman's Liberation in a Biblical Perspective," *Concern* 13, no. 5 (May–June 1971).
4. John S. Spong, *Into the Whirlwind* (San Francisco: Harper & Row, 1983), p. 189.

CHAPTER NINE

The Bible and Homosexuality

ow can you affirm what the Bible calls sin?"
Most people who think of themselves as
"Bible-believing Christians" are quite convinced
that they correctly know what the Bible says on
the issue of homosexuality. Homosexuality is wrong. It is an
evil perversion. It is a crime against nature. It is the most
heinous sin. Many other negative epithets are employed,
appearing to leave little room for debate on this issue. One
plaintive plea came from a Southern pastor who wrote
urging that I "be in repentance and sorrow for the
anti-scriptural stand on sexuality you have taken. The
thought of blessing the very same perversions that have
scripturally been promised due penalty is abhorrent to the
very mind of Christ."

Other letters that I have received quoted specific passages
from the Bible. There was a very repetitive quality about
these citations because the number of biblical references to
homosexuality is quite small. Compared to the sin of idolatry,
for example, or to the ritual details of temple worship, the
time spent on homosexuality by the biblical authors is
minuscule. There is not one reference to homosexuality in
any of the four Gospels. The argument from silence is not a
powerful one, but it does suggest that those who consider
this "the most heinous sin" must be terribly disturbed that

our Lord appears either to have ignored it completely or to have said so little on the subject that no part of what he said was remembered or recorded. Perhaps the judgment these people make expresses a hope and a wish, not very well substantiated but nonetheless vigorously claimed, that both God and Jesus might agree with them.

Certainly there are biblical passages that seem quite specific in their condemnation of homosexual activity. These passages will be examined in some detail. I will seek to identify their origin in history, to exegete their meaning to the community of faith that produced them, to place them into the context of their cultural and theological milieu, and to raise questions about both the scope of knowledge of those whose words were destined to become Scripture and the continuing truthfulness of their perceptions. Perhaps we will discover that everything written in the Bible is, first of all, not eternal and, second, not necessarily true.

The first presumed biblical reference to homosexuality is the story of the destruction of the towns of Sodom and Gomorrah. From the word "Sodom" have come the nouns "sodomy" and "sodomite" and the verb "to sodomize." Webster defines "sodomy" thus: "from the homosexual proclivities of the men of the city of Sodom in Genesis 19:1-11; carnal copulation with a member of the same sex or with an animal . . . the penetration of the male organ into the mouth or anus of another." The sodomite is the "one who practices sodomy." To sodomize is "to practice sodomy upon [another]." Despite the wide options offered by Webster, the primary understanding of sodomy in Western civilization is as a synonym for homosexuality and most especially for male homosexuality. Strangely enough, few people bother to read the complete text in Genesis 19. They are so sure they know what it means that they don't want to be confused with facts, especially biblical facts. This book, however, cannot luxuriate in such ignorance, so our focus now turns to that primary biblical passage so regularly quoted to condemn homosexuality.

The background to the Sodom episode begins in Genesis 18. Many, many years ago a man named Lot, who was nephew of the patriarch Abraham, lived in the city of Sodom. While Abraham was sitting at the door of his tent by the oaks of Mamre one afternoon, three men stood in front of him. One of the three seems to have been the Lord and the other two were called angels, but whether or not that word had supernatural connotations at that time is not clear. Abraham received his divine guests with all of the hospitality required in the Middle East. He washed their feet, invited them to stay with him, and began to prepare for them a meal of cakes, a tender roasted calf, and curds and milk. Abraham stood by them under the tree while they ate.

After dinner the guests inquired about Sarah, saying that when they returned in the spring Sarah would be the mother of a son. Since Sarah had long been barren and was now so advanced in age that "it had ceased to be with Sarah after the manner of women," she greeted this word by laughing out loud. "After I have grown old, and my husband is old, shall I have pleasure?" That is hardly the way the Puritans would have framed the question! Sarah's laughter was heard, and she was rebuked by the Lord with the question, "Is anything too hard for the Lord?"

The descendants of Abraham were now assured by Sarah's impending pregnancy. The divine promise to make of Abraham a great nation was intact. The visitors then turned their attention to the city of Sodom. Since Abraham was to become a great and mighty nation through which all the nations of the earth would be blessed, the Lord decided to confide in Abraham his plans for the city of Sodom. "Because the outcry against Sodom and Gomorrah is great and their sin is very grave, I will go down to see whether they have done altogether according to the outcry which has come to me; and if not I will know."

Two things are worthy of note in this passage. First, the sin of Sodom and Gomorrah is not identified. Second, the image of God is not only anthropomorphic but very limited. This "Lord" does not know what is going on in the world. He has heard reports, an "outcry" he calls it, and he has come down to check on those reports, to see whether or not they are accurate. There is certainly no omniscience here. The two men/angels turned and went toward Sodom while Abraham stood before the Lord and began the remarkable ritual of Middle Eastern bargaining designed to lower the price of a commodity, or in this case, the judgment of the deity.

"Wilt thou indeed destroy the righteous with the wicked?" Abraham began. "Suppose there are fifty righteous within the city; wilt thou then destroy the place and not spare it for the fifty righteous who are in it?" Abraham continued to lecture God, reminding God of the divine nature; "Far be it from thee to do such a thing, to slay the righteous with the wicked, so that the righteous fare as the wicked! Far be that from thee! Shall not the judge of all the earth do right?" The Lord, obviously moved by this rhetoric from Abraham, responded affirmatively, "If I find at Sodom fifty righteous in the city, I will spare the whole place for their sake."

Abraham, having won the initial skirmish, pressed his advantage. Suppose, he asked, there are but forty-five, or forty, or thirty, or twenty, or even just ten? In each case the divine promise was given, until finally, "for the sake of ten I will not destroy it." Then the Lord went his way and Abraham returned to his place. Abraham was concerned, at least by implication, about the welfare of his nephew Lot, a Sodomite, a term that at this point in history meant only a resident and citizen of the city of Sodom.

By this time the two divine messengers, no longer accompanied by the Lord, arrived at the gate of Sodom. Lot rose to meet them and to offer them the expected hospitality, without which no traveler would ever have survived. "Turn aside . . . to your servant's house," Lot entreated, "and spend the night, and wash your feet; then you may rise up early and go on your way." The visitors demurred at first, responding, "No, we will spend the night in the street." But Lot urged them, following the custom and language of hospitality, until he prevailed. So the visitors entered Lot's house, and he prepared a feast for them. He baked unleavened bread and they ate. As they prepared for sleep the men of the city, every one of them from the oldest to the youngest, surrounded Lot's house and demanded that Lot's guests be surrendered to them "that we may know them." There is no question that the Hebrew verb translated "know" carries the connotation of sexual intimacy. Earlier in the biblical text, at the end of the creation story when Adam and Eve were evicted from the garden, we read that "Adam *knew* Eve his wife, and she conceived" (Gen. 4:1). So it is certainly fair to assume that sexual interest was there in the gathering crowd of the male citizens of Sodom. It would be quite strange, however, for every single man of the city to be a homosexually oriented man, but the text is quite clear, the men of Sodom gathered "to the last man."

A study of Middle Eastern practices suggests a motivation somewhat different from sexual pleasure. These guests were aliens in a foreign city, subject to the will of its citizens, the recipients of their protection. An alien outside the security of his or her own tribe was totally at the mercy of the hospitality of another tribe. Being without rights, the alien could be befriended or abused by a city, as it chose. A popular way to insult the stranger was to force him to take the female role in the sex act. Nothing was more insulting to a man than to be treated like a woman, so an alien who was forced to act out the woman's role in sexual activity would receive the ultimate power insult that the male citizens of a city could administer. It would be a reminder of his weakness and vulnerability and of the strength and power of the citizenry. (Of course, in that day citizenship was a privilege extended only to men.) I propose that these were the realities behind the story. The men of Sodom wanted to abuse the guests of Lot by forcing them to take the woman's part in sexual acts. I suspect that in practice only a few of the men would perform sexually. The others would cheer and urge them on. Perhaps the few who did perform sexually were gay, and in this manner homosexual activity, patriotism, and mob violence combined to legitimize this misunderstood sexual desire.

In any event, Lot rescued his guests and shut them up safely inside his house. If they were in fact angels, they did not seem to possess any supernatural power. Lot also rebuked the men of Sodom: "I beg you my brothers, do not act so wickedly." That is as far as most people read. They know that the biblical tradition records that Sodom and Gomorrah were both destroyed by fire; that God judged them to be so wicked that there were not found even ten righteous persons inside the city. The implication is that homosexuality was the sin and that people guilty of this sin were deserving of divine wrath. But listen to the remainder of the story.

Lot, seeking to placate the mob at his door, went on to say, "Behold, I have two daughters who have not known man; let me bring them out to you, and do to them as you please; only do nothing to these men, for they have come under the shelter of my roof." How many of us can read this and say, "This is the word of the Lord!" Lot, the righteous man who would be spared by God, acting out of the custom and conviction of his day was willing to protect his guests at the price of offering his virgin daughters for sexual abuse.

To make the story even more confusing, the young men to whom Lot's daughters had been promised in marriage appear to have been members of that mob (Gen. 19:14), and they were subsequently invited by Lot to join his family in an escape from the destruction that would befall Sodom. These foolish young men thought Lot was jesting, so they declined and were destroyed. An additional, rather weird event in this narrative is that the angels sent Lot, his wife, and his two daughters out with instructions not to look back but to flee to the city of Zoar. The angels promised that the destruction of Sodom would be postponed until Lot and his family were safe. But Lot's wife disobeyed the command not to look back, and she was turned into a pillar of salt (Gen. 19:26), leaving only Lot and his two virgin daughters as successful escapees.

Lot was afraid of the men in the city of Zoar, and for good reason, since he was now the alien, so he went to live with his daughters in a cave in the hills. His daughters, fearful that they would never get married and have children, plotted to get their father drunk so that they could "lie with him." They did so on successive nights with resulting pregnancies. By this incestuous relationship the firstborn daughter had a son whom she named Moab, and the second daughter had a son whom she named Ammon or Ben-Ammi. Thus, in the view of the Hebrew Scriptures both the Moabites and the Ammonites came into being as the descendants of an incestuous relationship.

That is the full story of Sodom, quoted so often to prove that the Bible condemns homosexuality. What a strange text to use for such a purpose. The biblical narrative approves Lot's offer of his virgin daughters to satisfy the sexual demands of the angry mob. It suggests that incest is a legitimate way of impregnating women when there is no man around save the father of those women. What society would today be willing to incorporate either of these practices into its moral code? Who among us is willing to accept the definition of women implicit in this account? If we reject the denigration of women as property or the practice of incest, both being based upon an inadequate view of morality, are we not also free to reject this society's faulty understanding of homosexuality as being also based upon inadequate moral grounds?

Perhaps an even more important issue is the one of gang

rape, which seemed to be the intention of the men of Sodom. Is gang rape ever right, regardless of whether it is homosexual or heterosexual in nature? Lot seemed to think that homosexual gang rape was evil, especially since it violated the Middle Eastern law of hospitality, while the heterosexual gang rape of his daughters would be acceptable since no hospitality laws were at stake. Is it right for anyone to suggest that the condemnation of homosexual gang rape is to be equated with the condemnation of homosexuality per se? I think not, and I further believe that anyone who reads this biblical narrative with an open mind will discover that the real sin of Sodom was the unwillingness on the part of the men of the city to observe the laws of hospitality.

To make sure that this point is clear, the Bible repeats the Sodom and Gomorrah story in substantial detail in Judges 19, where once again the laws of hospitality are violated. A Levite and his concubine are given hospitality by an old man in the city of Gibeah. The men of that city gather, demanding that the guest be turned over to them for sexual degradation. The old man offers his virgin daughter and the Levite's concubine instead. If there is any doubt as to what was being proposed by the man of the house the text removes it, for that text has him say, "Here are my virgin daughter and [the] concubine. Let me bring them out now. Ravish them and do to them what seems good to you; but against this man do not do so vile a thing." Somehow the Bible did not seem to think it vile to abuse a woman sexually. The concubine alone was turned over to the men "and they knew her, and abused her all night until the morning." Her dead body was on the steps of the master's house when dawn broke. When the Bible is quoted literally to affirm a particular moral stance or to condemn specific behavior, it might be well for the one quoting to read the text in its entirety. Selective literalism is a very weak basis upon which to argue for the condemnation of anything. Morality will not ever be sustained by biblical ignorance.

There are other references to homosexuality in the Hebrew Scriptures where the English translation is simply in error and reflects the prejudice of the translator. A case in point is in Deuteronomy 23:17, which the King James Bible renders, "There shall be no whore of the daughters of Israel, nor a sodomite of the sons of Israel." The Hebrew word translated "whore" is *qedeshah,* and the Hebrew word rendered "sodomite" is the masculine form of the same word, or *qadesh.* These words mean quite simply a holy woman or a holy man and referred not to whoredom or homosexuality but to the cult of male and female temple prostitutes. The Revised Standard Version of the Bible renders this word as "cult prostitute" (for both genders), here and in several other places. But those who are certain that the King James Bible is the only true version of God's word find their prejudice against homosexual persons affirmed by this blatant mistranslation. The people of Israel had moved away from the agricultural and fertility gods of their neighbors. These cults worshiped fertility deities and both male and female prostitutes were part of their liturgical rites. It was not to be so for the worshipers of Yahweh, the book of Deuteronomy asserted. Even in ancient Canaan the temple prostitutes engaged in heterosexual activity leading to conception. Homosexual activity was never even hinted at, in the original texts of these passages.[1]

If one wants to make a case against homosexuality based on the Hebrew Scriptures, the best place to turn is to the Holiness Code of the book of Leviticus. This book, principally the work of the priestly writers during the late sixth or early fifth centuries B.C.E. while the Hebrew people were in the Babylonian exile, clearly and unmistakably condemns homosexual behavior, at least in its male manifestation. The major references are Leviticus 18:22 ("You shall not lie with a male as with a woman. It is an abomination.") and Leviticus 20:13 ("If a man lies with a male as with a woman, both of them have committed an abomination. They shall be put to death, their blood is upon them.").

Israel's call was to be different. This nation, as a response to its God, felt it had to "be holy, for [God is] holy" (Lev. 11:44-45). Its Scripture captured this theme when it asserted that God has "separated you from the peoples, that you should be mine" (Lev. 20:26). It was this sense of Israel's distinctiveness that kept her people separate from the Egyptians. A people that cannot be absorbed will finally split off in an exodus. This same distinctiveness led Israel to establish its identity as a unique people over against the Canaanites among whom they settled. Later it would keep them intact as a people through almost a century of exile in Babylon. This defining virtue of feeling called by God to be different is the background context of the Holiness Code in the book of Leviticus. It is here that homosexuality is condemned, but so are many other practices, such as child sacrifice, using mediums or sorcerers, incest, intercourse during menstruation, and bestiality. Activities that presumably had marked the life of the Canaanite people were not to be present in the people of the covenant.

The wording in Leviticus does not give us any clues as to the nature of the homosexual liaison being forbidden. Was this an aggressive act, the imposition of the will of a stronger man upon a weaker man? Was there any sense of mutuality? The penalty of death is to be imposed on both persons, which might imply an act of mutual consent, but the code also calls for death of both man and animal in cases of bestiality, and the animal could hardly be said to be a consenting participant.

It is also to be noted that the language of this text specifically confines it to male homosexual activity. Does this mean that the biblical writers did not know about female homosexuality? Or did they know about it and specifically not condemn it? Or was it that semen, the seed of life, was not wasted in the female homosexual act? During the exile the passion to reproduce, to guarantee the future of the exiled nation, was a very high priority and would have mitigated against any practices wherein the potential source of life was wasted.

This was not an age of population explosion. The same group of people who wrote the book of Leviticus also gave us the familiar seven-day creation narrative of Genesis 1. That narrative had God create the male and female together, both in God's image. The first words spoken to that man and woman were "Be fruitful and multiply and fill the earth" (Gen. 1:28). The writers were quite sure that the only sexual activity specifically blessed by God was that between male and female that led to procreation. The circumstances of that day, quite different from our own, determined their conclusions, but should they necessarily determine similar conclusions for our time? We need also to ask whether the authors of Leviticus had sufficient knowledge of the phenomenon of homosexuality to make an adequate judgment for all ages to come.

To determine answers to these questions, we must go even more deeply into Leviticus in particular and the entire Torah in general, and see whether there are other "truths" and "insights" there that have been abandoned instead of clung to, when new knowledge rendered them obsolete.

"Abomination," the word Leviticus uses to describe homosexuality, is a strong word and carries a sense of repulsive evil. It is noteworthy that the priestly writers use that same word to describe a menstruating woman. There is no question but that in many ancient traditions, including those described by the Bible, there was a deep fear of menstruation. Legends and superstitions that reflected that fear circulated freely. Cleansing rituals were required before the banished menstruating woman was allowed back into the life of the tribe. She was unclean and a presumed threat to male virility and to the health and well-being of the male sex organs. If a man had sexual relations with a menstruating woman, both were to be cut off from the people (Lev. 20:18).[2]

But the modern world has shed its fear of menstruation and now understands its natural role in procreation. Since it is clear we no longer agree with the biblical understanding of menstruation and do not feel bound to honor biblical injunctions concerning it, must we then be bound to honor the biblical understanding of homosexuality? What is it that makes us attribute to pre-modern Semites a universal wisdom, and makes us assume that their written words are free of ignorance, superstition, or prejudice?

Leviticus also gave instructions to Aaron as to who was to be disqualified from approaching God or acting as priest for the people. For us today, it is a strange list. The rejected were those who had a "blemish" (Lev. 21:17). A blemish was then defined among other things as being blind, lame, having a mutilated face, being a hunchback or a dwarf, or having scabs or crushed testicles (Lev. 21:18-20). The mentality of that age assumed that all these physical abnormalities were signs of the judgment and rejection of God. They did not understand that the polio virus could cause a fever that could leave one with a paralyzed limb. They could not comprehend astigmatism or cataracts, which can blind. The genetic origin of the dwarf or the hunchback was simply beyond their scope of knowledge. Undescended testicles would be considered crushed, and as we know today, the Klinefelter man who has the XXY genotype has empty scrotal sacs and no testicles in most instances, which would give the appearance of having crushed testicles.

None of these prohibitions or definitions are accepted today. They are clear examples of pre-modern ignorance. Not even the most vigorous fundamentalist would cite these texts to justify exclusion of such persons from any position today. The nature of prejudice is to condemn whatever is not understood, for ignorance always breeds fear and insecurity. Because there is still a large measure of both ignorance and fear abroad concerning the nature and origin of homosexuality, people seem quite willing still to quote this ancient source of Leviticus as the infallible and final word of God, because it validates and confirms as true their particular prejudice. If many of the other pronouncements of the priestly writers have been dismissed, then how valid is the claim that only in these isolated texts on homosexuality is the inerrant word of God spoken?

There are other sections in Leviticus that pose the same issue. Leviticus supports capital punishment. So do many conservative Christians, but I have yet to meet a conservative Christian who would advocate execution for cursing (Lev. 24:14), blasphemy (Lev. 24:16), being a false prophet (Deut. 13:5), worshiping a false god (Deut. 17:1-8), or cursing or dishonoring one's parents (Lev. 20:9). Though we have discarded these Torah injunctions, some still continue to presume that the Torah's condemnation of homosexuality is valid, that it is not based upon ignorance, and that it is still binding on the church today. That point of view simply will not hold. It cannot be sustained. Ignorance, no matter how buttressed by Scripture quotations, is finally still ignorance. The Levitical condemnation of homosexuality is a pre-modern illustration of ignorance. Since that judgment of ignorance has been made on hundreds of lesser Levitical prescriptions, it should not be difficult to add this one more.

There are many semi-fundamentalist Christians who are quite willing to surrender texts in what they call the Old Testament but will not do so in the New Testament. They are in fact unselfconscious Marcionites, followers of that second-century heretic Marcion who wanted to rid the church of its Hebrew heritage, including the Hebrew Scriptures. Being forced to abandon a word from the Torah is not traumatic for them, if they can establish their point of view out of the New Testament.

Most Christians in fact tend to value only the elements of

the Hebrew Scriptures that retain a sense of their ancient origins and religious understanding—creation, fall, flood, exodus, wilderness, promised land, exile, and messianic expectation. They also retain what they believe to be the moral essence of the law embodied in the Ten Commandments. Even when expounding the Ten Commandments, however, Christians show an amazing ability to forget history and tradition. The Sabbath day restriction, for example, is simply transferred willy-nilly to the first day of the week, the Christian Sunday.[3]

When we turn to the attitude of the Christian Scriptures toward homosexuality, the inconclusiveness found in the Hebrew Scriptures is still present. We have already observed that there is total silence on this issue in Matthew, Mark, Luke/Acts, and John. Paul is the most quoted source in the battle to condemn homosexuality.

Paul was quite clear. He wrote, "Their women exchanged natural relations for unnatural, and the men likewise gave up natural relations with women and were consumed with passion for one another, men committing shameless acts with men and receiving in their person the due penalty for their error" (Rom. 1:26-27). In this passage Paul certainly appears to be stating that homosexuality is evil.

Since every letter is a dialogue in which the reader is privy only to one side, and since the Epistles are letters of which we are neither the writer nor the intended recipient, it is important that we determine, first, to whom this letter was addressed and, second, the historical context in which the letter would have been heard and understood. Paul had never been to Rome. This letter was designed to introduce him and to prepare the Roman Christians to receive him and to become a supportive base for his planned missionary journeys to Spain (Rom. 15:22-24).

We can assume that the early tension between Jewish Christians and Gentile Christians found its way into the Roman Church also. We also know that under the reign of the emperor Claudius (41–54 C.E.) the Jews were expelled from Rome, including those Jews who had become Christians. Roman officials made no such subtle distinctions, and Luke, who would argue that Christians were both an extension and an expansion of the Jewish tradition and should therefore be given the same freedom from religious persecution accorded the Jews, was still some forty years into the future. With the Jewish Christians forced from the city, the Gentile Christians became dominant in the church. However under the emperor Nero, whose reign began in 54 C.E., the expulsion order against the Jews was repealed, and the Jewish Christians returned to Rome, renewing the tension in the church between the two groups.[4]

The Epistle to the Romans was written sometime before the year 58 C.E. The division in the Roman Christian community was uppermost in the mind of Paul as he wrote. In an attempt at reconciliation, he made an appeal for God from nature that was universal and not bound to the Jewish heritage (Rom. 1:20ff.). He also made an appeal for the primacy of the Jews in God's plan of salvation (Rom. 9–11).

It was within his apologia for universality that the verses that seem to condemn homosexuality were included. His argument was that in the worship of idols instead of the creator the worshiping creature became distorted. Truth was exchanged for a lie, and natural relations were confused with unnatural. Homosexual activity was regarded by Paul as a punishment visited upon the idolaters by God because of their unfaithfulness. In this letter women were included as equal partners in the sin of homosexuality. This is the only scriptural reference to lesbianism in the entire Bible.

For Paul, nature was not separate from God but was rather a creation of God. He was not suggesting that there was a natural norm that was broken by homosexuality, but rather that homosexuality was itself a punishment meted out to those who rejected the God of creation. When Paul used the metaphor of grafting the Gentile branch onto the Jewish tree, he suggested that God might violate the laws of nature to include both Israel and the Gentiles in God's kingdom (Rom. 11:24).

Homosexuality was thus for Paul not the sin but the punishment. The sin was unfaithfulness. This text was an indictment against faithlessness, with the suggestion that it would be punished with the identity confusion that manifested itself in homosexuality. If human beings could not discern the true God, they would be punished with undiscerning minds that would not discern other vital distinctions. It was an unnatural act for a heterosexual person to engage in homosexual behavior, he argued. He did not or perhaps could not imagine a life in which the affections of a male might be naturally directed to another male.

In I Corinthians 6:9-11 Paul gave a list of those who would not inherit the kingdom of God. That list included the immoral, idolators, adulterers, sexual perverts, thieves, the greedy, drunkards, revilers, and robbers. In I Corinthians 5:10 he had a similar list, but it included only the immoral, the greedy, robbers, and idolaters. In I Corinthians 5:11 Paul expanded that list by adding revilers and drunkards. In I Corinthians 6:9-11 sexual perverts, thieves, and adulterers are added. "Sexual perverts" is really a translation of two words: *malakos*, which literally means "soft" or "lacking in self-control" but was used to mean the effeminacy associated with homosexuality, and *arsenokoitus*, which literally means "a male lying" and probably referred to a male prostitute. The person with whom the male was lying was not mentioned, so presumably it could be either a male or a female. However, it was both possible and conceivable that the juxtaposition of *malakos*, the soft, effeminate word, with *arsenokoitus*, the word meaning male prostitute, was meant to refer to the passive and active males in a homosexual liaison, though that could not be proved and many scholars would dispute that conclusion.

These two references in Romans and I Corinthians exhaust the content of the Pauline corpus that specifically refers to homosexuality. Even with the context explained and the words analyzed, it still appears to me that Paul would not approve of homosexual behavior. It also appears to be obvious that Paul did not understand either the origin or the effects of a homosexual orientation. The fact that he viewed it not as sin but as punishment would cause one to question his assumptions.

What do we know about Paul that might help us to understand better the meaning of his words? He revealed much personal data in the epistles. He never married. He seemed incapable of relating to women in general, except to derogate them. His whole theological passion came out of an enormous sense of being unworthy and a sinner, a self-definition that had to be fed by some powerful self-negativity. His conversion experience was one of being loved while yet a sinner. God in Christ had accepted him, though he was sure he was unacceptable, and God had loved him into becoming a new creature in Christ. Paul described a war that went on within him, over which he had no control—a conflict in his being: "I do not do what I want, but I do the very thing I hate. . . . Nothing good dwells within me, that is, in my flesh. . . . Wretched man that I am! Who will deliver me from this body of death?" (Rom. 7:15, 18, 24). He talked of his "thorn in the flesh" that he prayed for God to remove without success (II Cor. 12:7-9). God's answer was "My grace is sufficient for you, for my power is made perfect in weakness." This was the portrait of a man who had known some inner conflict. Was that connected with Paul's understanding of himself, of his own sexuality? If homosexuality could be viewed by Paul as God's punishment, could not whatever it was that ate at Paul's soul also be seen that way?

Was Paul's opinion about homosexuality accurate, or was it limited by the lack of scientific knowledge available to him in his day and infected by the prejudice born of ignorance? An examination of some of Paul's other assumptions and conclusions will help answer this question.

Who today would share Paul's anti-Semitic attitude when he wrote, "God gave to [the Jews] a spirit of stupor,/eyes that should not see and ears that should not hear/down to this very day" (Rom. 11:8). These words now embarrass the ecumenical and interfaith community.

Paul believed that the authority vested in the state was instituted by God and was therefore not to be challenged by Christians (Rom. 13:1-2). Yet such people as the framers of the Magna Carta, George Washington, and Martin Luther King, Jr., believed that they had both a right and a duty to challenge the power of the established government. Paul believed that all women ought to be veiled (I Cor. 11:5-16). His sole support on this issue today comes from Moslem fundamentalists.

In these attitudes Paul's thinking has been challenged and transcended even by the church. Is Paul's commentary on homosexuality more absolute than some of his other antiquated, culturally conditioned ideas?

In the Pauline corpus the apostle did try to distinguish between that which was his opinion and that which was the revealed tradition of the church. He implied that the revealed tradition carried more authority than his opinion. Unfortunately, when Paul discussed many issues, including homosexuality, he did not always tell us whether this was personal opinion or revealed tradition. It really did not matter, though, for both personal opinion and revealed tradition are subject to change in the light of new knowledge and new insight. It is certainly possible, indeed probable in view of the now abandoned Pauline position on many issues, that what was articulated in Paul's writing was not God's unchanging word but Paul's ill-informed, culturally biased prejudices. Responsible Christians cannot close their minds to the knowledge explosion in the field of human sexuality by hiding behind a Pauline quotation and claiming that this is "the word of the Lord."

There are three other references in the New Testament to examine. One is in the pseudo-Pauline epistle to Timothy and the others are in the general epistles Jude and II Peter. I will not rehearse the reasons for the overwhelming consensus in the world of biblical scholars that I Timothy is not Pauline, but it lies primarily in the epistle's assumption of a highly developed church structure and the existence of a developed body of doctrine, both of which point to a time somewhat beyond the life of Paul. The purpose of the letter was to correct false teachers who were promoting speculative rather than authoritative teaching. The author listed the types of people who need to hear the law: immoral persons, *arsenokoitais* (translated as "sodomites" in the Revised Standard Version and as "them that defile themselves with mankind" in the King James Version), and kidnappers.

The argument was that correct teaching would issue in correct behavior, hence the presence of evil behavior revealed the presence of bad teaching. If "kidnappers" referred to people who enslaved young boys for the purpose of sexual exploitation, then the three words might be taken together to mean the male who desired sex with a young boy, the young boy himself, and the slave dealer who trapped the boy for sale. As such, this passage would refer to a particular type of exploitative sexual activity involving male sex slaves that is and should be condemned. But that should not be broadened to condemn the forms of love between consenting same-sex persons that are not exploitative but mutually life giving.

The references in Jude and II Peter are related to each other, so they really constitute a single source. Second Peter appears to be dependent on Jude. Neither is thought to have been written by the person whose name the epistle bears. Both are dated in a range from the end of the first century of the Christian era until well into the second century. Both use Sodom and Gomorrah as examples of those who receive the wrath of God for immorality. The main point of both passages is to show examples of God's destruction of people who do not believe (Jude) or who taught heresy (II Peter). They were emblematic of the increasing desire of the leadership of the Christian church to impose order and control on the life of the church. References to Sodom and Gomorrah were tantamount to threats of "hellfire" for those who did not mend their ways.

That is all that Scripture has to say about homosexuality. Even if one is a biblical literalist, the biblical references do not build an ironclad case for condemnation. If one is not a biblical literalist there is no case at all, nothing but the ever-present prejudice born out of a pervasive ignorance that attacks people whose only crime is to be born with an unchangeable sexual predisposition toward those of their own sex.

If new knowledge about the cause and meaning of homosexuality confronts us, then we must be willing to relinquish our prejudice and the prejudice of Holy Scripture and turn our attention to loving our gay and lesbian brothers and sisters, supporting them, and relating to them as a part of God's good creation. That will inevitably include accepting, affirming, and blessing those gay and lesbian relationships that, like all holy relationships, produce the fruits of the spirit—love, joy, peace, patience, and self-sacrifice—and to do so in the confidence that though this may not be in accordance with the literal letter of the biblical texts, it is in touch with the life-giving spirit that always breaks the bondage of literalism.

Notes

1. I am particularly indebted to Dr. Foster R. McCurley of the Lutheran Church, whose clear exposition of this text and others in the Lutheran publication *A Study of Issues Concerning Homosexuality* (New York:

Division for Mission in North America, Lutheran Chruch in America, 1986) was of great benefit to my own study.

2. For more details on the attitude toward menstruation, see John S. Spong, *Into the Whirlwind* (San Francisco: Harper & Row, 1983), chapter 5.

3. For fuller treatment of the Ten Commandments, see John S. Spong and Denise G. Haines, *Beyond Moralism* (San Francisco: Harper & Row, 1986).

4. Once again I express appreciation for the candid and vigorous treatment of New Testament texts in *A Study of Issues Concerning Homosexuality*. The Reverend Christian D. Von Dehsen wrote that part of the report. Interacting with it and checking its references was a positive exercise for me.

CHAPTER TEN

Through the Words to the Word

The harsh and prejudiced judgments of a Bible understood to be inerrant will not endure. A Bible so interpreted can hardly be a resource, as we have observed, in making decisions about issues of sexual ethics. That does not mean, however, that the Bible has nothing to say to these questions, or that the Bible should be abandoned. It does mean that if we take the Bible seriously we will not be able to take it literally, or as a fundamentalist might wish to do. It does mean that the truth of the Bible is neither frozen in some ancient pattern nor closed to the insights of the future. It does mean that the task of the Christian expositor of Scripture is to seek the living Word[1] that pours forth from the Bible, time after time, in generation after generation, with startling and converting power. That Word is not to be identified with the words of Scripture but is found in, with, through, and beyond these words.

This Word is heard in the biblical story of creation. It is not, however, to be identified with the account of seven literal days of creation that so enamored William Jennings Bryan in the famous Scopes trial in Tennessee in 1925. The Word is that which speaks of the goodness of creation. It is the Word proclaiming that life is good, that everything that is shares in the divine origin and must therefore be celebrated and affirmed.

Throughout history the dark shadows of dualism have constantly sought to cut away from the goodness of God's creation those things judged as evil or unworthy of the light of God's day or the skill of God's hand. Human fears erect barriers that we identify with God's will. Then our prejudice, instructed by those barriers, rejects the people or things that are outside our barriers or our understanding. But finally, the Word of God in creation breaks those barriers, demanding that the original goodness of creation continue to live. How can slavery or segregation be practiced when everything in God's creation is good? Yet if literalism is allowed then any number of specific texts are quotable to prove the rightness of slavery. The descendants of Ham were condemned to servitude (Gen. 9:20ff.), the Bible said. The Torah allowed slavery for non-Jews (Lev. 25:44ff.). Paul accepted slavery and sought to make it a bit more benign. He urged the runaway slave Onesimus to return to his master Philemon (Phil.) and directed masters to treat slaves kindly (Col. 4:1). The author of Ephesians described the proper relationship between slave and master (Eph. 6:5ff.). A literally interpreted Bible will support slavery, but the living Word, spoken in creation, will proclaim human freedom afresh in every age.

Every human movement toward freedom and inclusiveness, from the Magna Carta, to the Reformation, to the emancipation of slaves, to the condemnation of racism, to the awakening to the evils of sexism and homophobia, have all found support in that community of faith that believes in the Word spoken by God in creation. Life is good. It is to be cherished. Human beings are all of value and are meant to be loved. Holy people cannot be used or exploited by those who desire self-gratification at the expense of others. The God of creation will oppose that even if some of the literal texts of Scripture will not.

In creation God has called all people to live in God's presence as bearers of God's image. Yet history reveals that the beauty and wonder of the God of creation is regularly shrunk by small-minded human beings to the limits of their vision and the boundaries of their land. They rationalize whatever behavior it takes to establish their nation, to exterminate their enemies, to vindicate their tribal deity. The Word of God in creation, which will neither be circumscribed by human practice nor compromised by Holy Scripture, is heard anew whenever the barriers of prejudice fall or when national idolatry is shredded. For Israel that occurred in their exile, when the people learned that God was not bound to the limits of Israel, at least not the God of creation. For just a moment in that exile the vision of inclusiveness was imagined:

> Every valley shall be lifted up,
>   and every mountain and hill be made low;
> the uneven ground shall become level
>   and the rough places a plain.
> And the glory of the Lord shall be revealed
>   and all flesh shall see it together,
>   for the mouth of the Lord has spoken.
>
>   (Isa. 40:4, 5)

This lonely voice crying in the wilderness was the faithful echo of the Word of the Lord spoken first in creation. It breaks forth again and again to defy and shatter the barriers created by human beings to enable themselves to feel secure—even though they destroy the universality of the God of creation.

It takes the tragedy of the exile, or the disaster of a human epidemic like the bubonic plague in the fourteenth century or AIDS in the twentieth century, or a nuclear accident that threatens to poison our common environment, to lift the human being out of his or her security system and into the recognition that the human family is indivisible, sharing a common destiny, a common danger, and a common hope given to us all in the goodness of creation. In those moments the Word of God is heard, erupting through the very words of Scripture that once supported our nationalism. The God of creation speaks and declares, "I have looked out on *everything* I have made and 'behold, it [is] very good' " (Gen. 1:31).

God's word is also seen in the person of Jesus of Nazareth. Indeed, Christians have called that life "the Word of God incarnate." The literal words that describe this life, which we call the Gospels, are full of contradictions. The origin of the meaning and power of Jesus are debated in Scripture itself. There are two birth narratives in the Bible, whose details cannot be reconciled. In one, Joseph had to go to Bethlehem because of a census or enrollment, and Jesus was born in a stable there (Luke 2). In the other, Joseph and Mary lived in Bethlehem in a house to which the Magi journeyed to find the newborn king (Matt. 2:9-10). In Luke, Jesus was circumcised on the eighth day and presented in the temple in Jerusalem on the fortieth day, both in a rather leisurely fashion (Luke 2:21-39), but Matthew, at that very same time, had the holy family fleeing into Egypt to escape Herod. Luke had the holy family return to Nazareth, for that was their hometown (Luke 2:39). Matthew invented a story that forced Jesus to move to Nazareth, for Matthew was sure that his home was in Bethlehem (Matt. 2:20-23). Indeed, the two Gospel writers do not agree even on the name of Joseph's father. It was Heli or Eli, said Luke (Luke 3:23). It was Jacob, said Matthew (Matt. 1:16). What is the literal truth?

The event that opened the eyes of the disciples, and through them the people of the world, to the divine presence in Jesus was the resurrection. That crucial event is also widely disputed in the literal texts of the Gospels, as we observed in chapter 7.[2]

The specific words of the biblical narrative are so often confusing and contradictory that it is impossible to take them as literal truth, yet the Word of God in Jesus transcends the words and opens people to God's presence. The Word of God in Christ says that we are loved, valued, redeemed, and counted as precious no matter how we might value ourselves or be valued by a prejudiced world. Since the God of creation is perceived to be the God who calls creation good, then the Christ who is God's Word must make that goodness real and apparent. That is what salvation is all about. We see God and God's Word in Jesus because God is the source of life, and Jesus revealed this God in his very aliveness. I cannot worship the God in Christ unless I am willing to live fully, freely, and openly, scaling the barriers that inhibit life, escaping the straitjacket of someone else's or my own stereotype of who I am.

We see God and God's word in Jesus because God is the source of love, and the love that was apparent in that Jesus embraced all sorts and conditions of humanity. He was open to beggars (Mark 10:46ff.), prostitutes (Mark 14:3ff.), thieves (Luke 23:32ff.), lepers (Luke 17:11ff.), and the demon possessed (Mark 1:32ff.). His compassion washed over every life he confronted, transforming a cowardly Peter into a hero (John 21:15ff.); freeing James and John, the scheming sons of Zebedee (Mark 10:35ff.), one to be a martyr (Acts 12:2) and the other a beloved disciple (John 21:24);[3] opening the eyes of the reluctant Andrew until he could see the value of every gift, even the gift of five barley loaves and two fishes that a young lad offered to feed a multitude (John 6:8ff.); and accepting Matthew and Zacchaeus despite their collaboration with the Roman government (Luke 19:1ff.; Matt. 9:9). No one was apart from the love of this Jesus. The divisions that human beings create to determine worth were swept aside. A foreigner, an African from Cyrene, was compelled to carry Jesus' cross (Mark 15:21) and entered at once into the power of this man's love.

The Word of God in Jesus was not to be identified with the words people wrote about him but with the divine love that marked him and created life in those who confronted him. I cannot worship that Word of God in Jesus unless I am loving, accepting, and forgiving, as he has been to me and as I will be when I live in him. As Edmond Browning, the Presiding Bishop of The Episcopal Church in the United States, observed in his inaugural address to the church, "The ethics of the kingdom have to be grounded in the compassion of the Christ." By the life of the Christ no one was rejected, because no one was rejectable.

We see God and God's Word in Jesus because God is the ground of all being and Jesus dared to be himself—all of himself. I cannot worship the God in Christ unless I too have the courage to be all that God created me to be. The most appealing part of the Gospel portrait of Jesus, to me, is not the supernatural framework of miracles and cures; it is, rather, the remarkable integrity of his being. Under every conceivable set of circumstances Jesus had the courage to be himself. He gave himself away in every encounter. He was present to the Samaritan woman by the well (John 4:7ff.), who by all measures was a person of no status. He was also present to the rich young ruler (Mark 10:17ff.) who was endowed with much of this world's goods. Neither lack of status nor presence of status affected the being of Jesus. He was who he was.

One cannot give oneself away unless there is a self to give, a self that has been claimed, accepted, and courageously lived out. A self that is free to accept praise and to endure criticism, with no resulting change in essential being, is a self that is free. When I look at Jesus, who I believe is the Word of God, I see a free person who could accept the adulation of the Palm Sunday crowd without allowing the adulation to affect his being. I also see a free person hanging upon a cross, his life-force ebbing away, who could still accept the jeers of his tormentors without any trace of bitterness, defiance, or recrimination. His being was not changed by hostility and rejection any more than it was changed by praise. That is a portrait of freedom, the freedom of one who knows who he is and has the courage to be just that. We experience in him the incarnation of the ground of all being.

The Word of God in Jesus is a call to me to be myself, my whole self, without apology, without boasting. It is a call to dare, to risk, and to venture. That is what it means to me to worship the one who is the ground of all being and to feel empowered by this Christ to discover the courage to be the self I am in Christ.

God's Word is also seen and heard through the Spirit who calls us into community and who creates in us a sense of corporate identity that enhances and enriches our individuality. Spirit, biblically, is the life-giving breath or wind of God that animates and vitalizes the creation. It is a sanctifying presence, for life is made holy not by becoming self-righteous or pious but rather in the experience of becoming completed. As Irenaeus once observed, "The glory of God is man [or woman] fully alive." Life, full and free life, is always a product of community.

Spirit is always a group phenomenon. It is the experience of unity that does not require uniformity. It is that quality of being sustained as one is, while at the same time being called to extend one's imagination. It is both a celebration of one's individuality and a recognition of the deep and abiding interrelatedness and interdependence in all human life. When the writers of the Bible tried to capture this reality, they did so in pictures and images that, if literalized, become nonsensical. In the creation story the Spirit brooded over the waters of chaos (Gen. 1:2). The image is feminine, that of a nesting hen brooding and clucking over her eggs until new life appears. In the story of Adam the creating deity first molded Adam out of a clod of dirt, and then, stretching the divine presence upon this inert body as if to give it artificial respiration, poured into Adam the life-giving Spirit that called him into vitality and relationship.

In Ezekiel's vision of the valley of dry bones, it was the Spirit or wind of God that blew across that valley of death and caused those bones to come together and to be fleshed with life once more (Ezek. 37:1ff.). In the story of Jesus' birth, the Spirit was portrayed as coming upon Mary to present the world with a new creation (Luke 1:35). In the Pentecost narrative, it was the Spirit falling upon the bedraggled and scattered band of disciples that called them into life and power (Acts 2:1ff.). There was a mighty rushing wind, a tongue of refining fire, and the capacity to overcome any impediment to human community, which last was symbolized in the account by the ability of all to hear the story of God's love in whatever language they happened to speak. Beyond the literal words that distort there is the life-giving Word, creating, redeeming, sanctifying. This is the Word of God to which the words of Scripture point.

This divine Word is never quite so concrete nor so precise as we would like it to be. It does not remove from human beings the necessity of thinking, probing, wrestling, and seeking the elusive Word of God. It does not give answers so much as a context in which answers can be sought. It is open to hear a new Word that will cast a new light and force a new understanding on subjects that once were considered closed to discussion. It is a self-correcting Word and therefore does not bind us into the straitjackets of antiquity. Finally and always, the Word of God will break open all human pretensions to act as if that Word has been captured and tamed. It will call Christians of every variety and those who seek God in any tradition to enter the future, where the only thing certain will not be our faith formulations but the eternal Word of God that is always before us, creating and re-creating the people of God.

Faith is not an exact science. There are no changeless, eternal creeds or Bibles. There is only the changeless, eternal truth of God. The moment that truth is articulated or codified it becomes finite, limited, and in the end falsifying. Living with the eternal Word of God has about it the nature of being on a journey. The Bible is something like a travelogue. It moves from the Garden of Eden to the Eternal City by way of Ur, Egypt, Canaan, Babylon, Corinth, and Rome. The people of the covenant were traveling people. Tracing the adventures of our spiritual mothers and fathers shows us important landmarks for our own journeys. We learn from those faith stories how previous generations have walked. They inform us of the terrain that we must cover, dangerous pitfalls to avoid, the way stations of respite, and the occasions to celebrate. Their stories light and mark the paths to be chosen, but they do not and must not bind our course to the maps of yesterday.

We human beings have moved so many times in our religious history; surely we know that we will have to move again. We moved from fertility cults and nature religions to tribal deities who called us into exodus and bound our common life with a covenant and law. We moved from that tribal identity into an individualism that became so radical that we developed images of heaven and hell based on the good or bad deeds or specific persons, as if no one was responsible for anyone other than himself or herself. Now we are moving away from that individualism. We realize anew that we are all connected by such things as the collective unconscious that we carry within ourselves, the programming of the chromosomes of the ages, and the stamping of our personalities by prenatal forces. By this token the sexual values of today's religious systems must reflect today's understanding of life.

Those of us who have literalized the word of God, confining its creative power to a mold that accommodates only yesterday's wisdom, will not be able to adjust. In time that inability will force our faith to be rocked relentlessly until it is shattered and replaced either by a hysterical anti-intellectual retreat into an unreal world or by the despair of nothingness. On the other hand, those of us who know that the dynamic Word of God cannot be bounded will be able to change and grow, bringing to that Word our new questions, our new experiences, our new insights, our new perceptions of that eternal truth. The living Word of God will then be heard again, speaking in new accents, calling us to embrace new possibilities.

That is happening now in the sexual revolution. It will happen again and again in other areas, as we live into our scary and exciting future. God's Word is the Word beyond the words of Scripture, beyond the formulations of tradition, beyond the human attempt to capture or to literalize. It is rather the Word that by the grace of God is perceived as Spirit beyond letter.

Notes

1. I shall attempt to show the distinction between the Word of God and the words of Scripture by capitalizing "word" whenever it refers to the Spirit beyond the letter.
2. This point is detailed extensively in chapters 12–13 of my book *The Easter Moment* (San Francisco: Harper & Row, 1987).
3. I do not accept the identity of John Zebedee as *the* beloved disciple, but it is a common part of the church's tradition, and the author of John 21 claims the identity of being the disciple Jesus loved.

Part III

CHAPTER ELEVEN

Marriage and Celibacy: The Ideal and an Option

*T*he institution of marriage is in flux, evolving and changing in unique and unpredictable ways. It has its detractors and its supporters, and some elements of both points of view reside within me. I am ready to bid adieu to that patriarchal pattern of marriage that oppresses both partners in the name of a dying concept of masculinity, but I am not ready to abandon marriage. It continues to be, in my opinion, the single most important human relationship. A marriage faithfully entered and faithfully lived out is a profoundly life-enhancing experience that needs to be acknowledged, supported, and celebrated.

I also believe that celibacy can be a valid option to marriage for some people and should be explored and even encouraged in certain circumstances. I differ with the traditional moralists not on the values to be found in either marriage or in celibacy, but only in their desire to limit the definition of "moral behavior" to these two alternatives.

I do not believe that sexual morality can, in our day, be defined by or exhausted in the solitary options of faithful marriage or chaste celibacy. These options might well continue to be the stated ideals, the least complicated standards, and may even possess the greatest potential for fulfillment. But I have known too many non-marital relationships marked by the qualities of holiness to suggest that they are immoral because they are not within the narrow bands of legal marriage. I will try to define and defend these wider moral options in this section of this book. Before I do that it is important, however, to state powerfully and clearly my commitment to a faithful, monogamous lifetime marriage as the norm for the majority, and my sense that the chaste life of the celibate commends itself as a valid option for some.

This is not a new commitment for me. It is the opinion of a lifetime, undeterred by the pain of human brokenness. I stated it publicly in a book that I wrote in 1982: "In my deepest being I remain convinced of the truth that the highest development of human character and the greatest potential human joy are finally the results and by-products of the total commitment of one person to another in a holy marriage."[1] I still believe those words today.

A faithful, monogamous marriage has never been easy to achieve. It is perhaps even less easy to achieve now. The voices that speak for the values of a previous generation seem not always to comprehend either the pressures on young adults today or the radically different environment in which marriages are now consummated, compared to that of the past one or two generations.

We are bombarded with sex through the print and electronic media, on billboards, in novels and plays, and even in debates in the public arena. Sex, once considered an activity of the private domain, is no longer so, especially now that more and more of us are aware that sexual partners expose each other to infections carried by any sexual partner that either the man or the woman has had over the past decade. This new awakening to the potential danger of sexual activity has dampened the fires of the sexual revolution and has even caused the status of romance and marriage to rise. The peace demonstrator who once carried a placard proclaiming "Make love not war" is now not quite so sure about love. A widespread cultural retreat from promiscuous behavior is observable. The threat of herpes simplex and hepatitis type B, widely identified with heterosexual promiscuity, and acquired immune deficiency syndrome or AIDS, largely identified in this country with male homosexual promiscuity and with intravenous drug users, has chilled our enthusiasm for multiple sex partners. *Time* magazine, in 1984, went so far as to announce in a cover story that the sexual revolution was over. That may have been premature, but it was obvious that attitudes about sex and marriage had entered a new phase.

Sexual license has not brought, as some had hoped, only thrills, excitement, and fulfillment. Instead, many have found hurt, shallowness, disease, and even boredom. The human being is a creature that needs intimacy, continuity, commitment, and love. Sexual activity is a piece of that intimacy and love, or it becomes not much at all. Cheap thrills never last. As people have come to understand this, promiscuity is increasingly going out and commitment is coming in.

Conservative political and religious circles are rejoicing that faithful, monogamous marriage and a disciplined, self-chosen celibacy might be reestablished as the norms of this society—if not for moral reasons, at least for health reasons. They suggest that such a return to traditional morality alone will diminish the impact of these diseases. It is a powerful argument. Certainly the case can be made that promiscuous behavior, whether practiced by homosexual or heterosexual persons, is destructive to the soul and dangerous to the body.

James B. Nelson calls our attention to the many public debates which have thrust human sexuality into the forefront of our consciousness.[2] His list includes sexual justice issues such as equality in job opportunities and pay scales, abortion, family planning, population control, sexual abuse, television violence, pornography, prostitution, reproductive technologies, the now advertised use of condoms, and teenage pregnancy. Each of these issues is discussed freely in the media, indeed almost daily.

Dr. Nelson goes on to point out the sexual dimensions in violent crime, the arms race, and the economic and foreign policies of nations. All, he asserts, grow out of the alleged virtues associated with male dominance. These are related to and in some cases are the direct expression of the cult of winning, the uncritical commitment to competitiveness, and the dulling or, as Dr. Nelson expressively puts it, the "armoring" of emotions. These issues, he writes, are all the products of distortions stemming from the understanding of male sexuality lauded in the days of patriarchy. That understanding, however, is beginning to recede today.

Nelson further quotes James Weldon Johnson, who years ago observed that sexuality was implicated in the depths of our racial prejudice as well. In his paraphrase of Johnson's thoughts, he writes:

Historically, white males' categorization of women ("either virgins or whores") proceeded along racial lines: white women were symbols of delicacy and purity, whereas black women symbolized an animality which could be sexually and economically exploited. White male guilt was projected onto the black male, who was imagined as a dark, supersexual beast who must be punished and from whom white women must be protected. Black mothers nurtured their sons to be docile, hoping to protect them from white male wrath. That upbringing in turn complicated black marriages and led to certain destructive attempts to recover black "manliness." We are the heirs of a distorted racial history in which sexual dynamics have been a major force.[3]

These dimensions of our newly heightened sexual awareness, present in the social landscape, are illustrative of the paradigmatic shift that is abroad in our time. The values associated with the patriarchial era are dying in all of their manifestations. Couples choosing marriage choose it in this changing world. When the values, definitions, and images by which people live change, every institution in the social order will of necessity change also. Tomorrow's marriage will be vastly different from yesterday's marriage.

But whatever the character or shape of marriage, it will continue as the most popular option in the foreseeable future. This option needs to be supported by the whole society. The decision to marry is a central one. The marriage relationship is demanding; it takes effort to sustain it; but its rewards more than justify the time, energy, thought, and commitment that it requires. Marriage remains for me the ideal, the standard against which every other relationship must be measured. If that is so, an institution such as the church should commit its greatest energy and its primary resources to assist its people in the creation of healthy, faithful, monogamous relationships, with marriage being the norm to be encouraged.

If marriage is that important, it should be prepared for rigorously. Since it is so much more than a legitimization of genital sexual activity, there is some virtue in seeing the two separated, as they have been in recent years. Once the marriage bond is established, sex does need to be a sacred part of that relationship and an exclusive aspect of husband-wife intimacy not violated by the inclusion or intrusion of another person. No person should stand in public, either "before God and this company" or before a civil magistrate, and exchange the vows of marriage if this exclusive quality is not intended. If such a vow cannot be made in honesty, it should not be made at all. Both husband and wife need to have the security to trust that commitment, for only then can the depths that are possible in a human relationship be open to mutual exploration.

Contributing to the strengths and beauty of that marital relationship are shared memories. Foremost among our mental souvenirs of marriage are peak moments like the wedding itself, the honeymoon, the first residence, the celebration of various anniversaries or birthdays, special vacations, the first pregnancy, and the birth of each child.

Every couple could add their own special moments. Each of these memories constitutes a treasure not likely to be forgotten. Photograph albums are frequently kept to recall, even to relive, the ecstasy of those mountaintop heights.

There are also dark times that provide the ever-present shadows in human life but that, inside committed relationships, can also be powerful forgers of depth and unity. Sometimes the crisis is a physical move, perhaps not chosen but also not avoidable, that tears husband, wife, and children away from life-giving support networks of friends, making the members of the family aware of how important they are to each other. Sometimes the shadow is a failure that diminishes one or all but that nonetheless has to be borne corporately. Sometimes a sickness or death tests the strength of the marriage relationship. Studies show, for example, a sharply increased divorce rate among those couples who undergo the trauma of the death of a child. The transition moments like graduation, the marriage of a child, the arrival at the status of grandparent, and retirement add new dimensions. All of these things and many others feed the shared memory of a man and a woman who have committed themselves to each other "for better, for worse, in sickness and in health, until we are parted by death."

Then there are the little things, the family jokes, the mild put-downs, the idiosyncrasies, the personal likes and dislikes, the wide variety of human tastes in food, dress, entertainment, friends, that all become part of the family history. These are links that forge unity out of separateness. Nothing can open life to the depths of love, to the discovery of those hidden wells of personhood, more than a commitment intended for a lifetime in which two persons agree to share themselves fully and freely with each other and to grow together for all of their days.

If that relationship is interrupted by death or divorce, a second marriage might well ensue. It might even be a wonderful second marriage, but it will not have the time to develop the depth or form the memories that were at least potentially present when the first marriage was inaugurated. Time is essential to the sharing of life. A day lost is a day never recovered. Memories cannot be collected without the passage of time. The deeper and older the memories, the greater is the potential for self-discovery and self-giving. That is the hope and the joy of the lifetime commitment to marriage that makes it so special.

Marriage is a relationship in which vulnerability is present. Each partner is exposed to the other in many ways, from physical nakedness to emotional and mental nakedness. Just as the potential for fulfillment is at its greatest inside this lifelong commitment, so is the potential for pain at its greatest in the failure of a marriage. When two people who know each other well damage or reject each other, the pain is intense. There is nothing casual about divorce. Sometimes to endure the pain people bury their feelings, but the hurt lingers deep, creating sometimes bizarre compensatory behavior patterns. Sometimes no person is quite so foolish or quite so destructive as a newly divorced person looking for some way in which hurt can be stopped, wounds bound, and pain relieved. Alcohol, promiscuity, rebound relationships, drugs, and even suicide are the escape mechanisms employed.

Marriage is a powerful relationship. Powerful in its potential for life. Powerful in its potential for pain. It should not be entered lightly or left impulsively. Its importance is such that it deserves our best efforts, from forming a good union early, to the midlife crisis when priorities are always reevaluated, to a graceful aging. In the midst of the sexual revolution, I salute the faithful, monogamous, lifetime commitment of husband and wife as an ideal that has much, perhaps most, to offer and that is worthy of our best efforts, our vigilance, our constant nurturing, and our just plain hard work.

Though marriage must and will be part of our changing

world, some old assumptions about marriage will not endure. Flexibility has become a prime virtue in a marriage. Mutuality is replacing the old pattern of the dominant male and the submissive female. Dual careers are on the rise and have slowed down the high mobility that characterized since World War II the life of the family of the rising executive. Dual careers have also changed the pattern of childbirth.

The pressures of contemporary life are not supportive of families. The extended family, with its complex structure of interlocking relationships, has been replaced by the nuclear family, so that greater needs confront fewer emotional resources. The daily grind of the commuter, either in traffic as a driver or on public transportation as a rider, results in a desire to retreat from community into the isolation of an evening with two martinis, a television set, and no communication with one's spouse. If these pressures are not addressed, the long-range potential of many marriages will be in trouble.

One of the purposes of a religious institution is to help people feel rooted and to provide them with community. I covet for the church the role and vocation of being the extended family into which the nuclear family might fit, to the enrichment of both. I hope the training given to the pastors of today and tomorrow will include ways to strengthen family relationships. More effort must be made to enrich, sustain, encourage, undergird, transform, and bless the marriage bonds. If and when a marriage fails, other tactics are needed. But up until there is no hope left for a couple, both personal and corporate energy should be directed to the nourishing of their union. Marriage deserves nothing less.

If one is apprehensive or even certain that he or she cannot succeed in marriage, the celibate life should be looked at as an option. To many that will seem a strange suggestion, but I make it in all seriousness. I have known those who lived the celibate life openly and honestly. Some were heterosexual, some were homosexual. All chose this style of life as the best option for them. No one imposed it on them. Sometimes it was chosen after other options had been tried and had failed. Sometimes the loss of a spouse through death or the breakup of a relationship, or perhaps more tragically an accident or a sickness that incapacitated a spouse, presented the option of celibacy involuntarily, but then it was chosen freely as the best option at that time.

Sometimes the diversion of the energy of sexuality into another outlet, such as art, music, writing, or even gourmet cooking, permits a life-enriching creativity that compensates for the loss of intimacy and brings that person into the potential for wholeness that he or she might never have achieved otherwise. Sometimes a number of relationships of varying levels of friendship can sustain a life that is devoid of the primacy of that one special person. If one is committed to the life of celibacy, friendships with married persons of the opposite sex are not filled with threat to that person's marriage, seduction, or the innuendo of sex play, so that those relationships can be rich, life giving, and sustaining.

I do not believe that many people can, in fact, freely choose and then live out with integrity the celibate lifestyle. It is an option for a small minority at best. I do believe, however, that it ought to be considered as one way open at least to some as the best path to human wholeness, if not for a lifetime then at least for certain periods of one's life.

I would resist totally, however, a third party prescribing celibacy for someone else, as if morality required this as the sole alternative to marriage. I do believe that it can be for some another ideal and that as such it ought to be seriously presented and explored. It is, at the very least, far less complicated than some other options that might be chosen.

Although as a teacher of ethics my goal is not to coerce people to conform to societal norms under the guise of upholding morality, I do recognize that those norms developed because they served a valuable purpose in the common good. My primary ethical commitment is directed toward nurturing the fullness of life in individuals as well as society at large within whatever limits life places before them. The tensions between the one and the many result in an interplay between individual and corporate values. Marriage and celibacy do bridge the gap, as both are acceptable to society and, when freely chosen, to the involved individuals.

Before considering the possibilities of some of the other patterns of human relationships emerging today, which I believe fall inside the definition of a godly morality but about which there is vigorous debate, I wanted to salute the traditions. While disagreeing with those who believe that the two lifestyles of marriage and celibacy exhaust the categories of moral relationships, I do honor these lifestyles. I covet the treasures potentially present in marriage for the majority who will in fact seek the blessing of matrimony. I salute those who affirm and live out a celibate life. But having said that, I reach out to the others who do not fit these narrow definitions of morality.

What can we, as a body of Christians dedicated to the God who calls all people into the fullness of life, say to those sexually alive young people for whom marriage is not an option at this time? What do we say to our gay and lesbian brothers and sisters, for whom marriage has never been a legal or an ecclesiastical option? What do we say to those people whose marriages have ended either by death or divorce and who for many reasons—economic, emotional, or professional—cannot and will not enter again into the legal contract of matrimony? As one voice in the church, I am not prepared to condemn non-conventional sexual relationships that are issuing in enhanced life. I believe that there are other possibilities to which the church can respond with integrity. I present them now for discussion and debate. I have lived in the church long enough to be certain I shall generate both.

Notes

1. John S. Spong, *Into the Whirlwind* (San Francisco: Harper & Row, 1983).
2. James B. Nelson, "Reuniting Sexuality and Spirituality," *The Christian Century* 104, no. 6 (February 25, 1987): 187-90.
3. Ibid., p. 190.

CHAPTER TWELVE

Betrothal: An Idea Whose Time Has Come

I call on the churches of this land to revive a concept of betrothal and to install it as a valid option and a sign of a serious commitment, even though it falls short of the legal status of marriage. In many ancient societies a man and a woman were pledged long before they were married. That betrothal sometimes meant that they were bound in a relationship of commitment that, in some instances, permitted sexual intimacy. That institution of betrothal met very real social and economic needs in those ancient societies. There are today quite different social and economic needs in our society, which perhaps a newly defined and revived institution of betrothal would meet once again.

I am proposing that we revive the word, with a new definition. By "bethrothal" I mean a relationship that is faithful, committed, and public but not legal or necessarily for a lifetime. I prefer this word to "trial marriage" because I do not want to suggest that the ultimate commitment of marriage can be relativized. In fact, the contemporary practice among engaged people comes close to defining what I mean by betrothal. To make it a bit broader I would stretch engagement to include the somewhat more vague category of "an engagement to be engaged." Such a betrothal may, for some young couples, be a stage of life preliminary to marriage, or it may be for others a relationship complete in and of itself and that has meaning for both partners in a particular context in which a lifetime vow is neither expected nor required.

A liturgical form for such a betrothal would be fitting. That liturgy would include a declaration that the couple intends to live together in love and faithfulness for a period of time in a bonding relationship. This commitment would be recognized by the general public and by the church as serious, not shallow; as open, not hidden; and as creating a sense of mutual responsibility by which each partner is willing to be bound. The conception and birth of children would not be appropriate to this relationship of betrothal. A child born of both intention and love deserves to have the nurture available in and the security provided by a legal bond of marriage, with permanence of commitment being the expectation of both the father and the mother.

The success of a betrothal would be determined in large measure by the willingness of the individuals involved to abide by these agreements. Clarity about the importance of these understandings would be a major part of the agenda in pre-betrothal counseling sessions between the pastor and the prospective young man and woman.

This idea is not new. It is not even new as a proposal from someone in the hierarchy of the church. The Most Reverend and Right Honorable Geoffrey Fisher, a former Archbishop of Canterbury (1945–1961), after his retirement called on the Church of England to develop some liturgical service of mutual dedication for a couple to enable them with the church's blessing to enter something he called a "trial marriage."[1] Needless to say, his conservative ecclesiastical colleagues dismissed the idea of their former Primate as the product of an aging mind bordering on senility. One wonders how it was that the archbishop could have been so far ahead of the thinking of his own time. I believe this is an idea whose time has now come.

Alvin Toffler, from a completely secular point of view, came up with much the same idea in his book *Future Shock,* when he wrote that the future of marriage might be defined in terms of three separate commitments designed for three separate stages of life.[2] Stage one, said Toffler, would be the stage of young love, trial marriage, and a commitment to live together, made while the young adults were still in that unsettled period of preparation for life. Stage two would be inaugurated when one chose a partner with whom a home would be built and by whom the conception, birth, nurture, and growth to maturity of children would be accomplished. The proposed termination of this phase of the marital contract would be something like the departure of the last child from home or the graduation of the last child from college. Stage three, Toffler concluded, would begin with the choice of a partner with whom one desired to share the mature years, the one with whom to grow old. This mate would be a friend with whom one would share the common interests that create life-giving unity. Toffler did not rule out the possibility that each of these marriage commitments might well be entered into by the same two people. He did see the requirements and mutual needs of the prospective partners at each separate stage to be so unique that honesty demanded the possibility of a new commitment at the point of transition.

Neither Archbishop Fisher nor Alvin Toffler could have made their proposals a century ago. The circumstances were such that such options were not even conceivable. But times have changed, as has been chronicled in chapter 3. Legitimizing trial marriages or revising the concept of a betrothal could not be considered without the historical occasion of such factors as the lowering of the age of puberty, the raising of the age at which marriage occurs, the changes in the meaning of marriage produced by the feminist awakening, and the lengthening span of life.

Is it a legitimate demand of a moral society to say to the

brightest and the best of the new generation that they are to suppress their sexual drives from puberty, at perhaps age twelve, to the time of finishing law school, for example, at age twenty-five? Or is that a naïve expectation based upon the moral code of a different era being applied uncritically to a new age? Can an ethical standard completely out of touch with biological reality be expected to survive? The fact is that the standard has not survived. The guilt that helped undergird and enforce this standard of virginity prior to marriage has survived and continues to wear down its victims' feelings of integrity. With each passing day, however, the power of that guilt is weakening along with the institution that has historically used guilt to maintain its position: the church.

Guilt, described by someone as "the gift that keeps on giving," has long been the major weapon in the arsenal of the church. Its primary use is behavior control. The first step in that process was to convince the general population that the church alone had the power to forgive sins. Citing a text like Matthew 16:18-19 from holy and authoritative Scripture helped: "And I tell you, you are Peter, and on this rock I will build my church, and the powers of death shall not prevail against it. I will give you the keys of the kingdom of heaven, and whatever you bind on earth shall be bound in heaven, and whatever you loose on earth shall be loosed in heaven." It was easy to interpret binding and loosing in terms of withholding or granting forgiveness. There followed the identification of the ecclesiastical hierarchy as the legitimate heirs to the power promised to Peter. The articulate spokesman for the hierarchy called himself the Vicar of Christ on Earth and Peter's heir, the Bishop of Rome. When the church added the reward of heaven to its power of forgiveness and the punishment of hell to its power of withholding forgiveness, the levers of guilt moved the population to obedience. A powerful system of behavior control then was able to come into being. This system was managed by the church and is still unmatched in Western history for its effectiveness.

The final step in the construction of this control system was to connect guilt with some common aspect of humanity. Sex was the obvious candidate for this honor. Sexual intercourse was characterized as evil, base, defiling, animal in nature, appealing only to the lower self, and provided by God solely as a means to procreation. Women were taught by the church that the perfect woman was a virgin who produced a son without sexual activity. If a virgin mother was the perfect woman, no other woman could achieve perfection, or, conversely, every other woman would be clothed in guilt. The two qualities upheld for women were then split by the church. Human virtue in a woman could be achieved either as a virgin nun or as a prolific mother. Out of this mentality came both the call to the nunnery and the condemnation of any artificial means of birth control. Sex was an evil that was rendered virtuous either in prohibition, or failing that, in the procreative task. To impede the reproductive function even in marriage was, therefore, to participate in sin.

Guilt was elicited in men by the church's condemnation of all sexual desire. Since the desire itself was evil, the woman who aroused that desire in men was thought to be particularly evil. Nonetheless, when a man experienced sexual desire, as universal and God given as this was and is, that man was called a sinner. He was guilty before God. He had to go to a representative of mother church, make confession, and receive forgiveness. Guilt was thus attached to sexual desire and sexual activity, making sexual sins from that moment on the obsessive concern of the church. Thus it has ever been.

As a consequence of this yoking of sex with guilt, the sexual revolution of recent history has also been in many ways a revolution against the church. Eager to regain its ancient control, the church predictably met this challenge by trying to reestablish and reinforce its usual standards. The Vatican still condemns birth control and joins with most other Christian churches in labeling all human sexual activity that falls outside the institution of marriage as evil. Undiscerning guilt is the primary emotion that the church continues to attach to human sexuality. That guilt is being thrown off, but before the day of complete emancipation comes, misplaced guilt will do its destructive work on the human psyche, as it always has in the past.

It is past time to strike a mortal blow against this debilitating guilt. If there is a way that the church can uphold the goodness of sexuality and affirm responsible and discriminating uses of that godly gift, then we should do so. Reviving the institution of a formal betrothal is the proposal I recommend to accomplish this dual purpose.

Betrothal is appropriate today for other reasons. Into that increased gap of time between puberty and marriage our society has added to the sexual equation one major factor that encourages experimentation, and at the same time we have taken away another factor that used to discourage experimentation. Through a combination of biological knowledge and technological genius, effective and safe birth control devices are readily available. The world has come a long way since that day in 1873 when an ovum was first seen under the microscope. With conception safely separated from sexual activity, the consuming fear that was a major inhibitor of sexual relationships outside of marriage was removed. The primary reason that people had been taught to refrain from sex save inside the bonds of marriage had lost its force. Birth control is not yet 100 percent effective nor is it without risk, especially to women, but the ability to prevent pregnancy is statistically high. The potency of that controlling fear of pregnancy has been dissipated. To that extended period between puberty and marriage the means of controlling conception effectively has been added.

At the same time, society discontinued the practice of

chaperoning proper young ladies. Opportunities for privacy have thus been dramatically increased. In earlier generations amorous young people found it more difficult to elude the strict, watchful eyes of parents, guardians, maiden aunts, younger siblings, or house mothers who took the task of chaperoning female college students with vengeful seriousness. Even young women who had finished college were once required to live under rigid rules in the community where they taught or nursed. If they were unmarried they discovered that adulthood and a profession did not free them to come and go as they pleased. In the early years of this century the Barbizon Hotel in New York City did not allow males beyond the lobby. Many a young woman out to seek her fortune was allowed to leave home only if she made her residence in the Barbizon. Malicious gossip could ruin the reputation and end the career of a woman who did not keep up appearances. Sinclair Lewis's turn-of-the-century novel, *Main Street,* chronicled that process in dramatic detail.

But all this was before the general availability of automobiles and the rise of a mobile society. It was before the anonymity of suburban housing developments and gigantic shopping malls. It was before the pattern of early one-on-one dating, "going steady," cruising, parking, baby-sitting, and all the other opportunities young people now have to explore physical intimacy with one another. It was before the proliferation of coeducational colleges, coeducational dormitories, and coeducational roommates. It was before explicit sex in movies, novels, television programs, and advertisements became commonplace. It was before all-night beach and bar parties in Florida during school spring break, and before the lowering of the age of the draft and in some states the age of drinking alcoholic beverages to eighteen.

Can anyone today imagine sending 25,000 eighteen- to twenty-two-year-old men and women (in roughly equal numbers) away from their homes, placing them on the unstructured and unchaperoned campus of a great university, making the means of birth control readily available, and still expecting them to live in sexual abstinence? If we as a society really opposed sex outside of marriage, would we allow social and educational patterns such as these to form? Can the same society that makes the opportunity for sexual promiscuity available be surprised when sexual promiscuity develops? The real surprise, in my opinion, is not the presence of promiscuous people but rather the fact that with little or no help from either the society at large or from their elders in particular, young men and women have developed standards of their own that are enforced by the pressure of their own peer groups. These standards are not the ones by which their great-grandparents lived, but they are standards nonetheless. Basically, today's young adults believe that sex outside not a marriage but outside a meaningful relationship is wrong. What constitutes a meaningful relationship is not easily defined, of course, and varies widely.

This contemporary standard, like every human standard, is violated with some frequency. There are also a minority of young people who refuse to be bound by this or any other standard and are promiscuous. For most young people, however, promiscuity is not part of their system of values. Exploratory testing of a relationship is a part of their system. When commitment reaches a certain point, a genital sexual relationship is inaugurated. Sometimes it is quite destructive; sometimes it is affirming, loving, and life giving. My sense is that the church should offer to these younger citizens the possibility that when that relationship reaches a certain intensity, when it is committed and exclusive, when their peers begin to relate to them as a couple, and when they want to begin a trial period of living together, then such a relationship might be blessed by their church because that relationship carries with it the possibility of life-giving holiness.

A moment of transition as serious and intense as the commitment to live together, with each offering to the other his or her vulnerability, needs to be marked by a liturgical observance, a public celebration. The proposed couple needs to stand before God and in the presence of families and friends and say to each other what it is that they are doing, note its possibilities and its limitations, and promise to treat the other with sensitivity and love so that each might grow because of their life together. Such a solemn and important moment of transition needs to be prepared for carefully, to be anticipated joyously, and to be remembered always. So setting a date and undergoing preparation through counselling with a pastor who is open enough and sensitive enough to enter their lives and appreciate their hopes and their fears become essential ingredients. When the relationship ends, that termination also needs to be marked in some appropriate fashion.

Some relationships are not destined to last a lifetime, but that does not mean they are to be denigrated. Most of us have had close relationships that ended in time. How many of our high school friends still remain primary to any of us? Does this lack of longevity render that which once had great meaning of no value now? Of course not! It means only that each relationship in a lifetime meets us where we are at the moment it is begun. It shapes and forms us in powerful ways for its duration and then it leaves us with the residual effects of its meaning, enabling us to draw on that meaning forever. Are those relationships rendered evil because they were born, bloomed brightly for a time, then faded and died? Why do we imagine that a relationship of even greater intensity, born of real love if not of ultimate commitment, and lived out in sensitivity, responsibility, and vulnerability, is somehow without lasting significance if it turns out to be less than eternal? If a trial marriage, or a relationship of betrothal, as I prefer to call it, convinces two people that marriage is not for them, is that a tragedy? Would not the hurt and the wounds that the break-up of such a relationship of betrothal creates be easier and quicker to heal than those from a divorce, with its legal ramifications and its still virulent social stigma?

The revival of the institution of betrothal as a recognized relationship, committed and responsible but not legally binding, would in fact help to order and to make holy the world of sexual testing that now marks the lives of so many single young adults. It would signal a new attitude in the life of the church, a willingness to abandon moral preachments and to enter into the vulnerability of actual life, where decisions are made from among real options, not ideal or impossible options, and where the presence of the church allows the wisdom of the wider community to be a part of decision making. It would also be a means whereby the power of human sexuality would be respected and not condemned, disciplined and not rejected, celebrated and not denied. The guilt of the ages, so long experienced as a weapon in the hands of the church, would be overturned, and the beauty of holiness would be seen in an arena where so often nothing has been allowed save the voices of control and judgment.

A relationship of betrothal would honor the power of sex by taking it seriously. It would offer a channel through which that power could be affirmed; it would make sacred the relationship in which that sexual gift could be shared. It would offer an option to casual sex, and a challenge to promiscuity. Most of all, it would suggest that sexual activity divorced from significant commitment is a shallow and destructive way to experience a powerful and holy emotion. When young lovers would move in together they would not do so casually, for shared life is never casual—it is always profound. A liturgy of betrothal would guarantee the seriousness and the profundity of this decision.

A society that offers marriage or celibacy as the only options for all of life will simply not touch the masses of the post-pubescent but not yet married single generation.

Forced to reject the relentless judgment they hear from the church, they will also reject the message out of which that judgment flows. The radical suggestion that the institution of betrothal should be revised and offered by the church as a symbol of responsible commitment will send shock waves through a generation that is quite sure that religion in general and the church in particular has nothing of substance to offer their lives. If the church combined that daring suggestion with some degree of public honesty about the authority of its Scripture, as I have attempted to do in this volume, then the audacity of its integrity would at the very least demand attention, and the power of our gospel might once again be allowed to enter some hearts and minds from which it has been shut out for some long time.

I propose this revival of betrothal, and I call the church to consider it seriously and to be willing to adopt it publicly if its wisdom can be demonstrated. The debate, however, needs to be with the secular world, not simply within the church, which usually pits liberal tradition-bound Christians against conservative tradition-bound Christians. It is not surprising that this procedure only allows the church the option of backing slowly into the future. Our times call for more than that—more initiative, more courage, more willingness to risk, more honesty, less fear. Time alone will reveal whether or not the Christian church has enough elasticity to survive.

Betrothal, with appreciation to one Geoffrey Fisher, I dare to suggest is an idea whose time has come again.

Notes

1. John S. Spong, *Into the Whirlwind* (San Francisco: Harper & Row, 1983), p. 142.
2. Alvin Toffler, *Future Shock* (New York: Bantam Books, 1971).

CHAPTER THIRTEEN

Should the Church Bless Divorce?

What would it mean to have the church offer a liturgical service to mark the end of a marriage? Would it serve, as some suggest, only to encourage people to seek divorces? Would it bring a note of grace and redemption to one of life's moments of brokenness? Would it enable people who were not able to keep the marriage vows to experience more forgiveness than guilt? Does the church really want to lessen guilt, or is it the conscious or unconscious fear of all ecclesiastical structures that if guilt is lessened so also will be motivation and control? What would such a service look like, feel like, and accomplish?

These were my questions when I was invited to attend such a service, designed to mark the end of a marriage of two people, both of whom I admired and counted as friends. I could not, before that service, have answered any of the questions posed above. The experience was for me a profound one, to which my mind has returned time and again. In this chapter I will try first to enable my readers to enter the experience, before attempting to draw from it possibilities for future ministry in our world of revolutionary values.

It was not an unusual setting. A man and a woman stood before the altar, which was properly dressed with flowers, candles, and the elements necessary to celebrate the Eucharist. A priest and a lay reader were in the sanctuary, fully vested.

A small congregation of some twenty-five people gathered in the chancel to share this moment of worship. They were invited guests, close friends in many instances of both the man and the woman. To be present with both of them at this service was the sole purpose for which they had come. A couple who may have been the closest personal friends of this man and this woman came in just before the service started and took their places, the man beside the man, the woman beside the woman, as if to play the roles of best man and matron of honor.

But this was not a marriage. It was rather something called "A Service for the Recognition of the End of a Marriage." It was, in fact, a liturgy designed to offer to God the pain of a divorce.

This man and this woman once stood before the altar and exchanged their solemn vows "to love and to cherish until we are parted by death." It was a vow that they could not or did not keep.

Theirs was the not unfamiliar experience of a growing alienation. There was more hurt than healing in their marriage. There was more offense than forgiveness. There was an increasing inability to communicate that seemed to emerge out of the radically different life paths that each partner was taking.

Finally there came the realization that there was no more life or potential for life in their relationship. Nor was there any more capacity to try again. So the drama of these two lives played out the scenes of the decision to part, the actual separation, the provisions to care for the children, the division of property, and the divorce.

Both the man and the woman were and are committed Christians, and the church that had been a central focus of their marriage somehow also had to be the focus of their separation. Hence, this service—painful, traumatic, but intensely real—was planned to offer this all-too-human reality called divorce to God, and to seek healing and new directions from this God for these lives.

The opening hymn, "Abide with Me," announced firmly that this would be no pollyannish attempt to gloss over human pain. The eventide of death had fallen on this relationship. This couple had experienced the deepening darkness of human brokenness. They had sought help—it had failed. So we sang, "Help of the helpless, O abide with me."

The Call to Worship used words from the Psalter (Ps. 130) that spoke of God as shelter and strength in the time of a shaking earth, when mountains fall into the ocean depths.

The liturgist spoke: "This man and this woman have decided after much effort, pain, and anger that they will no longer be husband and wife. They wish to be friends and to respect and care about each other. They are now and will continue to be parents to their children, and they wish to be responsible for each of them."[1]

The gathered friends responded: "In this difficult time we join with you as your friends. We have been with you in your joys, your struggles, and your tears. We have not always known how to be helpful. Although we may not fully understand, we honor your decision. We care and we give you our love."

Then we joined in a confession asking God to "embrace us when frustration and failure leave us hollow and empty. . . . in the confession of our lips show us now the promise of a new day, the springtime of the forgiven."

The lessons followed. Isaiah exhorted us to "remember not the former things." The psalmist proclaimed the reality of the God who hears when we call "out of the depths." Paul reminded us that nothing in either life or death "can separate us from the love of God," and John echoed Jesus' words that when we trust in God we can "let not our hearts be troubled."

Then the man and the woman stood and faced each other and spoke. They spoke of pain and failure, and the inexorable nature of separation. They spoke of loneliness and the need to learn new ways of relating. They spoke of death, which clearly both were experiencing. They asked each other for forgiveness. They pledged themselves to be friends, to stand united when relating to their children, to be civil and responsible to each other. They thanked their friends for the willingness to share that moment of pain.

It was painful—the excruciating pain of human brokenness, the irrevocable fracture in a relationship that once had brought joy and fulfillment to each. Both the man and the woman wept, and so did every member of that gathered group. Hearts cried out for an easy answer, for an embrace, for someone to say that this bad dream would depart and the past would be restored. But this service took place in life, not in Hollywood. The pain was real and it had to be endured and transformed. It could not be removed.

The man and the woman returned to their seats, and we sat in an aching silence for what seemed an interminable length of time. Some prayed. Some tried to dry their tears. Some wished they had never come. But all remained.

Finally we rose and said together: "We affirm you in the new covenant you have made; one that finds you separated but still caring for each other and wishing each other good will; one that enables you to support and love your children; one that helps to heal the pain you feel. Count on God's presence. Trust our support and begin anew."

Then we prayed the Prayers of the People, which culminated in these words that the congregation spoke together: "On behalf of the church which blessed your marriage, we now recognize the end of that marriage. We affirm you as single persons among us and we pledge you our support as you continue to seek God's help and guidance for the new life you have undertaken in faith."

Then came the Peace, in which the healing power of the embrace of friends washed over each of us.

We then made Eucharist together as a holy community of people who had shared an experience that would never be forgotten.

The closing hymn pointed us to new beginnings:

> When our hearts are wintry, grieving, or in pain,
> Thy touch can call us back to life again;
> Fields of our hearts that dead and bare have been;
> Love is come again like wheat that springeth green.

When the service was over, wine and cheese were offered in the social parlor. But that amenity added little to the evening and was short lived. Before many minutes passed each of us had departed into the night to contemplate the reality of human pain that we had experienced and to wonder if its power was really touched in this service of worship.

I was left with many impressions. First, pain and death are present in divorce for both the husband and the wife, whether acknowledged liturgically or not. Second, it takes courage, maturity, and a willingness to endure enormous vulnerability to stand up, even among an invited group of close friends, and confess failure and ask forgiveness. Third, sometimes the fracture of separation and divorce is so bitter that one or both partners could not and would not choose such an experience. Fourth, a funeral service for someone you love is also painful and difficult, but it is a pain and a difficulty that enables you to grow. Sometimes healing does not begin in the bereavement process until the funeral ritual is over. Yet divorce, which is certainly a death experience, is frequently allowed to run on interminably through a masochistic legal process, until all emotional reserves are exhausted and all personal dignity is spent. The final divorce decree is a rather impersonal piece of paper that offers no therapeutic possibility to the lives that have been hurt in the process. Fifth, every common experience is a bonding experience in which lives and relationships are redefined. This service enabled this man and this woman to begin the process of relating to each other in a new way that had the possibility for friendship within it. Somehow the bitterness of rejection was not total, and the pain of failure was not complete. Finally, sharing in this service enabled those of us who had been friends to both the man and the woman to continue separate friendships with each without the sense of having taken sides in their domestic dispute. Those who had once related to this couple as a couple could now relate to both persons as individuals without feeling disloyal to either. So one price that divorce frequently exacts did not have to be paid. The community did not have to choose sides and add to one or the other an additional dimension of rejection.

My conclusion after weeks of processing feelings was a powerful yes for this proposed liturgy. Such a service is needed by the church as a pastoral tool, to be used in appropriate situations to bring the grace, love, and forgiveness of God to a common human experience of brokenness and pain. It would also be a symbol of the church's willingness to surrender its power position as the dispenser of moral judgment and the custodian of community standards. It would place the church where I think the church should be—in the midst of human pain, brokenness, and failure. "Those who are well have no need of a physician," said our Lord (Mark 2:17). But throughout history the church has seemed far more content to be the arbiter of human righteousness than to be present in the midst of the brokenness of human sin.

We do not live in an ideal world. Our visions of perfection are constantly compromised, and our ultimate hopes and dreams are never achieved. It is in those moments when we fail that the church needs to meet us in our pain, enable us to stand even though we have fallen, and give us courage to live again, to love again, to risk again.

No one should abandon a sacred relationship like a

marriage without making every effort to heal and transform the brokenness. Not to struggle to preserve that which is a sacred trust is to reveal a shallowness that will continue to plague one's life. But when that struggle has been engaged deeply and honestly and still has not succeeded, then the church must reach out to her hurting people with a faith that embraces the past in forgiveness and opens the future in hope.

Without compromising the essential commitment to the ideal of faithful, monogamous marriage, the church needs to proclaim that divorce is sometimes the alternative which gives hope for life, and that marriage is sometimes the alternative which delivers only death.

The fullness of life for each of God's creatures is the ultimate goal for human life that the Christian church upholds. When marriage serves that goal, it is the most beautiful and complete human relationship. When marriage does not, or cannot, serve that goal, it becomes less than ultimate and may well prove less than eternal.

In that case the church on every official level needs to accept the reality and the pain that separation and divorce bring to God's people and to help redeem and transform that reality and that pain.

I am convinced that no divorced couple could walk through the service for "A Recognition of the End of a Marriage" without knowing that in the searing pain of human brokenness there is redemption, forgiveness, hope, and the opportunity to seek new fulfillment along a new path.

There are many detours on the road through life. We frequently do not travel the best route, the most direct route. But we Christians serve a God who can bring resurrection out of crucifixion, life out of death, joy out of sorrow, redemption out of pain. Perhaps this God can also bring us to fulfillment despite our detours, to wholeness despite our brokenness.

In that hope we live.

Notes

1. Much of this liturgy was adapted by the couple involved from a proposed trial service of the United Church of Christ.

CHAPTER FOURTEEN

Blessing Gay and Lesbian Commitments

*D*ear Friends in Christ: We have come together in the presence of God to witness and bless the union of these persons in a lifelong commitment of love. The calling to live in the bond of a covenant is a gift from God, in whose image we are created and by whom we are called to love, to reason, to work and play, and to live in harmony with God and one another. In celebrating this covenant we are reminded of our highest vocation: to love God and to love our neighbor.

"Patricia Hollingsworth and Valerie Miller are here to bear witness to their love for each other and to their intention to embody Christ's love in their relationship. Each has found the other to be a gift of God in the midst of a broken and sinful world. We are now called to share in their happiness and to witness this exchange of vows, because we believe God, who is love and truth, sees into their hearts and accepts the offering they are making.

"The joining of two persons in heart, body, and mind is intended by God for their mutual joy, for the help and comfort given one another in prosperity and adversity, and for the greater manifestation of love in the lives of all whom they encounter. Therefore this commitment is to be undertaken and affirmed seriously, reverently, deliberately, and in accordance with God's intention for us."[1]

These words are from one of many proposed rites to bless a same-sex union. It was prepared as a study document and has no official liturgical status in any ecclesiastical jurisdiction. It is, however, symbolic of efforts going on in numerous branches of the Christian church as Christian leaders begin to look at the reality of homosexuality with more loving and understanding eyes than church leaders possessed even a decade ago.

I have quoted its opening declaration at length, adding only fictitious names, to make it obvious that this is a covenant being entered into by two people of the same gender. I chose female rather than male names because cultural attitudes surrounding lesbian couples are not as hostile as for the unions of gay men. Prejudice is so strange and irrational. To some degree our cultural homophobia is another expression of the patriarchal bias that has marked civilization for thousands of years and that has visibly begun to recede only in this century. Men, whose dominant position is assumed in a patriarchal world, express their values in an abhorrence of those males who, in their judgment, willfully choose to love another man instead of a woman. But that hostile response changes to a more benign disbelief at the thought that a woman might not choose a man as the object of her affection. There is even the suggestion, widely assumed and articulated by males, that if a "real man," presumably someone like the person speaking, courted a lesbian, the misdirected affection could be cured. This male prejudice also surfaces in the judgment made so frequently by preachers and politicians alike that AIDS is a plague visited by God on homosexual persons as a punishment for the evil of their lives. There is in this conclusion a willful and even blissful ignorance of the fact that up to half of the population of homosexual persons is female, and AIDS is almost unknown among lesbians. If these voices of judgment were consistent in their reasoning, they might decide that the absence of AIDS among homosexual women is a sure sign of God's favor. But, of course, prejudice is not consistent.

So I chose female names. I wonder what emotions and images were elicited in the minds and hearts of my readers as they read the words of the service. Because they are appropriate to a wedding, the reader probably just skims placidly through them, until the realization strikes that the prime participants in this liturgy are not a man and a woman but rather two women. Then the words might well elicit strange emotions and evoke strange images. My suggestion is that the emotions and images would have been stronger and more hostile still if the names had been George Ligon and Stan King. (Again I hasten to add that these names are also fictitious.) Part of my task in writing this book is to temper those emotions and unload those images, for I regard the blessing of gay or lesbian couples by the church to be inevitable, right, and a positive good.

Everything I now know about homosexuality, through conversations with gay and lesbian people, the books I have read, and the experts with whom I have talked, has led me to the conclusion that a homosexual orientation is a minority but perfectly natural characteristic on the human spectrum of sexuality. It is not something one chooses, it is something one is. It is set before birth and is abnormal only in the sense that it is a minority orientation and not the statistical norm for our society. The evidence for this I have noted in chapter 5. Gays and lesbians, like all people, have unique gifts and contributions to offer the human family, some of which might well be present in them because of, not in spite of, their sexual orientation. But it is hard to discover gifts that celebrate one's being when the atmosphere in which one lives is laced with a murderous, oppressive hostility toward who one is.

When people are oppressed by either the external bonds of slavery or the internal bonds of prejudice, their natural creativity is inhibited. It is suffocated in the struggle just to survive. To the ancient Egyptians, Jewish slaves were inconsequential, dull people to whom the lowest of menial tasks were assigned. Jews were considered by their oppressors to be unfit for anything else. How surprised the Egyptians would have been to discover that in the Jewish people they enslaved lurked the genes that would produce two of the world's great religions; the genius minds of Albert Einstein, Sigmund Freud, and Karl Marx; and the life-giving gifts of Eddie Cantor, Jack Benny, Itzhak Perlman, Leon Uris, and Herman Wouk. But the world could not be the beneficiary of these gifts until that slavery was ended. One wonders what genius and grace has been denied the world because of our prejudice against homosexuals. What might have been gained is hinted at by considering that such extraordinary people as Leonardo da Vinci, Michelangelo, Christopher Marlowe, Erasmus, Dostoyevsky, Tchaikovsky, Francis Bacon, W. H. Auden, Richard the Lion Hearted, Lord Byron, Herman Melville, Maynard Keynes, Walt Whitman, and, some would argue, John Milton were gay.

If my conclusions about gay and lesbian people are valid, then the whole of society must be seen as guilty of a cruel oppression of this courageous minority. The time has surely come not just to tolerate, or even to accept, but to celebrate and welcome the presence among us of our gay and lesbian fellow human beings.

One way to do that is for the church to admit publicly its own complicity in their oppression, based on its vast ignorance and prejudice. It is time to overcome that dark chapter of church history by living new chapters with an attitude that embraces yesterday's exile, practices the inclusiveness of God's love, and celebrates the unique gifts of all of God's diverse children. The one act that above all others will best show a serious intention to change the church's attitude will be for the church to state its willingness and eager desire to bless and affirm the love that binds two persons of the same gender into a life-giving relationship of mutual commitment. That ritual act alone will announce to the homosexual world and to ourselves a shift that will be believed. No matter how that liturgy is discussed or defined, the media, the critics, and the world at large will hear it and talk about it as the marriage of homosexuals. But before we decide what to call this service, we need to understand what it is and what it is not. The central clue to this is to discover what the church does and does not do in marriage.

The church does not, in fact, marry anyone. People marry each other. The state, not the church, defines the nature of legal marriage. It does so by giving to married couples the right of joint property ownership. It is not within the power of the church to change this legal fact, though its implications need to be addressed. What the church does in holy matrimony is hear people's public vows to love each other, to live in a faithful relationship, and to be mutually supportive and caring in all of life's vicissitudes. Then the church adds to that vow of commitment its blessing. That blessing is really the church's only contribution. The church blesses the commitment to be a couple that issues from the vows of the two people who stand before "God and this company." That blessing conveys ecclesiastical sanction on the relationship and the official willingness of the church and, through the church, of society to support, undergird, and stabilize in every way possible the life of the newly formed couple. The hope of the church is that this sanction and the resultant public support might enable the vows exchanged in good faith before the altar to have an increased chance of being kept.

If the conveying of blessing and official approval is the church's gift to give, then surely that can be given to any relationship of love, fidelity, commitment, and trust that issues in life for the two people involved. We have not in the past as a church withheld blessing from many things. We have blessed fields when crops were planted, houses when newly occupied, pets in honor of Saint Francis, and even the hounds at a Virginia fox hunt. We have blessed MX missiles called "Peacemakers" and warships whose sole purpose was to kill and destroy, calling them, in at least one instance, *Corpus Christi*—the Body of Christ. Why would it occur to us to withhold our blessing from a human relationship that produces a more complete person in each of the partners, because of their life together? Surely the only possible answer to that question is that the church has shared in the habitual prejudice of the ages. Now I call on the church to step out of this prejudice and bless relationships between human beings that are marked by love, fidelity, and the hope of a lifetime of mutual responsibility. What this service is called can then be left to the people involved, and they can then urge the state to accord such relationships the legal benefits of marriage.

Only when official and public sanction is given to gay and lesbian couples will our society begin to think of them as units rather than as individuals and begin to relate to them in a way that enforces and undergirds that unity. Such simple things as inviting gay and lesbian couples to social functions and to family gatherings and sharing in the celebration of the anniversaries and other holy moments that mark their lives together would solidify the gay or lesbian couple just as it does the heterosexual married couple. Many gay and lesbian couples feel compelled to limit their associations to other homosexual persons with whom they can live their private lives in comfort.

Heterosexual marriages today, as this book has already noted, are under great duress. They are shattering in one out of two instances. That is so despite all the energy expended by the church and society to recognize, bless, and affirm those marriage unions. It is an enormous tribute to the commitment of gay and lesbian people to recognize that they have succeeded in forging long-lasting and in some cases permanent bonds without the support of church, state, or society; indeed in most cases they have done so in the face of active hostility from all three sources.

The heterosexual community needs to see and experience homosexual unions that are marked by integrity and caring and are filled with grace and beauty. The heterosexual majority seems to assume that the only form homosexual lovemaking takes is the promiscuous life of gay bars, pornography, and one-night stands. They are ever ready to condemn that behavior pattern as morally unacceptable— and so it is. But two things seem to have been overlooked by those who make these judgments. First, promiscuity, pick-up bars, pornography, and one-night stands are not unknown in the heterosexual world. That kind of behavior is destructive no matter what the sexual orientation of those who live out that style of life. Second, heterosexual people have the publicly accepted, blessed, and affirmed alternative of marriage that has as yet not been available to the homosexual population. If there is no such positive alternative for homosexual persons, then what is the church's expectation for them? If the church or society refuses to recognize or promote any positive alternative in which love and intimacy can sustain a gay or lesbian couple, then those institutions are guilty of contributing to the very promiscuity that they condemn.

A willingness on the part of church and society to accept, bless, affirm, and encourage long-term faithful relationships among gay and lesbian people would be just and proper. But above all it would indicate to the homosexual minority that there is a recognized alternative to the loneliness of celibacy on the one hand and the irresponsibility of sexual promiscuity on the other.

The fact is that the homosexual population has recognized and supported committed couples, long ahead of the church. In numbers far greater than the "straight" majority suspects, gay people have forged this alternative for themselves with no official help or sanction from anyone. Though those homosexual persons alienated from the church might not welcome the church's Johnny-come-lately arrival on this scene, I believe that the vast majority who crave a sign of society's acceptance of their existence would, if not for themselves then for others. But whether welcomed or not, this is a step the church must take *for the church's sake*. We need to be cleansed from our sin. Then we can send a message to the homosexual population that, first, we have recognized our need for repentance and, second, we are ready at last to offer our resources to turn the attitude of the world away from its traditional stance of rejection, away from intolerance, away even from a grudging acceptance, until finally we can begin to celebrate the presence and the contributions of gay people and of gay couples as well as heterosexual people and couples in our common life.

Being public and articulate about what we believe concerning gay couples and designing a liturgy to place those convictions into the context of public worship is, in my opinion, a major mandate for justice before the church today. Unbeknownst to figures in the hierarchy of the church, the blessing of gay unions is being conducted as a private pastoral rite in congregations of all traditions across this land, at this very moment. In Canada, I am told, the gay and lesbian population invites pastors to do house blessings for them, which includes a blessing of those who live therein. For gay and lesbian couples there, this has served as the church's blessing upon their relationships. It is both a clandestine and an ingenious ploy, but in the future the church will need to be more open and more honest about its participation in it. The grapevine is quite active in informing the gay population of where they can go to receive this ministry of the church.

Gay and lesbian clergy are themselves opening the doors of their churches to their brothers and sisters. None of the proposed liturgies being developed today has yet received the sanction of any ecclesiastical tradition, save the Universal Fellowship of Metropolitan Community Churches, a relatively new denomination founded to minister primarily but not exclusively to gay men and lesbians. Given the virulent negativity that still exists, it may well take another decade before official acceptance is accorded. But ten years is an astonishingly brief time for a change of this magnitude. It will be a signal achievement to achieve it in a decade or less. Until that time I hope that the debate this proposal receives will be a factor in the continuing process of consciousness-raising, and I hope more ordained clergy will be bold enough to add this resource to their private pastoral ministries, until the day arrives when it becomes part of the church's public liturgy.

People do change, and the knowledge explosion continues each day. I am a living example of these facts. Ten years ago I would have been shocked and aghast at the things I am writing at this moment. Five years ago I still had to be pushed to take an inclusive position. However, scientific data that made me aware that my prejudice grew out of ignorance combined with the witness of gay and lesbian people, some of whom were clergy, to educate me. When I became open to new possibilities, then the humanity of representatives of the homosexual world was able to touch my humanity. They loved me and they invited me into the integrity and life-giving power present in their relationships. It was my recognition of the meaning and validity at work in their mutually committed lives that enabled me to accept the new data and to walk slowly but surely away from the prejudice of a lifetime.

If I can make such a journey, so can the church. If not this year, then next year, but it is inevitable that it will come. I only know that when we finally free ourselves from our prejudices we will have a hard time understanding how we had been so blind in the first place. Can anyone imagine a world that would say that Willie Mays, Hank Aaron, or David

Winfield cannot play major league baseball because they are black? Well, Jackie Robinson and Satchel Paige could imagine that, for they experienced it first hand. Can anyone imagine the Metropolitan Opera without Leontyne Price? The negativity toward blessing gay and lesbian unions will someday be like the assumption that baseball is a game for white males only, or that a black woman from Mississippi could not hope to sing at the Met. That stance will die and be one more embarrassing relic in the museum of cultural and ecclesiastical prejudices. I look forward to that day. I hope I contribute to its early arrival.

The time to move in this direction is certainly now. The witness of contemporary theology is stimulating us to think about liberation and self-affirmation. The insights of contemporary psychology encourage the expression of natural and basic human drives through creative and responsible outlets. Contemporary health concerns demand the redefinition of responsible social behavior. The growing body of data about sexual orientation charges us to rethink our assumptions. We need only to add the courageous and responsible voice of the official church. That voice will affirm God's Word in creation that "it is not good for man [woman] to live alone." It will affirm God's Word in Jesus Christ that all are invited to come unto him to find the rest of acceptance. It will affirm God's Word in the Spirit that in the body of Christ, whatever language we understand will be the language through which God's love will be proclaimed to us (Acts 2). It is this Word of God that calls us to act now.

———————————— +++++ ————————————

"In the name of God, I, George, take you, Stan, to be my companion; and I solemnly promise here before God and these witnesses that I will stand beside you and with you always, in times of celebration and of sadness, in times of pleasure and of anger, in times of sickness and of health; I will care for you and love you so long as we both shall live."

"Now that George and Stan have pledged themselves to each other by solemn vows, by joining hands, and by giving and receiving rings, I declare that they are united to one another in a solemn covenant of love, in the name of God: Creator, Redeemer, and Sustainer.

"Let us uphold them in this covenant."

And the people respond: "Amen."[2]

———————————— +++++ ————————————

I suspect that these words will remain strange and shocking to many. All words that announce new life sound foreign to the ear, at least until experience illumines understanding.

The original Jewish Christians must have recoiled when someone first suggested that Gentile Christians should be welcomed into the church without their having to obey Jewish law.

Western Christians in both Europe and America must have cringed when someone first suggested that non-white members of ethnic minorities must be welcomed into the life of the church as equal brother and sisters.

The rigid ecclesiastical hierarchy, so sure that they spoke for God, must have thought it strange and shocking when someone first suggested that a left-handed person was not evil and might well serve as a priest.

The male priesthood, certain that only men could be symbolic representatives of the deity, must have thought it outrageous when someone first said that women too are called to be pastors, priests, and bishops, and that ordination must be opened to include them.

The proposal that the church bless and affirm publicly the union forged in love by two persons of the same gender will also be received as strange and shocking. That too will pass, and the practice will become in time quite commonplace.

"In Christ," said Paul, "shall all be made alive." Yes, *all*, including the gay and lesbian couples who have become in Christ one flesh. *Now* is the appointed time to break the bondage of this prejudice that prevents that gift of life promised to all by the Christ from being realized.

Notes

1. Adapted from a study liturgy circulated in the Diocese of California, 1986.
2. Ibid., slightly adapted.

CHAPTER FIFTEEN

Post-Married Singles and Holy Sex

*B*eing single is not abnormal. It may not even be the minority lifestyle. Almost everyone, if their years of being single were counted up, would discover that a minimum of one-third of his or her life had been spent in that status. We were all born single. Even twins are two single persons. Many people will end their lives single, for even the best of marriages will leave one partner or the other alone for some time as widow or widower. My mother is now in the ninth decade of life. She was married for only fifteen years before being widowed, so she has been single for more than four-fifths of her years thus far.

The percentage of years spent in single status has increased in this century, and particularly so in Western civilization. The rising demand for higher education has been a factor. The emancipation of women from the domestic stereotypes of the past has been another factor. The combination of these two factors has created a third, namely the entry of women into the professional sphere and into the executive level of corporate business. The additional years of preparation and the fulfillment found in a career itself have challenged marriage as the woman's primary option, or at least lifted career goals to parity with marriage goals. The result has been a higher percentage of singleness in our population. Still another contributor to this trend has been the fact that many more marriages end in divorce today than was true in the nineteenth century. Those divorced people have swelled the ranks of single people. Singleness is a significant part of the whole of many lives and, therefore, is a major experience of human beings in our time.

Yet the Christian church continues to assume that marriage is the norm of life and that singleness is either a sign of immaturity, or of sexual perversion, or of failure, or of extreme sadness, or of some tragic fate. Since singleness is not trusted save inside the rare vows of religious celibacy, the single person is regarded as a kind of loose cannon that threatens the marital fidelity of others. There is, therefore, a not-so-veiled negativity toward the "non-vowed" single person that emanates regularly from the voices and precepts of the church.

Young unmarried single people are told by official church statements that they are not yet mature or whole. Most specifically, they are reminded that one aspect of their being, namely their sexuality, is reserved for married life alone and that there are to be no alternatives to that moral requirement despite the tremendous social shifts I have previously chronicled. Those who are married, and as such safely removed from a dangerous singleness, are told that divorce is a sin and a failure, and if divorced they cannot remarry with the church's blessing unless various demeaning procedures are followed in order to secure that holy permission. Those who are by virtue of law single because they are gay or lesbian persons are told that sexual celibacy is for them the only legitimate lifestyle that can be called moral. Those who are widowed are told that part of their grief and burden will be the loss of sexual intimacy that must be endured unless remarriage becomes a possibility at some date in the unforeseen future.

In all of these prohibitions there is that familiar echo of judgment and condemnation that derives from a definition of human sexuality as dangerous and evil unless it occurs inside marriage, the one socially approved relationship in which sexual intimacy sheds its connotation of sin.

There will always be individuals who will test the boundaries of any rule, but in our generation the rules have become so out of touch with reality that they are simply disregarded. The tide of change always begins with the trickle of a few nonconformists, and then it grows into a veritable flood as increasing numbers of people abandon the convictions of the past. That, I have argued, is the situation we face today.

I have looked at what the changing circumstances mean to young unmarrieds and to homosexual people. I have suggested that the rising divorce rate is not always a tragedy but represents in some cases mature decisions to change or to grow, and might itself receive something other than blanket condemnation from the church.

Now, I turn to look at the lives of mature single people, most of them post-married people, many of whom are not interested in remarriage ever again, or at least not at this time. Does their single status require sexual abstinence? I think not. I do believe, however, that their single status and their personal integrity do require a keen understanding of responsible and appropriate sexual activity.

To suggest that abstinence is not mandatory is not to suggest that "anything goes." Sex is still powerful. Where sex enhances life, I am prepared to call it good. Where sex destroys or diminishes life, I am prepared to call it evil. I seek a pattern in which sex can be holy for the mature, post-married adult.

The sexual revolution and its aftermath have created a sort of sexual schizophrenia. The voices still wedded to fading traditions shout with increasing frenzy, "You shall not!" The voices of the new age, however, say through every conceivable medium, "You shall! Indeed, you should!"

The traditional voices are still tinged with fear. If the fear of pregnancy has faded, then the fear of infection has become its successor. There is also the genuine fear of moral anarchy, and the fear of the loss of power by those institutions who loved the role of moral arbiter. Those fears make all talk of sex sound negative.

The voices of change, on the other hand, remind us that the fear of pregnancy is over, that love is what counts, that women are liberated, that virginity is an expression of an evil system of repression, and that sexual activity, far from being defiling, is in fact healthy and pleasurable. Books on how to do sex, and do it well, abound on best-seller lists. Indeed, so many "how-to" books have been published in recent years that the *New York Times Book Review* section has created a new best-seller list other than fiction and nonfiction: "Advice, How-to, and Miscellaneous." In addition to volumes specifically on sexuality, there are diet and exercise "how-to" books that are intrinsically related to sexuality.

As the fury of the sexual revolution reached its crescendo, the fear that once deterred sexual activity was replaced by pressure to engage in sexual activity, to do it right, to enjoy it, and even to tell the world how you are doing it. Nowhere are these realities more at work than among mature singles. These people are in a very different place from their younger counterparts. The romantic relationship that drives toward marriage may well not be appropriate to their place in life. A marriage and subsequent divorce may have left them so hurt, so devastated, that they are not capable of making another lifetime commitment. The death of a spouse may have been so draining emotionally that both their grief work and their own personal rehabilitation may take years. They may be left with dependent children and so few economic resources as to make the addition of a new relationship all but impossible. Their lives may be complicated by the restrictions of someone else's last will and testament, the insensitivity of Social Security laws, or financial commitments previously made to their children. They might be in careers that require high mobility and regular transfers to varying regions of the country or world, making a commitment to the permanency of a relationship with another career-minded person very problematic. There are doubtless other reasons that could be stated, but these are sufficient to make us aware that marriage or remarriage is not, and in some cases cannot ever be, the solitary answer for all post-married people.

Yet the need for companionship with a member of the opposite sex does not disappear. That companionship can be on many levels—from a working relationship or a brief social connection to a deep friendship in which time is invested, life is shared, and intimate moments are spent together. Is sex to be ruled out by the guardians of public morality from all of these relationships, because they each fall short of the solitary standard of marriage? On the other hand, is sex to be expected and anticipated by a hedonistic society in every male-female encounter that confronts the single adult?

There are voices that would say yes to both questions. I would like to propose that no is the proper and only moral answer to both questions. But that answer must be accompanied by an attempt to delineate the circumstances that might justify both the no to total abstinence and the no to indiscriminate sexual activity.

Karen LeBacqz, a professor of Christian ethics at the Pacific School of Religion in Berkeley, California, has proposed that the basis for developing a sexual ethic for singles might be found in what she calls "appropriate vulnerability."[1] She argues that when pregnancy is separated from sexual activity, one of the two primary historical purposes of sex is removed. Procreation and the pleasure of union have been considered the dual sexual legitimizers. It was the procreation aspect, not the union aspect, that demanded marriage as the context of sex. With procreation removed, either by effective birth control or by longevity that stretches past the fertile years, the basis of sexual decision making shifts from marriage to the quality of the human relationship, including its level of investment, commitment, and vulnerability. Dr. LeBacqz leans heavily on the insight captured in the biblical account of creation in the verse, "The man and his wife were both naked, and were not ashamed" (Gen. 2:25). To be "naked," she argues, is a metaphor for being vulnerable, and to "feel no shame" is a metaphor for appropriateness. If that interpretation of the Genesis story is accurate, then the Word of God that we hear spoken in the creation narrative proclaims that appropriate vulnerability is "the purpose of the creation of man and woman as sexual beings who unite with one another to form one flesh."[2]

This view is supported by the fact noted earlier that the Hebrews used the verb "to know" as a synonym for sexual intercourse. It places sex into a relationship that is deep and significant, for no one can really know another unless the other reveals himself or herself. Self-revelation opens us to hurt, to wounds, to abuse, as well as to love and to trust. No relationship can grow without vulnerability, without the openness of mutual revelation and mutual acceptance of that revelation. In the creation story Adam and Eve chose to abandon that stance of vulnerability in exchange for the quest for power. They were enticed by the hope that they might "be like gods" (Gen. 3:5), rather than continuing in the status of vulnerability. The desire to possess godlike power over another is a manifestation of the hardening of "the heart of vulnerability."[3] It is interesting to note that the climax of the Christian story is in the affirmation not of power but of powerlessness, which is nothing other than the willingness to be vulnerable. How else can one read the story of the cross?[4]

Dr. LeBacqz proceeds to draw the conclusion that "any exercise of sexuality that violates appropriate vulnerability is wrong. This includes violations of the partners' vulnerability and violations of one's own vulnerability."[5] The rapist, for example, is one who refuses to be vulnerable. So also, Dr.

LeBacqz dismisses as not moral seduction, prostitution, promiscuity, and any sexual encounter in which another is hurt. Sex, she argues, "is not just for fun, for play, for physical release, for showing off, or for any of a host of other emotions that are often attached to sexuality. It is for the appropriate expression of vulnerability." Without that, she concludes, "the sexual expression is not proper."[6]

Nothing about the argument for vulnerability suggests that marriage is the only context in which sex is deemed appropriate. Premarital, or gay or lesbian unions, might well fall within the boundaries of appropriate vulnerability. At the same time, sexual activity even inside a marriage might not be "an appropriate expression of vulnerability."

This understanding of sexual activity grounded in vulnerability offers to older singles new options that go beyond abstinence as the only legitimate moral response to their single status, while at the same time ruling out manipulative and self-serving sexual liaisons. This means that the traditional basis for determining the issue of whether a sexual relationship is good or bad, whether it should be given a yes or a no, is no longer confined to the issue of marriage. Nor does it mean that all standards or the structures that protected vulnerable people must be abandoned.

It does mean that the church must give up its elevated stance of righteousness and enter with its people into the more difficult gray areas of life to seek a basis for decision making that is life giving, not life destroying, and is appropriate to the age and circumstances of the people involved. It does open the possibility that the same activity that is pronounced good in one relationship or at one age can be destructive in another relationship or at another age. It does move us away from rigid rules and into the freedom of relativity.

In 1977 the United Church of Christ put out a "preliminary study" on human sexuality. Within that study was the recommendation that "the physical expression of one's sexuality in relation to another ought to be appropriate to the level of loving commitment within the relationship."[7] This principle suggests that human relationships exist on a continuum, and that physical expressions of love ought to be related to the location, the meaning, and the intensity on that continuum. Something as innocent as holding hands might well not be appropriate in many relationships. Though the report did not use the word, the implication was nonetheless present that commitment and vulnerability are deeply related. Commitment requires a willingness to be vulnerable. Shallow commitment requires little vulnerability. Deep commitment presupposes great vulnerability. At some point on the scale of commitment, this principle of proportionality would admit the appropriateness of sexual activity. It recognizes, as Dr. LeBacqz points out, that "the more sexual involvement there is to be the more there needs to be a context that protects and safeguards that vulnerability."[8]

Being single lacks the protection that marriage gives to our vulnerability. Age and experience would seem to indicate that older people might require less of a protective structure than younger people. To the degree that men still have more power than women, greater consideration must be given to the greater vulnerability of the woman. In the midst of these shifting guidelines, we struggle to live into a proper sexual ethic for post-married single people. We are no longer children who must do as we are told. We are rather adults who have to learn to be responsible. Celibacy is not the answer for most and has in practice been largely set aside as no longer appropriate. Promiscuity and casual sex also are not the answers.

I believe that sex outside of marriage can be holy and life giving under some circumstances, but it can also be evil and life diminishing under other circumstances. I offer for debate the following proposal for the structure necessary to make sex holy if it occurs outside the bond of marriage among older post-married adults.

1. The sexual relationship between single adults must be just that—a relationship between *single* adults. It must not be a violation of either person's marital bond. If one's marital vow is broken by a sexual affair, that affair becomes an expression of dishonesty and will finally be destructive to both the marriage and the character of the violating person.

2. A sexual relationship between single adults must be a union of love and caring, not just a union of convenience or desire.

3. A sexual relationship does not appropriately initiate a relationship. Rather, a sexual relationship must grow out of the bond that two people build together over a period of time. Sex is not properly shared until many other things are shared, such as time, values, life stories, friendship, communication, and a sense of deep trust and responsibility. In other words, sex is not appropriate until there is a structure that will protect each person's vulnerability.

4. Intimacy is by its nature an intensely private and discreet human activity. Appropriate vulnerability requires that it must be kept that way. If both partners are not willing to protect the vulnerability of the other, the relationship becomes hurtful, hateful, and destructive. The sacred, exclusive quality of those special moments cannot be compromised by gossip, by indiscretion, or, even after the relationship has come to an end, by an expression of one person's anger. The unwillingness to make this commitment, or to carry through on it once made, would argue that the relationship was built on the power of ego needs and not the vulnerability of personhood.

5. The relationship in which sex is shared by single adults needs to be exclusive. It may not turn out to be eternal, but while it is active it does need to be exclusive. Multiple sex partners at the same time is a violation of vulnerability, commitment, honesty, and the reality of caring.

There may be other guidelines that need to be added. I am

certain I have not exhausted the list of things necessary to create holiness. I do not, however, want to overburden human beings with directives, warnings, and structures. I do respect the human ability not to allow behavior patterns that are finally self-destructive to go on forever unchecked. Nor will human beings forever deny to themselves behavior patterns that promise to enrich, fulfill, and expand their lives.

Yes, there can be holy sex in the life of a mature single adult. Not all sexual activity among mature single adults is holy. Finally, a warning needs to be issued to those institutional representatives of organized religion who still claim the power to define morality. The church must abandon its irrelevant ethical judgments that arise from realities that no longer exist and enter the arenas where life is lived, where people are hurt, where love is experienced, where ideals are compromised, where people awaken from their dreams, and be a part of the debate that will separate the ethics of life from the ethics of death. The prohibitions of the past have been abandoned, not because people are evil "secular modernists" but because life has changed and those prohibitions are simply no longer appropriate. To expend ecclesiastical energy clinging to those prohibitions, to pass resolutions recalling people to those prohibitions, to seek to revivify those prohibitions, will prove an exercise in futility. Finally, such activities will so discredit the church that whatever moral authority it has in other areas of life will be dissipated as well.

Our new world is here because gigantic shifts in consciousness, values, and human power equations have taken place. Like every dramatic shift in history, this one has excesses that need to be curbed. Like every great transition of consciousness, this one must be directed and guided, even though this is like riding a whirlwind. Like every new vision or paradigmatic change, this one has gained its power because positions against which it protests were frozen and defended far beyond the time when their credibility had disappeared. Even at this late date the Christian church needs to hear the call to stand with its people in the real world of human choices and there to separate the wheat from the chaff.

Notes

1. Karen LeBacqz, "Appropriate Vulnerability—A Sexual Ethic for Singles," *The Christian Century* 104, no. 5 (May 1987): 435-38.
2. Ibid., p. 437.
3. Ibid.
4. I developed this thought in more detail in an article entitled "The Powerlessness of Christ," *The Witness* 69, no. 3 (March 1986): 6-8.
5. LeBacqz, "Appropriate Vulnerability," p. 437.
6. Ibid.
7. The United Church of Christ, *Human Sexuality—A Preliminary Study* (New York: United Church Press, 1977), p. 103.
8. LeBacqz, "Appropriate Vulnerability," p. 437.

CHAPTER SIXTEEN

Women in the Episcopate: Symbol of a New Day for the Church

hroughout this book I have implied that in the defining of sexual issues and values the most powerful institution in Western civilization has been the Christian church. The church has claimed that power effectively, and the Christian world at large has delegated it almost unquestioningly to the church. The sexual revolution that challenged the church's authority to delineate right and wrong has been accomplished in an era when the authority of the church in all areas has been widely questioned. One of the reasons for this loss of power has been the church's built-in resistance to the paradigmatic shift away from patriarchy into mutuality.

Perhaps the most sexist institution left in Western civilization is the church. It continues to hold before the world a God imaged almost exclusively as masculine. The implication of this divine imaging is that only the male is capable of reflecting and symbolizing the deity—a stance that affirms patriarchy. Overwhelmingly, the ranks of the ordained are filled by men. Only in recent years has the ordination of women been a legal possibility in most churches. Very few women have yet achieved in any Christian tradition significant positions of power and influence. Women are still categorically denied ordination in the Roman Catholic and Orthodox traditions, the two largest Christian bodies in the world. Women are also denied ordination in many fundamentalist churches, which still operate on the anti-female prejudices found in those biblical texts discussed in detail in chapter 8. There are, as of this date, no female bishops in the Anglican communion or in the Lutheran churches of the world.

Since at the highest levels of decision making the liturgical churches of the world are all male, sexual mores have been set from a position of overwhelming male bias. The patriarchal world view has been identified with the patriarchal God, as defined by the patriarchal hierarchy of the patriarchal church. So the language of the liturgies of the church is for the most part the language of male dominance. The words of our hymns ("Faith of Our *Fathers*," "Turn Back, O *Man*," "Lead Us Heavenly *Father*, Lead Us") and creeds ("for us *men* and for our salvation he came down from heaven") and the categories of Christian theology (God is *Father, Son,* and Holy Spirit) make this obvious. If Professor Elaine Pagels is accurate in her understanding of church history, male dominance and theological orthodoxy were merged in the struggles to rout the heretical thinking of the democratizing Gnostics, who were open to women, and to consolidate ecclesiastical power in the hands of men only.[1]

When the ideal woman was defined for the Christian West as a perpetual virgin, few people noticed that those doing the defining were all celibate men. To whom is a perpetual virgin an ideal woman except a celibate man? Guilt, inadequacy, and the desacralization of human sexuality were the inevitable by-products. If sexuality per se was thought to be evil, then female sexuality was believed to be particularly evil. Tertullian, an early church father, spoke for this rising ecclesiastical rejection of women when he said, "It is not permitted for a woman to speak in church, nor is it permitted for her to teach, nor to baptize, nor to offer the Eucharist, nor to claim for herself a share in any masculine function, least of all in the priestly office."[2]

Jerome, in the fourth century, added to the negativity when he wrote, "Nothing is so unclean as a woman in her periods. What she touches she causes to be unclean."[3] Jerome later wrote, "When a woman wishes to serve Christ more than the world, she will cease to be a woman and will be called a man."[4] To be a man was, in Jerome's mind, a major improvement. Cyprian, Tertullian, and Jerome all urged women to remain virgins as the only means to escape the consequences of the fall.[5] Ambrose likened the loss of a woman's virginity to a defacement of creation.[6] Marriage, Jerome argued, was acceptable only because from it "more virgins were born."[7] A thirteenth-century church breviary blamed women for the evil sexual desires that males were incapable of repressing. This explanation was simple: "Satan, in order to make men suffer bitterly makes them adore women, for instead of loving the creator they sinfully love women."[8]

Through the ages a patriarchal, chauvinistic church has been the environment in which sexual ethics were formed, sexual stereotypes were defined, and sexual values were stated. It is not lost on today's generation of women that the churches that believe the use of contraceptives to be sinful are the churches with an all-male clerical hierarchy in which celibacy is still required for membership.

For many sessions of the House of Bishops of The Episcopal Church I have watched this all-male hierarchy, made up in large measure of postmenopausal males, deliberate on the evils of abortion. There is something unethical about people of one gender determining the fate of the other. Abortion laws affect primarily poor, young women. The Episcopal bishops are none of these. For the present and the foreseeable future, the changing patterns of sexual morality will be a major agenda item for debate in that House. There will be no women bishops present to temper the maleness of that discussion. In the past it has been an all-male hierarchy that has deliberated on whether or not divorced persons could be remarried, the morality of such things as artificial insemination or in vitro fertilization, and on the many other sex-related issues brought before us by the rapid advances in biomedical technology.

In the seminaries of all the mainline Protestant traditions, however, the gender balance of the student bodies has shifted in the last two decades from a negligible female presence to a female enrollment that averages 30 to 40 percent of the student body. Some seminaries now have female majorities. A change is obviously on the way. It will take perhaps another decade for these candidates to overcome the conscious and unconscious prejudice that is the residue from the past, and to claim for themselves more and more positions of power, authority, and public note.

The church today needs symbols that will force a change in consciousness among its people. The most important symbol, in my opinion, will be the presence of women in the office of bishop in those churches that claim that office, particularly the Anglicans (i.e., Episcopalians), the Roman Catholics, the Orthodox, the Lutherans, and the United Methodists. The United Methodists have already broken the episcopal sex barrier by electing some outstanding women of ability as bishops, but because the episcopacy in that tradition, as in the case of American Lutheranism, constitutes only an office and not a unique sacerdotal order of ministry as in the Catholic traditions, the necessary consciousness-raising publicity that accompanied that transition has been minimal for the church and society at large.

In The Episcopal Church women were not seated with voice and vote in national conventions until 1970, the same year that ordination of women to the diaconate, the first step in Holy Orders, was approved. Ordination of women to the priesthood was denied as late as 1973. An irregular ordination of eleven women to the priesthood in Philadelphia in 1974 created apoplexy in the House of Bishops. The three retired bishops who performed these ordinations were censured not once but twice. They were denied seat and vote with their brothers in the House. It was a chaotic and hostile time. The anger was in direct proportion to the threat. Male power and male control in the church were made vulnerable.

Finally, in 1976 the ordination of women to the priesthood was affirmed by The Episcopal Church and took effect canonically on January 1, 1977. Today more than one thousand women are numbered in the ranks of the ordained ministry of The Episcopal Church. That expansion of ordination to include women became the occasion for some clergy and congregations to move into schism. Splinter groups began to appear, calling themselves The Anglican Catholic Church or The Continuing Anglican Church or some variation of that title. The names were meant to imply that they alone were the bearers of the true faith, which included the unbroken tradition of male supremacy. Time has not been kind to those splinter groups; it seldom is to movements of negativity. Today they are not a significant force in American Christianity or even in the awareness of Episcopalians or the nation at large.

In the meantime women priests in The Episcopal Church have joined seminary faculties as professors and chaplains and have taken their places as rectors of larger and larger parishes. One woman priest is now the senior archdeacon in a diocese, overseeing the work of more than forty churches and administering a budget larger than the total budget of many dioceses. Another is a cathedral dean.

It will not be long before the all-male Episcopal House of Bishops will come to an end, and women will be in decision-making positions in that church, taking part in defining God, producing liturgies, reinterpreting creeds, developing new sexual images, and determining the boundaries of moral and immoral behavior, most especially in the area of sexual ethics. It will be a new day welcomed with joy by the growing majority, and deplored, castigated, and resisted to the dying breath by the defenders of the receding patriarchy.

In the dawn of that new day people will laugh at the threadbare explanations used by defenders of the patriarchal patterns of the past. When John Paul II asserted in 1986 that women would never be ordained to the priesthood of the Roman Catholic church, he rationalized that ban by noting that Jesus did not choose any female disciples. Somehow the truth of that argument was supposed to be self-evident. A closer look, however, reveals it to be self-serving and irrelevant. Jesus did not choose any Polish males to be disciples either, but no one has suggested to this former Polish cardinal that being Polish might be a barrier to the priesthood. Jesus did not choose any Gentiles, or people of color, or one-eyed people, or people who were lame or hard of hearing, or people in any of a thousand other categories. Yet the church was not limited in its choice of leaders by such stringent literalism. A prominent bishop in the Church of England recently stated that women should remain in the traditional roles of wives and mothers. It somehow escaped his notice that Elizabeth II reigns over that kingdom and that Margaret Thatcher runs its government.

Not the Pope, the orthodox tradition, the prejudice of any male ecclesiastical figure, nor any other force under heaven will stop the movement away from patriarchy toward mutuality, and the sooner the churches of Christendom place women into positions of decision-making authority, the sooner this wonderful but sexually antiquated institution will begin to right the wrongs of the ages and to lift from both men and women the stereotypes of the past. The election of a woman bishop in those churches that have none as yet, and the election of more women bishops in those churches that now have a few, will indicate that some parts of the Christian church are ready to move beyond the sexist limitations of yesterday.

In time every church will follow. Those who take too long

to arrive at this decision will lose their influence. In a very short time the lines of battle and debate will be so far beyond this issue that some churches will look like those few Japanese guerrilla fighters discovered on Pacific islands long after World War II was over, who had been cut off from the main body of their forces. Years later they were still in battle readiness, flailing away in the cause of their emperor and wondering why no one was taking them seriously. For once, just once, it would be exhilarating to see the church greet the future with enthusiasm rather than to follow our usual pattern of being dragged, screaming and kicking, into it.

The election of women to the office of bishop will announce to the world that the Christian church has finally read the signs and that we rejoice to be part of a new day. Amen. So let it be.

Notes

1. Elaine Pagels, *The Gnostic Gospels* (New York: Random House, 1979).
2. Ibid., p. 60.
3. Marina Warner, *Alone of All Her Sex* (New York: Alfred A. Knopf, 1976), p. 76.
4. Ibid., p. 73.
5. Ibid.
6. Ibid.
7. Ibid.
8. Ibid, p.153.

EPILOGUE

Enduring the Present to Claim the Future

*M*y case is now argued. I have deliberately done it with both passion and provocation. This book is not a call to immorality, as some critics will inevitably charge. It is rather a call to a new and rigorous morality inside a set of parameters different from those of the past. It lays its emphasis not on the law, not on the socially recognized institution of marriage, but on commitment, vulnerability, and reality.

My assumption is that sexual activity is designed by the Creator not just for procreation but also for the enhancement of human life. We no longer need to be anxious about the human ability to procreate sufficiently. Indeed, unless we learn to curb procreation, overpopulation may turn out to be the path to human genocide. Our focus today must rather be on the ways that sex can enhance life in the circumstances of this century. To bring together sexual activity and the fullness of life is the task before the church in our time. The enhancement of life does not come through controlling guilt or through prejudicial stereotypes. It comes through responsible action that is honest, non-manipulative, sensitive, and life giving. It comes through a loving human relationship that does not violate any commitments the involved persons have previously made that are still operative. It comes through the acceptance of the self that one is, and the willingness of two persons in mutual acceptance to share themselves with each other.

As I close this book my hope is that its ideas will be debated on their merits and amended, adapted, adopted, or even rejected. Better ideas may well sweep my proposals from the field of consideration. However, my experience in the church is that this "community of the Holy Spirit" more often responds to non-traditional suggestions not by interacting rationally but by killing or attempting to discredit the messenger. Many persons in the history of this institution have gone to the stake without the opportunity to see the church adopting, within a century of their deaths, the very concepts for which the originators were martyred. The early reformers John Hus and John Wycliffe were not allowed to see their ideas come to fruition, but the reformation that they began changed the face of Western history. Copernicus was excommunicated for suggesting that the earth was not the center of the universe. Galileo was forced by the church to recant scientific insights that are today universally accepted. By the time of Charles Darwin the power of the church to determine what was to be called the truth was greatly diminished. Nonetheless, Bishop William Wilberforce made a public career out of attacking Darwin. In Darwin's day that debate was thought to be between two equally matched adversaries, but today all recognize the name of Darwin while few can recall any of Wilberforce's now abandoned conclusions or, in most cases, even his name.

It has not been different in recent history. One has only to read books like *A Time for Christian Candor* and *If This Be Heresy,* by the late, controversial, and persecuted Bishop James A. Pike, to realize that what seemed wildly sensational a quarter of a century ago is commonly accepted today. When the great English Bishop John A. T. Robinson wrote *Honest to God* in 1963, his book was trumpeted in all the secular newspapers of England as a scandalous attack on orthodoxy. As a result, it sold more copies than any religious book since *Pilgrim's Progress*. Its insights, however, would hardly stir any response today. They have become rather conventional.

The church, in my opinion, has for too long catered only to those who remain inside its hallowed walls. To keep them safe and secure, church leaders have not shared with this faithful remnant the insights of biblical scholarship, for fear that "their faith would be offended." One bishop, attacking Bishop Pike in the sixties, reminded him of all the "little people" who were upset by the things he was saying. Bishop Pike responded by saying that most of the "little people" were growing up, asking questions the church could not or would not answer, and consequently leaving the church in droves.

It is these people who have departed from the church who need to be called to its attention today. These "church alumni" are the ones who must be engaged in significant conversation. In large measure this book is designed to educate the people still in the pews to the presence of those who have departed, and to say to those who have stepped away that something new is happening in the churches. I want it to be recognized by this group that some parts of the church are discussing sex in ways that do not produce guilt, and being publicly honest about what the Bible is and is not, what it says and does not say. That is a new thing. Christian voices from within the church are daring to challenge the conventional, closed-minded religious mentality that is so often perceived as the church's only public voice.

I am convinced that if this book escapes the ranks of the church and is heard in the secular society, it will make a genuine contribution. If it is read only by the faithful remnant and those ecclesiastical persons who work to keep that remnant secure, then it will face attack, ridicule, and deliberate misinterpretation. Its author will bear the abuse of those who, unable to deal with the content, decide to ignore the content and attack the credibility of the content's source.

We live today in a gentler world. I am not likely to be burned at the stake. More importantly, the world moves more rapidly today, and I am still young enough to watch the church change dramatically. I can take consolation from the fact that people like me who love the church and who yet dare to question the church's conventional wisdom can, over a long enough period of time, make a vital difference.

Leaven changes the dough from within, and it cannot be found once its work has been done. Salt also loses its identity, but its presence is recognized in the taste of the soup. I hope this book is the leaven in the lump and the salt in the soup. I also hope that any debate it engenders will give to the church a yeasty quality and a new flavor.

APPENDIX

**Report of the Task Force on Changing Patterns
of Sexuality and Family Life**

Prepared at the Request of the 111th Convention
of the Diocese of Newark

By the Task Force on Changing Patterns
of Sexuality and Family Life

The Rev. Dr. Nelson S. T. Thayer, Chair
The Rev. Cynthia Black
Ms. Ella Dubose
The Rev. Abigail Hamilton
Ms. Diane Holland
Mr. Thomas Kebba
Mr. Townsend Lucas
Dr. Teresa Marciano
The Rev. Gerard Pisani
The Rev. Gerald Riley
Ms. Sara Sobol
The Rev. Walter Sobol

Introduction

Following the mandate of the Diocesan Convention on January, 1985, the Task Force on Changing Patterns of Sexuality and Family Life has been meeting for study and discussion, focusing its attention on three groups of persons representative of some of the changing patterns of sexuality and family life: (1) young people who choose to live together without being married; (2) older persons who choose not to marry or who may be divorced or widowed; (3) homosexual couples. All three kinds of relationships are widely represented in the Diocese Newark, and it has been recognized that the Church's understanding of and ministry among the people involved has not been adequate.

The aim of the Task Force has not been original social scientific research. Members of the Task Force have engaged in Biblical, theological, historical, sociological and psychological study, and in extensive discussion of the issues raised. The intent of the Task Force has been two-fold: to prepare a document that would help the clergy and laity of the diocese to think about the issues, and to suggest broad guidelines for the Church's pastoral response to persons in the three groups and to those not in those groups but who are concerned about the issues raised.

The process of study and discussion engaged the members at the deepest levels of their self-understanding as human beings and as Christians. We sometimes found ourselves confused, angry, hurt, uncertain. The subject brought up basic fears and prejudices which members had to struggle with corporately and privately. We became more deeply aware of our own fallibility and of our need for each other's response, correction and support. Each member is a distinct person with her or his own distinct experience and viewpoint; complete uniformity was neither sought nor attained.

But the Task Force became and remains convinced that such a process of search and person-to-person engagement is essential for the Church to respond to the social, cultural and personal realities involved in the changing patterns of sexuality and family life. Appropriate response to these issues requires the willingness to confront within ourselves some of our most deeply formed impulses and assumptions, and some of our tradition's most firmly embedded attitudes. This can only occur in a context of conversation with others whose experience and viewpoints enable our own to be transformed.

We understand the Church to be a community in search, not a

community in perfection. As a community in search, the Church must recognize the needs among its members, among all Christians, indeed among all persons, for loving support, for mutual trust, and for growth through learning from each other. As one contemporary writer has put it, "as such a *community* the Church is of prime significance in making love a reality in human life—incarnating the Incarnate Love . . . These images affirm not only intimacy and mutuality but also inclusiveness; there are implications for a diversity of sexual patterns within a congregation. Different sexual lifestyles being lived out with integrity and in Christianly humanizing ways need not simply be tolerated—they can be positively supported. The 'family of God' can ill afford to make the nuclear family its sole model." (James Nelson, *Embodiment*. Minneapolis: Augsburg Publishing House, 1978, p. 260.)

This report crystallizes the Task Force's perspective on these issues. It does not summarize each discussion, nor does it present all the research and data that informed these discussions. The report is offered to the Diocese of Newark to stimulate our corporate thinking and discussion. The Task Force's major recommendation is that discussion continue on an intentional, diocese-wide basis. This and other recommendations are offered in the final section.

I. The Cultural Situation

The social and cultural changes that have occurred in American society over the past half-century are increasingly being reflected in the changing attitudes of members of the Anglican communion regarding some of the basic moral values and assumptions which have long been taken for granted. Profound changes have occurred in our understanding and practices in areas involving sexuality and family life. Traditionally, the Church has provided, virtually unchallenged, direction and guidance on these matters that deeply affect the individual, the family unit and the community at large. Today, the Church is no longer the single arbiter in these matters, which were once thought to be within its sacred province. Some of the factors that have led to the diminution of this status are:

1. Secularization of American society as it moved from a predominately rural background at the turn of the century to today's predominately urban setting. This has produced new and competing centers of values and morality.

2. Social, economic and geographical mobility that has individually and collectively loosened structures traditionally provided by the community, church and family. These structures tended to channel and constrict values, choices and behavior in the areas involving sexuality, marriage and family life.

3. Advances of technology, which have provided means of disease control and birth control, which have effectively separated the act of sexual intercourse from procreation.

4. Reduction of the age at which puberty begins. This confronts children with issues of sexuality earlier than in the past.

5. Adolescent dating without chaperonage. This removes a powerful external structure of control of sexual behavior.

6. Many in contemporary culture begin and establish a career at a later age than formerly. Marriage also tends to occur later. These two developments combined with convenient methods of birth control, the earlier onset of puberty and the absence of chaperonage, significantly lengthen the period when sexuality will be expressed outside of marriage.

7. The gradual but perceptible changes in attitude regarding what constitutes a "complete" human being: the human body and sex are no longer considered something to be ashamed of, and these physical realities as well as intellect and spirituality constitute essential elements in the development of a complete human being.

8. The decline of exclusive male economic hegemony, which has resulted in a realignment of the male/female relationships in society.

9. The existence of a better educated society, which does not depend upon authorities to determine "what is right" on issues such as nuclear war or power plants, abortion, birth control, poverty, environment, etc.

10. The intensifying clash between the claims of traditional authority as demanded by the family, church and society and the aims of twentieth century men and women to seek their own fulfillment in ways that were not necessarily acceptable in the past. This is, of course, an ancient tension; it gains its particular contemporary character in American society from the dissolution of the degree of ethical consensus as the society has become increasingly pluralistic.

The Church needs to think clearly about these social, cultural and ethical realities. It must order its teachings and corporate life so as to guide and sustain all persons whose lives are touched by these realities. The challenges that these realities pose to our beliefs and practices must be examined and responded to.

As indicated in the introduction, this report is intended to contribute to the Church's understanding of these issues, and to offer perspective on and suggestions for the Church's response.

II. Biblical and Theological Considerations

A. *Tradition and Interpretation*

The Judeo-Christian tradition is a tradition precisely because, in every historical and social circumstance, the thinking faithful have brought to bear their best interpretation of the current realities in correlation with their interpretation of the tradition as they have inherited it. Thus, truth in the Judeo-Christian tradition is a dynamic process to be discerned and formulated rather than a static structure to be received.

The Bible is misunderstood and misused when approached as a book of moral prescriptions directly applicable to all moral dilemmas. Rather, the Bible is the record of the response to the word of God addressed to Israel and to the Church throughout centuries of changing social, historical and cultural conditions. The faithful responded within the realities of their particular situation, guided by the direction of previous revelation, but not captive to it.

The text must always be understood in context: first in the historical context of the particular Biblical situation and then in our own particular social and historical context. The word of God addresses us through scripture. It is not freeze-dried in prepackaged moral prescriptions, but is actively calling for faithful response within the realities of our particular time. Any particular prescription in scripture, any teaching of the law, must be evaluated according to the overarching direction of the Bible's witness to God, culminating in the grace of Christ.

B. *The Centrality of Christ and the Realm of God*

The central point of reference for the thinking Christian is the life, ministry, death and resurrection of Jesus Christ. The history of interpretations of the meaning of that event begins in scripture itself and continues into our immediate present. The central fact about Jesus's life and teaching is that he manifested in his relationships, acts and words the imminent and future Kingdom of God, which will be referred to as the Realm of God.

The Realm of God as presented by Jesus in his relationships and in his parables is characterized by loving action on behalf of all men and women including especially the poor, the sick, the weak, the oppressed and the despised, the outcast and those on the margins of life. The Realm of God presents us with both the fulfillment and the transcendence of the inherited law. The Realm of God presents us with an overturning—even a reversal—of the structures by which humans attempt to establish their own righteousness, which inevitably oppresses or exploits, or marginalizes others.

The challenge to the Church to respond creatively to changing patterns of sexuality and family life in America must be seen as an instance of the Holy Spirit leading us to respond to the blessing and claim of the Realm of God foreshadowed and made continually present by the life of Christ Jesus. In his death Jesus exemplifies sacrificial love that is faithful to his vision of the Realm of God. In the resurrection we know God's ultimate faithfulness and sovereignty.

It is in response to this central example and teaching of Jesus regarding the Realm of God that we attempt to discern what should be the Church's response to changing patterns of sexuality and family life. We discover in the actions and parables of Jesus that the Realm of God manifests grace unfettered by legalistic obligation to tradition and "the law." When the choice is between observance of the law or active, inclusive love, Jesus embodies and teaches love. It is in the light of this fundamental principle of God's active reconciling love that any religious law or dogma, social or economic arrangement is to be assessed.

C. The Realm of God and Human Social Structures

The specific instances of changing patterns of sexuality and family life that this Task Force addresses do not occur in a cultural vacuum but in the cultural turmoil marked by the ten developments noted in the opening section of this document. Not one of these developments is morally unambiguous. All of them are marked—as has been every development of social history—by the human propensity for self-deception and self-aggrandizement at the expense of others, which Christians call "sin."

Jesus's radical claim is that in his person the Realm of God confronts us, in every age, with our bondage to sin. Included in sin's manifestations are the social norms and arrangements by which we conventionally order our lives. In parable after parable Jesus presents us with the need to see historical relativity, the need to examine the arbitrariness and the maintenance of power by traditional structures. The Church itself and the authority of its traditional teachings is subject to judgment by the ongoing activity of the Realm of God.

Judged by the grace of God starkly presented by the parables, Jesus's preaching and his actions show us that response to the Realm of God requires us to be ready to perceive and modify these structures in our society that hurt and alienate others rather than heal and extend love to those in circumstances different from our own.

With this consciousness we hear the challenges to our conventional attitudes and practices regarding sexuality and the family and try to discern how these challenges should influence our understanding of our traditional values and our response to new realities. We engage in this process knowing (and discovering anew) that all our thoughts are laced with our desire for self-justification, our need for self-aggrandizement, and the willingness to hurt those whom we see as opposing us. Sin is our human condition; it permeates all our institutions, all our traditions, and all our relationships; so it has always been for humankind; so it has always been in the Church.

D. Historical Relativity

Recalling our sinful condition causes us to look critically both at the Church's conventions and at the demands for change put forward by various groups in our culture. The relativizing impact of the Realm of God enables us to see more clearly what Biblical and historical research discloses: that beliefs and practices surrounding marriage and sexuality have varied according to time, culture and necessity. We tend to sacralize the familiar and project into the past our current practices and beliefs and the rationales supporting them.

Such is the case with our assumptions about marriage. We tend to project into early Biblical times a twentieth century model of monogamous self-chosen marriage when clearly, at various periods in the Old Testament records, polygamy was assumed (at least for the wealthy). Even into the Middle Ages a marriage was an economic event, perhaps an alliance, between two families or clans.

Marriage was not given the status of a sacrament by the Church until 1439. And not until 1563 did the Church require the presence of a priest at the event. And even then marriage functioned to solemnize an agreement which had been entered into more for reasons of procreation, the channeling of sexuality, and economic benefit to the families than as a means of preexisting love between the two persons to develop and flourish, as we expect of present-day marriage.

In the Bible and in our own Western heritage, sexuality outside of marriage has been proscribed for women—not men. When women were found adulterous, the violation was of property rights rather than of sexual morality as we tend to conceive it, because women were viewed as property of fathers, and then of their husbands.

Homosexual behavior was condemned because it was part of pagan religious practices from which Israel sought always to differentiate itself. Biblical scholarship maintains that in the story of Sodom and Gomorrah, Lot's concern was not with the homosexual nature of the implied rape of his guests, but with such behavior as a violation of rules of hospitality. Homosexuality as a fundamental human orientation is not addressed in scripture; and Jesus himself was entirely silent on the subject.

E. Revised Understanding of the Person

A major change in perspective is occurring in religious thinking regarding sexuality and the body. Greek philosophical and agnostic thought had great influence on the early development of Christianity. Since that time the Church has tended to teach that the body is a dangerous vessel, subject to temptation and sin, which temporarily houses the superior soul or spirit. Whereas the Greeks regarded the mind or spirit as able to reach its triumph only by freeing itself from the corrupting captivity of the physical body, the Hebrews knew no such separation. In Hebraic thought one does not *have* a body, one *is* a body. What we today refer to as body, mind, and spirit were—in Hebraic thought—dimensions of an indivisible unity.

The contemporary, more Hebraic understanding of the person runs counter to the traditional dualistic teaching of the Church, which has tended either to try to ignore the fact that humans are embodied selves, or has looked at the physical, sexual body as the root of sin. The contemporary attitude views sexuality as more than genital sex having as its purpose procreation, physical pleasure and release of tension. Sexuality includes sex, but it is a more comprehensive concept.

Sexuality is not simply a matter of behavior. Our sexuality goes to the heart of our identity as persons. Our self-understanding, our experience of ourselves as male or female, our ways of experiencing and relating to others, are all reflective of our being as sexual persons.

We do not have *bodies,* we *are* bodies, and the doctrine of the Incarnation reminds us that God comes to us and we know God in the flesh. We come to know God through our experience of other embodied selves. Thus our sexual identity and behavior are means for our experience and knowledge of God. This theological perspective means that issues of homosexuality, divorce and sexual relations between unmarried persons involve not only matters of ethics but have to do with how persons know and experience God.

It is our conclusion that by suppressing our sexuality and by condemning all sex which occurs outside of traditional marriage, the Church has thereby obstructed a vitally important means for persons to know and celebrate their relatedness to God. The teachings of the Church have tended to make us embarrassed about rather than grateful for our bodies. As means of communion with other persons our bodies sacramentally become means of communion with God.

III. Ethical Essentials

From the perspective of Jesus's teaching regarding the Realm of God, all heterosexual and homosexual relationships are subject to the same criteria of ethical assessment—the degree to which the persons and relationships reflect mutuality, love and justice. The Task Force does not in any way advocate or condone promiscuous behavior which by its very definition exploits the other for one's own aggrandizement. The commitment to mutuality, love and justice which marks our ideal picture of heterosexual unions is also the ideal for homosexual unions. Those who would say homosexuality by its very nature precludes such commitment must face the fact that such unions do in fact occur, have occurred and will continue to occur. The Church must decide how to respond to such unions.

It is becoming clear that many persons—single, divorced or widowed—may not seek long-term unions, while some commit themselves to such unions without being formally married. The overriding issue is not the formality of the social/legal arrangement, or even a scriptural formula, but the quality of the relationship in terms of our understanding of the ethical and moral direction pointed to by Jesus in the symbol of the Realm of God.

The challenge to the Church is to discern and support the marks of the Realm of God in all these relationships. The Church should be that community above all which is marked by its inclusion of persons who are seeking to grow in their capacity for love and justice in their relationships and in their relation to their world-neighbors. The Church should actively work against those social and economic arrangements which militate against the establishment of such relationships.

IV. Marriage and Alternative Forms of Relationship

Our nation has been described as a "highly nuptial" civilization. This means that for whatever reasons many Americans see marriage as a vehicle for happiness and satisfaction. Life-long marriage offers the possibility of profound intimacy, mutuality, personal development and self-fulfillment throughout the years of the life cycle. On the other hand, of course, a marriage can be marked with the sin of self-centeredness and exploitation of the other, and by the estrangements of male from female, weaker from stronger.

Ideally, marriage can be a context in which children can develop their identities by drawing on both male and female ways of being a person. It can therefore provide a uniquely rich context for the formation of children into adults who cherish and intend the qualities of the Realm of God—love and justice—in the context of ongoing relationships marked by sacrifice, forgiveness, joy and reconciliation. It can also give to parents the opportunity to mature and develop their own capacities for caring generativity.

The Church must continue to sustain persons in the fulfillment of traditional marriage relationships both for the well-being of the marriage partners and because such marriage provides the most stable institution that we have known for the nurturing and protection of children. But the Church must also recognize that fully intended marriage vows are fraught with risks. Belief that deeper knowledge each of each in marriage will enable the original intentions of love and devotion is not always fulfilled. Persons living through the dissolution of marriage need especially at that time the support of an understanding and inclusive community. Such is true obviously also for divorced persons, whether living singly or in new relationships.

One of the Church's present deficiencies is its exclusionary posture toward those who have "failed" in the conventional arrangement of marriage and family and the conventional understanding (and avoidance) of sexuality has blinded us to present reality. The Church needs actively to include separating and divorced individuals and single parents.

The Church must take seriously that Jesus's teaching and manifesting of the Realm of God were concerned not with the formal arrangements of our lives but with our responsiveness to the vision of the Realm of God. Admittedly, this confronts all of us with a relativization of all personal, social and economic arrangements by which we live. We cannot live without structure in our relationships; but these structures are subject to continual correction by the image of the Realm of God. If the Church is to err it must err on the side of inclusiveness rather than exclusiveness.

Marriage has served as a stabilizing force in American society, channeling sexuality in socially acceptable directions, providing a structure for the procreation and nurturing of children, and enabling enduring companionship between a man and a woman by defining the legal and spiritual responsibilities of the married couple. Although marriage has taken many forms in human society, it has been a central, constant building block of human society in all cultures. The power of sexuality both to attract persons, and satisfy persons, and to disrupt the social order has been recognized in the practices, mythologies and laws of all cultures.

Marriage has bound the family, clan and tribe to customs and traditions which insure survival and identification of a people as a people. The church must consider the consequences of calling into question institutional relationships which have permitted the Church to flourish and survive. However, our contemporary consciousness of racial, sexual and economic domination and exploitation has raised our culture's consciousness about some of the oppressive, repressive and exploitative dimensions of marriage and family arrangements. This heightened sensitivity, combined with a cultural ethos that favors self-fulfillment over the dutiful but self-abnegating adherence to conventional marriage and family arrangements, has caused many to deny that life-long monogamous, heterosexual marriage is the sole legitimate structure for the satisfaction of our human need for sexuality and intimacy.

There are those who think that even though the forms have been enormously diverse, the pervasive human tendency to union with an individual of the opposite sex in a committed relationship and the universal presence of family structure in some form evidences something fundamental about the nature of the created human order itself. Biologically, this has been the only option for the perpetuation of the human race as we know it. While other arrangements may be appropriate to the given nature of particular individuals, monogamous, life-long marriage and family organization ought not to be thereby relativized as simply one option among others.

Given the Church's traditional view of the exclusive primacy of marriage and the nuclear family and the (relative) opprobrium with which the Church has viewed other options, the Church must learn how to continue to affirm the conventional without denigrating alternative sexual and family arrangements. Again, the criteria are the quality of the relationships and their potential for developing persons responsive to the Realm of God. The Church must find ways genuinely to affirm persons as they faithfully and responsibly choose and live out other modes of relationship.

We live after the Fall. The metaphor of the Realm of God reinforces the realization of brokenness and finitude in all our human arrangements and relationships. We sin daily in our self-deception, self-centeredness, self-justification and readiness to exploit and oppress others for our own material and emotional self-aggrandizement. And this is clearly seen in our readiness to interpret scripture and tradition to reinforce what we perceive as our own best interests so that we appear righteous and those who differ from us appear unrighteous.

The dynamic process of God's incarnational truth has brought us to a time in history when the critical consciousness made possible by modern forms of knowledge—including Biblical scholarship—enables us to see the Realm of God as a present reality relativizing all human knowledge and social arrangements. We are therefore suspicious of the invocation of tradition even while we believe that in God's ongoing creation not all relational arrangements are equally aligned with a caring God's purposes for humankind.

Those who believe that the heterosexual family unit headed by monogamous heterosexual partners offers the best possibility for the development of children who will become confident, loving, compassionate and creative adults must acknowledge the historical fallibility of the family in accomplishing such results. All sexual and family arrangements must be judged by the same criteria suggested by the metaphor of the Realm of God.

Ultimately, do couples (of whatever orientation) and families (of whatever constitution) exist for the sake of their own self-fulfillment? The Gospel does not support such an individualistic possibility. Nor does it support promiscuous behavior, which by its very nature uses the other person simply for one's self-aggrandizement, whether mere sexual release, as compensation for feelings of inadequacy or to express hostility. Theologically, patterns of sexual and family arrangements are to be judged according to the degree to which they reflect and contribute to the realization of the Realm of God. Since this is a dynamic not a static reality, continual diversity, exploration, experimentation and discernment will mark the life of the faithful Church.

In the absence of set rules, great demands are thus placed on clergy and others who counsel persons regarding these issues. We believe that at the level of congregational life, the Church ought not focus its concern on this or that particular pattern. The Church's focus ought to be on persons as they seek to understand and order their lives and relationships. All relationships and arrangements are to be assessed in terms of their capacity to manifest marks of the Realm of God: healing, reconciliation, compassion, mutuality, concern for others both within and beyond one's immediate circle of intimacy.

V. Considerations Regarding the Three Alternate Patterns

As indicated in the Introduction, the Task Force decided to address specifically the Church's response to young adults who choose to live together unmarried, adults who never married or who are "post-marriage," due to divorce or the death of their spouse, and homosexual couples. We do not address the subject of adolescent sexuality, although we agree on the need for more thorough-going education of adolescents within the Church regarding sexuality and relationships.

We believe that certain questions of context are appropriate whenever persons consider beginning a sexual relationship: (a) Will the relationship strengthen the pair for greater discipleship in the wider context? Will they be better enabled to love others? Will their relationship be a beneficial influence on those around them? (b) Will the needs and values of others in the larger context be recognized and respected, especially the needs of their own children (if any), their parents, and their parish community? Since an ongoing sexual relationship between two persons occurs within a network of relationships to parents, children (perhaps adult children), colleagues and fellow parishioners, such a relationship needs to be conducted with sensitivity to the possible emotional and relational effects on these other persons. (c) What is the couple's intention regarding the procreation and/or raising of children?

Regarding the relationship itself, the following considerations are appropriate: (a) The relationship should be life-enhancing for both partners and exploitative of neither. (b) The relationship should be grounded in sexual fidelity and not involve promiscuity. (c) The relationship should be founded on love and valued for the strengthening, joy, support and benefit of the couple and those to whom they are related.

A. *Young Adults*

One of the issues facing the Church in our time comes under the broad category of what used to be called "pre-marital sex." The issue for the Church to which attention is given in the following discussion is specifically defined as that of young adults of the opposite sex living together and in a sexual relationship without ecclesiastical or civil ceremony. (Of course, many young adults, for economic and social reasons share housing without having a sexual relationship. We do not address these relationships in what follows.)

From an historical perspective, such relationships are not unfamiliar to our culture. For many years common-law marriage had legal validity for purposes of property and inheritance settlements. Attitudes concerning careers, emotional and sexual commitments and intimacy, marital economics, and experiences (either through observation or background) all contribute to decisions concerning the form of relationship a man and a woman choose. In the contemporary world, young adults may live together to deepen their relationships, as a trial period prior to a commitment to marriage, or as a temporary or a permanent alternative to marriage.

In order to maintain the sacredness of the marital relationship in the sacrament of Holy Matrimony, the Church has generally been opposed to the actions of couples choosing to live together without ecclesiastical or civil ceremony. Opposition has been and is expressed both in direct statement and by silent tolerance. The effect of the opposition has been to separate those couples from the ministry of the Church, to the detriment of the quality of their relationship, of the spiritual growth of the individuals, of their involvement in the mutual ministry of the Church, of their contribution to the building up of the Christian community. Current research documents that persons living under these circumstances are less likely to profess an affiliation with an established religion or to attend church. And yet these persons might well benefit from a church affiliation.

To minister to or engage in ministry with those who choose to live together without marriage does not denigrate the institution of marriage and life-long commitments. Rather it is an effort to recognize and support those who choose, by virtue of the circumstances of their lives, not to marry but to live in alternative relationships enabling growth and love.

In a community in search, all benefit from mutual support and concern. Although living among persons of differing lifestyles can be threatening, it can provide those who have committed themselves to a life-long relationship in marriage the opportunity to renew, to reform, to recreate their loyalties and vows in an atmosphere of alternative possibilities.

We emphasize that the Church's focus should be on persons as they seek to understand and order their lives and relationships. All relationships are to be assessed in terms of their capacity to manifest marks of the Realm of God: healing, reconciliation, compassion, mutuality, concern for others both within and beyond one's immediate circle of intimacy. Extending the image of the Church as a community of persons in search raises pastoral implications. A community in search seeks wisdom, understanding and truth in the experience and hopes of each of its members and from those (too often ignored) who choose not to participate in that community.

Both at the diocesan and congregational levels, the Church can actively engage in education and discussion on all issues of sexuality. Members of the congregation, persons from specific disciplines in the secular world, and persons who have in their own lives wrestled with pertinent issues can all be asked to participate in such efforts. Congregations should encourage open, caring conversation, leading to trust and mutual, supportive acceptance. This makes more credible the Church's claim to faithfulness to the Realm of God.

Persons who have been ignored or rejected by the Church's ministry, or who have assumed such rejection, can only be reached and loved by a community that witnesses in *deed* to its faith that God calls all people to new hopes, to new possibilities, by a community that knows it does not have all the answers and in which each member contributes to its growth and future wholeness in the Realm of God.

B. "Post-Married" Adults

Some mature persons, by life-long choice or because of divorce or the death of a spouse, find themselves unmarried but desiring an intimate relationship. We affirm that there can be life-enhancing meaning and value for some adult single persons in sexual relationships other than marriage. Economic realities may militate against traditional marriage arrangements. For example Social Security payments are reduced for two individuals who marry; channeling inheritances for children can become legally expensive and complicated where re-marriage occurs; maintaining a one-person household is for many persons prohibitively costly.

The choice of celibacy or estrangement from the Church for such persons who choose not to marry is not consonant with the Church's hope of wholeness for all persons in the Realm of God. Our understanding of the Church is one of inclusiveness. As we struggle to understand what the Church is called to in our time, one of our goals is inclusion in the Christian body of persons who have thoughtfully chosen lifestyles different from that of the mainstream.

Because we are whole human beings, and not, in the last analysis, separate compartments of body and soul, therefore the spiritual, mental, emotional, physical and sexual aspects of our personalities are all to be nurtured and expressed in responsible ways if we are to continue to grow towards wholeness in our mature years. We are created sexual beings, and our spiritual health, no less than any other aspect of health, is therefore linked to sexuality. When, therefore, mature single adults choose to celebrate their love and live their lives together outside of marriage, provided that they have considered and responded sensitively to the public and personal issues involved, we believe that their decision will indeed be blessed by God and can be affirmed as morally acceptable and responsible by the Church.

C. Homosexual Couples

Changing patterns of sexuality and family life confront pastors and congregations with new challenges and opportunities for understanding and for ministry. Rather than arguing about these issues we need first to listen to the experience of those who are most directly involved. Where homosexuality is concerned, fear, rejection, and avoidance by the heterosexual community is common and entrenched; we believe that pastors and congregations must meet members of the homosexual community person to person. The first step toward understanding and ministry is listening.

We need as much as is possible to bracket our judgements and listen to persons as they are. The Church needs to acknowledge that its historic tendency to view homosexual persons as homosexual rather than as persons has intensified the suffering of this 5%-10% of our population. A congregation's willingness to listen is a first step toward redeeming our homophobic past.

Listening is also a first step toward acknowledging that our own understanding needs ministry. Those of us fearful and angry regarding homosexuality need liberation, and this can only come through person to person communication. So the Church's response includes permitting itself to be ministered to by the homosexual community.

This process will help the Church recognize that whatever our historical experience, we encounter each other as we are with all our many limitations and potentialities. What we may become is a function of our open meeting of each other and of the reconciling, empowering spirit of God active in such open meeting.

Such person to person meeting, by means of open forums, small group discussions, and one to one conversations, needs to be accompanied by the study of Biblical, historical, theological and social scientific perspectives. Accurate information and informed opinion are important counterbalances to the fear and distortion which have so often inhibited the Church's ability to respond appropriately.

Listening opens the door of hospitality, which has so long been firmly shut. Such words as ministry and hospitality, however, still suggest a relationship of inequality, we and they. As such they perpetuate the image of the Church as separate from the homosexual community. In fact, however, we believe that the Church should be as inclusive of homosexual persons as it is of heterosexual persons. In this light, all the normal avenues of inclusion should be available to homosexual persons.

Criteria for membership, for participation in church committees, choirs, education, vestries, etc. and for ordination should be no different for any given group. Some persons express fear that including homosexual persons in the full round of church life will influence others—especially children—to become homosexual. In fact, we know of no evidence or experience to confirm that such association can bring about a homosexual orientation.

Ideally, homosexual couples would find within the community of the congregation the same recognition and affirmation which nurtures and sustains heterosexual couples in their relationship, including, where appropriate, liturgies which recognize and bless such relationships.

D. Recommendations

Sexuality is an integral part of our God-given humanity. The Church must devote more attention to sexuality in its child, adolescent and adult educational programming. As we understand more about the nature and meaning of our sexuality we will learn how to respond more appropriately to persons of many different circumstances.

Change in the Church's life is an ongoing process. We therefore urge education and discussion at all levels of diocesan life.

Specifically we recommend the following:

1. That all collegial groups such as the Commission on Ministry, the Newark Clergy Association, and all other regular commissions and committees of the diocese address these issues as they impact their areas of responsibility and concern.

2. That the March/April Clergy day, 1987, and the June, 1987, Religious Education Conference include sexuality among the issues to be considered.

3. That Congregations develop programs appropriate to their setting and circumstances which enable education and discussion regarding issues of sexuality and the Church's response to changing patterns of sexuality and family life. In addition to providing structured educational programs, the Church should be a community where persons can discuss their experience and clarify their self-understanding relationships and courses of action. We would urge congregations to provide space and time, for example, for parent groups whose children are gay or lesbian and who want to discuss the implication of this for their own lives. Likewise, gay and lesbian couples may want to meet with each other or non-gays for support and friendship.

4. That Convocations support and perhaps sponsor such programs as suggested above.

5. That a group similar to this Task Force be established to facilitate discussion at the congregational level, to monitor the process, and to report to the Diocesan Convention of 1988, perhaps with recommendations or resolutions.

BIBLIOGRAPHY

Adler, Alfred. *Cooperation Between the Sexes: Writings on Women, Love, Marriage, Sexuality, and Its Disorders.* Garden City, N.Y.: Anchor Books, 1978.

Advisory Committee of Issues Relating to Homosexuality. *A Study of Issues Concerning Homosexuality: Report of the Advisory Committee of Issues Relating to Homosexuality.* New York: Division for Mission in North America, Lutheran Church in America, 1986.

Allport, Gordon W. *Personality and Social Encounter.* Boston: Beacon Press, 1960.

Auel, Jean M. *The Clan of the Cave Bear.* New York: Crown, 1980.

_____. *The Valley of the Horses.* New York: Crown, 1982.

_____. *The Mammoth Hunters.* New York: Crown, 1985.

Bainton, Roland H. *Erasmus of Christendom.* New York: Charles Scribner's Sons, 1969.

Batchelor, Edward J., Jr. *Homosexuality and Ethics.* New York: Pilgrim Press, 1980.

Berne, Eric, M.D. *Sex in Human Loving.* New York: Simon & Schuster, 1973.

Boswell, John. *Christianity, Social Tradition, and Homosexuality.* Chicago: University of Chicago Press, 1980.

Bowers, Margaretta. *Conflicts of the Clergy.* New York: Thomas Nelson, 1963.

Brooten, B. *Women Priests.* New York: L. and A. Swidler, 1977.

Burnhouse, Ruth Tiffany. "Homosexuality?" *The Episcopalian,* April 1987.

Burton, Robert. *The Mating Game*. New York: Crown, 1976.

Capra, Fritjof. *The Tao of Physics*. Berkeley, Cal.: Shambhala, 1975.

_____. *The Turning Point*. New York: Simon & Schuster, 1982.

Chapman, A. H. *Harry Stack Sullivan*. New York: G. P. Putman & Sons, 1976.

Coats, William. "Sex and the Mature Single Adult." *The Episcopalian*, May 1987.

Delaney, Janice, Emily Toth, and Mary Jane Lupton. *The Curse: A Cultural History of Menstruation*. New York: Dutton, 1976.

Durden-Smith, Jo, and Diane de Simone. *Sex and the Brain*. New York: Arbor House, 1983.

Erickson, Erik H. *Identity and the Life Cycle*. New York: International University Press, 1959.

Fortunato, John E. "Should the Church Bless and Affirm Committed Gay Relationships?" *The Episcopalian*, April 1987.

Freud, Sigmund. *Three Contributions to the Theory of Sex*. New York: Dutton, 1962.

_____. *Totem and Taboo*. New York: Vintage Press, 1946.

Friedman, Richard E. *Who Wrote the Bible?* New York: Summit Books, 1987.

Fuller, R. Buckminster. *The Critical Path*. New York: St. Martin's, 1981.

Haines, Denise G. "Should the Church Bless Committed But Not Married Sexually Active Relationships?" *The Episcopalian*, March 1987.

Heywood, Carter. *Our Passion for Justice*. New York: Pilgrim Press, 1984.

Hick, John. *God and the Universe of Faith*. London: Macmillan, 1973.

Horney, Karen. *Feminine Psychology*. New York: Norton, 1967.

Jones, Clinton R. *Homosexuality and Counseling*. Philadelphia: Fortress Press, 1974.

_____. *What About Homosexuality?* New York: Thomas Nelson, 1972.

Kinsey, Alfred C. et al. *Sexual Behavior in the Human Female*. Philadelphia: Saunders, 1953.

_____. *Sexual Behavior in the Human Male*. Philadelphia: Saunders, 1948.

Kolbenschlag, Madonna. *Kiss Sleeping Beauty Good-Bye*. San Francisco: Harper & Row, 1988.

LeBacqz, Karen. "Appropriate Vulnerability—A Sexual Ethic for Singles." *The Christian Century* 104, no. 5 (May 1987): 435-38.

Mace, David R. *The Christian Response to the Sexual Revolution*. Nashville: Abingdon Press, 1970.

Mace, David R., and Vera Mace. *The Sacred Fire*. Nashville: Abingdon Press, 1986.

Maslow, Abraham. *Toward a Psychology of Being*. Princeton, N.J.: Van Nostrand, 1952.

McNeill, John J. "Homosexuality—The Challenge to the Church." *The Christian Century* 104, no. 8 (March 1987): 242-46.

Nelson, James B. "Reuniting Sexuality and Spirituality." *The Christian Century* 104, no. 6 (February 1987): 187-90.

Pagels, Elaine. *The Gnostic Gospels*. New York: Random House, 1979.

Parrinder, Geoffrey. *Sex in the World's Religions*. New York: Oxford University Press, 1980.

Philips, J. A. *Eve—The History of an Idea*. San Francisco: Harper & Row, 1984.

Pike, James A. *A Time for Christian Candor*. San Francisco: Harper & Row, 1964.

―――. *If This Be Heresy*. San Francisco: Harper & Row, 1967.

Pittenger, W. Norman. *Making Sexuality Human*. New York: Pilgrim Press, 1970.

Reik, Theodor. *Psychology of Sex Relations*. Westport, N.Y.: Greenwood Press, 1975.

Richardson, Herbert W. T. *Nun, Witch and Playmate—The Americanization of Sex*. New York: Edwin Mellen Press, 1971.

Robinson, John A. T. *Honest to God*. Philadelphia: Westminster Press, 1963.

Rogers, Carl R. *Becoming Partners*. New York: Delacorte Press, 1972.

Rouse, A. L. *Homosexuals in History*. New York: Dorset Press, 1977.

Russell, Letty M. "Woman's Liberation in a Biblical Perspective." *Concern* 13, no. 5 (May–June 1971).

Rutledge, Fleming. "No Covenants on Trial." *The Episcopalian*, March 1987.

Spong, John S. "Sexual Ethics: No Longer a Matter of Black and White." *The Episcopalian,* February 1987.

_____. "The Bible and Sexual Ethics." *The Living Church* 194, no. 22 (May 31, 1987): 8-11.

_____. "Changing Patterns in Human Sexuality." *The Living Church* 194, no. 17 (April 26, 1987): 10-13.

_____. *Into the Whirlwind—The Future of the Church.* San Francisco: Harper & Row, 1983.

_____. *The Easter Moment.* San Francisco: Harper & Row, 1987.

_____. *This Hebrew Lord.* San Francisco: Harper & Row, 1987.

Spong, John S., and Denise G. Haines. *Beyond Moralism.* San Francisco: Harper & Row, 1986.

Stone, Merlin. *When God Was a Woman.* New York: Harcourt, Brace, Jovanovich, 1976.

Sullivan, Harry Stack. *The Interpersonal Theory of Psychiatry.* New York: W. W. Norton, 1953.

Szymanski, Walter L., and Horace Lethbridge. "The Blessing of Same Gender Couples—A Rochester, New York Experiment." Unpublished paper. 1972.

Teilhard de Chardin, Pierre. *How I Believe.* San Francisco: Harper & Row, 1969.

_____. *The Phenomenon of Man.* San Francisco: Harper & Row, 1976.

Toffler, Alvin. *Future Shock.* New York: Bantam Books, 1971.

Toynbee, Arnold J. *Christianity Among the Religions of the World.* New York: Charles Scribner's Sons, 1957.

United Church of Christ. *Human Sexuality—A Preliminary Study.* New York: United Church Press, 1977.

Von Rad, Gerhard. *Old Testament Theology.* San Francisco: Harper & Row, 1965.

Wantland, William C. "The Bible and Sexual Ethics." *The Living Church* 194, no. 22 (May 31, 1987): 8-11.

_____. "Changing Patterns of Sexuality." *The Living Church* 194, no. 17 (April 26, 1987): 10-13.

Warner, Marina. *Alone of All Her Sex.* New York: Alfred A. Knopf, 1976.

Winter, Gibson. *Social Ethics.* San Francisco: Harper & Row, 1968.

Yates, John W., II. "Sex and Older Singles." *The Episcopalian,* May 1987.

INDEX

"Abomination" in Leviticus, 145-46
Abortion, 221
Abraham, 97-98, 112, 117, 123-24, 129-30, 137-38. *See also* God
Adam, 139, 162, 213
Adultery, 131
AIDS, 197-98
Appropriate vulnerability, 212-15
Arsenokoitus, 150, 153
Asherah, 119, 124

Baal worship, 113, 117-20, 124
Bathsheba, 100, 127
Betrothal, 177-87
Bible, the, 25, 28-39, 90-93, 98-100, 106, 108, 113-15, 117-18, 163-64. *See also* Homosexuality; Language; Paul; Prejudice; Sodom and Gomorrah
as a weapon, 115-16
conflict between reason and nature, 128
and homosexuality, 88, 115-16, 135-55
inconsistencies in, 105-6, 108, 110-12, 159
inerrancy, 25, 112, 156-57, 162
and menstruation, 145-46
and rape, 141-42
Birth control, 50-51, 181-82
Bi-theism, 125

Celibacy, 12, 83-84, 166-75, 210
Christianity, 25, 120
Chromosomes, 77-78
Church, the, 25, 38, 66, 91, 219, 225. *See also* Prejudice
behavior control, 180-81
challenge to, 240-46
divorce, 63-64, 188-95
future of, 225, 227-30
and God, 38-39
guilt, 180-81
and homosexuals, 12, 70, 81-88, 116, 196-207
inclusiveness, 37
marriage, 173, 200
ordination of homosexuals, 86-88
prejudice, 25, 38-39
science, 78-79
sex, 14, 39, 86, 116, 181-82, 209-10, 214, 217-18, 227
sexism, 219-25
sexual revolution, 52-53
singles, 209, 217-18
Clergy
homosexual, 86-88
recognizing homosexual unions, 203-5